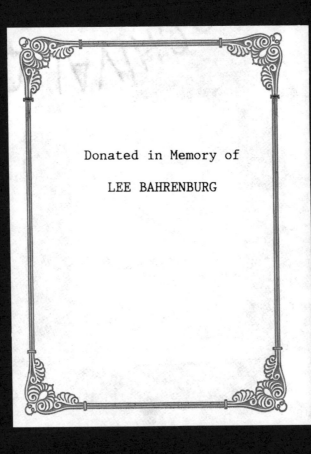

Donated in Memory of

LEE BAHRENBURG

Pickup Artists

A HAYMARKET BOOK

PICKUP ARTISTS

Street Basketball in America

LARS ANDERSON

AND

CHAD MILLMAN

VERSO

London · New York

First published by Verso 1998
© Lars Anderson and Chad Millman 1998
All rights reserved

Verso
UK: 6 Meard Street, London W1V 3HR
USA: 180 Varick Street, 10th Floor, New York, NY 10014-4606

Verso is the imprint of New Left Books

ISBN 1 85984 235 6

British Library Cataloguing in Publication Data
A catalogue record for this book is available from the British Library

Library of Congress Cataloging-in-Publication Data
A catalog record for this book is available from the Library of Congress

Typeset in Dante by NorthStar, San Francisco, California
Printed and bound in the USA by R. R. Donnelly & Sons Co.

Contents

Acknowledgements

We would be remiss if we did not thank the numerous people who helped us along the way. We are in their debt.

Our editor, Mark Mravic of *Sports Illustrated,* lent a graceful hand with his edits and could always be counted on to lighten the mood with his quick wit. Our literary agent, David Vigliano, believed in the project when no one else did. Our respective bosses at *Sports Illustrated* and CNNSI, JB Morris and Stefanie Krasnow, understood when we needed time away from the office to work on this project. Alexander Wolff, a senior writer at *Sports Illustrated,* guided us and allowed us to tap his expertise on the subject. Sandy Padwe, the associate dean of Columbia University's Graduate School of Journalism, helped shape the idea at the very beginning. John Huet, a photographer, graciously donated his wonderful pictures to what he felt was a worthy cause. Susie Ter-Jung gave us her time and talent with a camera. And the *Sports Illustrated* library staff – Linda Ronan, Joy Birdsong, Angel Morales, Natasha Simon and Linda Wachtel – always pointed us in the right direction.

Finally, to Verso's finest. Steve Hiatt's attention to detail helped us sleep at night and Colin Robinson's leadership kept the project moving forward.

Foreword

My favorite hoops utterance of all time issued from the mouth of Bobby Hunter, the New York City playground regular and former Harlem Globetrotter. He was asked about Earl "the Goat" Manigault's legendary take-off-from-the-foul-line, two-full-revolutions-in-flight throwdown at the 135th Street Playground in 1963, the moment to which all of modern playground culture might be faithfully traced.

"I myself have never seen its equal," Hunter said of that dunk. "And I was in Detroit at the time."

That comment perfectly captures the yin and yang, the defense and the offense, that goes into the making of a book like the one you hold in your hands. On the one hand, writing a history of playground ball is a hugely ambitious undertaking. Part of the untidy essence of the schoolyard game is that facts don't sit still for those trying to chronicle them. Moments after its execution, a simple move to the hoop can easily become a full-court slalom through five defenders, then six, then seven. Not even boxing is as steeped in braggadocio as the world of pickup basketball; not even fishing is as subject to so much embellishment; not even Babe Ruth's called shot has spawned so many bogus witnesses.

On the other hand, as the whole sprawling story of the Goat and other legends illustrates, a payoff awaits those willing to sort out the hyperbole from the fact. Lars Anderson and Chad Millman have proven this with their passionately but conscientiously assembled book. Riveting profiles give life to figures both forgotten and never heard of, while a long-overdue history of basketball's most elemental version is a valuable contribution to the game's bookshelf.

Some folks – the kind who take any exuberant young talent and try to truss it up in a blazer – sneer at basketball in its freest form. Those people would not have an ally in the inventor of the game. Dr. James Naismith was delighted at how basketball goals began to crop up all over the American landscape as the nineteenth century spilled into the twentieth. He collected pictures of the most exotic places he found them. The original Doctor J also said, "Basketball is a game that cannot be coached. It can only be played." The authors have paid homage to that maxim.

Much about playground basketball has changed since Chuck Wielgus and I tried to capture it in 1980 in *The In-Your-Face Basketball Book*. But the essence of the game remains the same. It's still a dream game. Fate and tragedy still suffuse too much of it. And there's still the endless transaction between the game's culture – its language and folkways and fashions – and the culture at large. You're going to enjoy this evocation of where we've been, where we're at and, because anticipation is a quality highly prized inside the chain-link fence, at least a hint of where we're going.

Alexander Wolff,
Senior Writer, *Sports Illustrated,*
New York City, Summer 1997

In memory of Amy Nicolle Johnson
of Rockford, Minnesota. Your soft smile is still
remembered, every day. — L.A.

To Stacy, for her support, her sacrifices and, most of all, for
her inspiration. Thank you. — C.M.

1

Straight Out of Brooklyn

Outside Holcombe Rucker Park at 155th Street and Eighth Avenue in Harlem, a group of about 250 holds a vigil along a rusted fence. The crowd is not one you'd expect to see this far north in Manhattan. Yes, the usual suspects are there, dressed in their Nike shirts with matching shorts and hi-tops, but there are also pockets of fans in Birkenstocks and dreadlocks, in loafers and business suits. The people in the crowd are black, white, Latino, Chinese. They are, simply, basketball fans.

This eclectic bunch has been waiting three hours for seats at the Entertainers Classic. They wait as a red-orange late-summer sun sinks behind the Polo Grounds housing projects across the street from the court. They wait, impatiently, as car lights and street lamps begin to burn in the gloaming. They wait as a train on elevated tracks rumbles past in the distance, sending the quintessential sound of the city through the heavy air. They wait as police officers, dozens and dozens of them, mill around the court or guard the barricades, stone-faced and anxious.

Then, suddenly, the wait is rewarded as they see what they have come to see: James "Speedy" Williams has arrived.

As Speedy, flanked by two voluptuous women with delicate features and long legs, slinks into the park, three of the cops begin chanting his name – *Speedy, Speedy, SPEEDY* – their voices rising with each syllable.

The three cops know him. All the cops do. Speedy nears the court, and many in the crowd join the chant. He smiles softly, sweetly, at this Messiah's welcome. It's a sublime smile, one of complete confidence, one of knowing, somehow, that you are in a place where you are in total control. Speedy slaps nearly every hand in the line, does everything but kiss the babies, then steps onto the court. A canopy of darkness has unfurled across the clear, star-lit sky. It's time to play ball.

The barricades are removed, the gates opened and the spectators let in. The bleachers fill in a matter of seconds. But a major problem develops – the referees haven't shown up. The Entertainers Classic is the biggest street basketball tournament in the United States. It's been going on all summer at this fabled Harlem park, and tonight the semifinals of the tournament's most elite division are scheduled to take place. But no referees means no games. And so, with a look of bewilderment spread across his face, the tournament director announces that the games will have to be postponed until tomorrow. If it were not for the police presence, the place would erupt.

"I'm still getting paid for this," says Speedy as he walks back to his friend's car. "I usually get paid eight hundred dollars a game, but I'll settle for two hundred dollars tonight. I got expenses that need to be taken care of. And, man, my time is money."

Speedy jumps in the car and heads to a corner in south-central Harlem. It sits atop a high-arching hill, offering a spectacular vista to the south of the pulsing lights that illuminate the New York night. The ethereal view contrasts with the reality of this part of the city. At night, this night, this corner on Amsterdam Avenue can be perilous. Hopelessness lives here, alongside the bug-eyed junkies and the short-skirted prostitutes. "I'm going in to talk to my man," says Speedy, as he gets out of the car.

The man Speedy is about to meet is the sponsor of the best street basketball team in New York City. He is young, in his twenties, very wealthy, and he allowed Speedy to bring a reporter to this meeting on the condition that he remain anonymous. He owns five new cars that gleam as if they've just been driven off the lot, vehicles that stick out sharply in this run-down neighborhood. No one will say absolutely that this person is a drug dealer – such things aren't discussed openly in the neighborhood – but more than a few of his players have suggested it. For him, the glory of being associated with a team that dominates playground tournaments up and down the East Coast is well worth the tens of thousands of dollars he has spent this summer as its sponsor. The team's victories are good for business. Whatever that business is.

"I'm under contract for eight hundred dollars a game," says Speedy. "But think about it. We have fifteen guys on the team, the top players in the city, who are all under contract. We play, like, four games a week, all summer long. That means my man is paying a hell of a lot of money to be our sponsor and to get the street cred that goes with it."

The sponser is in a restaurant, and he greets Speedy with a handshake that quickly melts into a hug. "No game tonight, huh?" he says to Speedy. "That's OK. We'll kick some ass tomorrow. Here's two hundred for the effort. Go get yourself something nice."

"Thanks, bro," Speedy says. He walks back out into the cool darkness of the night, jumps in the car and heads home to Brooklyn.

So ends another day in the life of James "Speedy" Williams – one of the best basketball players you've never heard of.

Speedy, twenty-nine, is as close to a professional playground basketball player as you'll find. Like the other great pickup artists on the street, he is almost certainly talented enough to play in the NBA. But for a variety of reasons, he never has – and never will – sign a million-dollar contract. Speedy makes his living playing basketball for drug dealers.

The most dangerous game he ever participated in took place in the summer of 1995. The money Speedy would earn – more than $1,500 – made palatable the idea of playing in a basketball game that was as dicey as Russian roulette, but it was nevertheless with a heavy sense of dread that he stepped onto the basketball court at Hoffman Park in Queens that August day. He knew that many of the 300 people who had gathered to watch the game were carrying weapons. He knew that with a total of $20,000 riding on the outcome, every move he made – every drive to the basket, every jump shot, every pass – would be carefully and critically analyzed by every spectator. But most important, Speedy knew that if he didn't lead his team to victory, the consequences might be devastating. Even deadly.

"You never know what's going to happen when you're playing for twenty thousand dollars," says Speedy. "If somebody thinks you're dogging it or not trying your hardest – well, it could be life-threaten-ing."

Speedy doesn't use drugs and he rarely drinks alcohol, but he often plays basketball for drug dealers. In 1995, the dealer of Speedy's choice went by the handle of Pooch. Drug games – games in which dealers wager large sums of money on teams that they recruit, assemble and subsidize – are as much a part of life in New York as three-card monte scams. A dealer operates on the principle that a basketball team that can dominate his competitors' teams will enhance his reputation and his image among the clientele. But to get the best players, dealers must proffer thick wads of money, expensive clothes and top-of-the-line bas-ketball shoes. The lure of lucre has become so great in these games that some Division I college players who have returned home to New York for the summer have been known to participate.

Speedy plays because he needs the money to survive. Dealers like Pooch have been pandering to Speedy for nearly a decade, and though Speedy understands that there is no honor in playing among thieves, he is nevertheless willing to compromise his ideals in order to support his family. "I know that it's wrong to play in these games," says Speedy, "But, hey, I got people who deal in some shady business looking out for me. If I need anything, all I have to do is ask them for it."

In that 1995 game at Hoffman Park, Pooch's team raced out to a double-digit lead, with Speedy scoring about half the team's points. Like most drug games, this one would end when one side reached 100. Halfway through the game it became clear that Speedy's team was going to win easily, and the game quickly devolved into a war of attri-tion. "The other team figured the only way they could win was to hurt us," says Speedy. "We only had six guys on our team, so if two get hurt, it's over. We have to forfeit."

With his team leading 90–72, Speedy drove hard to the basket. Leav-ing a defender in his wake with a cross-over dribble Tim Hardaway would envy, Speedy slithered into the lane, then took off, climbing the invisible staircase. When his jump reached its apex, Speedy flicked the ball toward the basket. Just as it left his hand, a defender slid over and undercut him with his shoulder. Speedy landed flat on his back as the ball trickled through the net.

His legs tingled. He couldn't breathe. If he had been unable to go on, Pooch's team would have had to forfeit despite its double-digit lead. "I really didn't think I'd be able to get up," Speedy says. "But we only needed a few more buckets, so I was able to stick it out. It was rough, but we ended up winning. Even though my body ended up losing."

What wasn't rough was the paycheck. For about ninety minutes of basketball and an assortment of bumps and bruises, Speedy was handed fifteen $100 bills.

"Speedy is a genius, an absolute genius on the court," says Nick Murphy, former head coach at Medgar Evers College in Brooklyn, where Speedy played for two years. "The NBA should be laughed at for not picking up this guy. I've been judging talent for a long, long time, and I can say without hesitation that a player of Speedy's caliber only comes along every ten or fifteen years in the entire country. He's *that* good.

"I saw Speedy attend a Knicks camp at SUNY-Purchase. With my own two eyes I saw [former Knicks point guard] Derek Harper grab Speedy's jersey when he was guarding him. Harper, one of the top point guards in the league, couldn't guard Speedy. What is the NBA thinking?"

A good question. If nothing else, Speedy Williams certainly *looks* like a professional basketball player. He has big, soulful brown eyes. When he smiles, which is often, light flickers off his gold-capped left front tooth. His legs, though chicken-wire thin, are firm and muscular, and he's quick as a jackrabbit (hence the nickname). But the most impressive feature of his physique is his upper body, which bursts with muscles in places most people don't even have places. Though Speedy stands just five-foot-eleven, with that muscular torso he's strong enough to push around bigger, taller players.

Such strength is the essence of a New York playground player. In the Big Apple, where the outside shot became extinct about the time Robert Moses was ruling the city, you have to have upper-body strength to survive in the Darwinian world of street basketball. Most playground games are decided by the team that dominates the four-foot triangle under the basket, placing primacy on those elements of the game that involve brute force, such as rebounding and positioning.

Without question, though, Speedy's demeanor is what makes him the pure embodiment of New York basketball. His hubris makes Allen

Iverson's on-court attitude look like monkish humility. When Speedy goes one-on-one, he doesn't want merely to win; he wants to embarrass his opponent, make him look like a fool. He dribbles the ball between the other guy's legs at every opportunity. He calls each of his shots, just to let everyone within earshot know he can't be stopped. And, of course, while Speedy plays, an incessant cacophony of trash talk cascades from his mouth. *You got nothing. No game. Show me, cuz. Bring it. C'mon now, bring it. I've been waiting for you all my life.* And on and on. With Speedy, basketball is perpetual motion.

"I probably make around fifty thousand dollars a year playing ball," says Speedy. "Most of it comes during the summer when I play guys one-on-one out in the streets, or playing in big money games, like the one in Queens. But I play every day of the year, and I'll take anybody on one-on-one at any time."

That $50,000 a year doesn't seem to take Speedy very far. The wooden stairs leading up to his fourth-floor two-bedroom apartment in the Crown Heights section of Brooklyn creak when ascended, as if to warn tenants that someone is coming. It's the only alarm Speedy has for his fiancée, Nicole King, and their baby, Jasmine. The apartment shakes as a subway train rumbles by on the track just a quarter-block away. The baby screams. Nicole asks Speedy to calm Jasmine. This is not Norman Rockwell's vision of America. And it is certainly not how Speedy, when he was a young boy, envisioned his life at age twenty-nine.

"I never thought we would have to live here," says Speedy in a rare serious tone. "I always thought I'd be able to get out of the poor neighborhoods and buy a real nice house. I still think I can. Nicole and I are saving money so we can move. I want my daughter to grow up in a nice neighborhood and in a nice house. We have big dreams for Jasmine, and this isn't the right place for her to grow up."

The baby's room also serves as storage space for nearly two dozen of Speedy's trophies, some as tall as six feet, which are clustered in one corner. In another corner is a stack of newspaper articles detailing Speedy's exploits. But something doesn't feel quite right in this room. The legend-in-waiting deserves a grander pantheon. These trophies and these articles seem more like an afterthought, pushed to the side like old clothes. Looking at the trophies, you wonder if Speedy will end up like John Updike's Rabbit Angstrom, an aging basketball star who has outlived his legend, an athlete whose promise has turned to regret. Perhaps in time Speedy will gain mythic status in New York basketball lore – perhaps he will become his generation's version of Earl "the Goat" Manigault, the Harlem hero who dominated the streets of New York in the 1960s. But for now, in this room, the legend is stuffed into a corner.

Speedy grew up in the Forrest housing projects in the Bronx, an armada of high-rises at 149th Street and Park Avenue. His father, James Sr., worked at Lennox Hill Hospital as a respiratory oxygen technician, and his mother, Ernestine, worked at Columbia Presbyterian Hospital in Manhattan as a nurse. Speedy's parents preached a not uncommon sermon – one of a strong work ethic and academic vigilance. Sometimes the message sank in; sometimes it didn't. At Morris High in the Bronx, Speedy showed an interest in photography, but not always in his schoolwork, or even in basketball.

"The coach wanted me to play varsity my freshman year, but to put it bluntly, I wasn't that good of a kid when I was in high school," says Speedy. "I was really into photography and I also was into hanging out with my friends late at night. I didn't have the discipline to play ball. I preferred to cruise around and tour the city with my friends. The worst thing we ever did was graffiti a few times, but we were basically up to no good most of the time."

Nearly every player who makes it to the NBA begins his journey to basketball nirvana by junior high school at the latest. The pre–high school years are a crucial developmental stage, one in which players learn discipline and respect for the game. Speedy had a prime opportunity to gain such experience by playing for the Gauchos, a prestigious youth team in New York that has bred such players as Rod Strickland and Kenny Anderson. But though he harbored dreams of playing in the NBA, Speedy turned down the chance.

"I wanted to be the main man," he says. "When I play on a team I want to be the one everyone looks to at crunch time. I could have played for the Gauchos, but I probably would've had to share time and start on the bench because I didn't have a big reputation at that time. I can't handle that. It's hard to admit, but I want to be the one you look to to carry the team."

Although Speedy passed on the opportunity to play for the Gauchos when he was in junior high, he didn't pass when the chance came to earn a quick buck by bamboozling someone on the court. After sampling the basketball hustler's life just one time, he became addicted to playing for money.

Speedy says he'll never forget the first time he played for cash: The memory is seared in his mind like that of a first kiss. It was a late fall afternoon in 1984. Speedy, sixteen at the time, was going one-on-one on a neighborhood court, flashing that smile of his as he demolished all comers. This didn't sit well with a man named Tyrone who was looking on, because it was the residents of Tyrone's apartment building whom Speedy was making look like fodder for the Harlem Globetrotters. Speedy, in effect, was "dissing" Tyrone's entire building. Tyrone took umbrage and challenged Speedy to a money game, one-on-one. Only the street ethics of the Bronx can spawn such an event.

One-on-one money games normally go to 15 points – 1 point per basket – and when you score a basket, you keep the ball. These days Speedy usually plays for $200 a game, though occasionally the wager reaches as high as $1,000. The bet this time was $250, and the game was to 11.

Accepting the challenge, Speedy hurried back to his building to round up his share of the wager. But as word of the game spread, residents began pouring out onto the street to watch and support Speedy in the unfolding melodrama. Nearly fifty residents from Speedy's building showed up, as did about the same number from Tyrone's. Everyone was betting. Everyone was yelling. As he walked into this combustible atmosphere, Speedy couldn't stop smiling. This, he realized, was his idea of paradise.

"Nobody really thought I had a chance," recalls Speedy. "Tyrone was, like, six-foot-seven, with a great vertical jump, so everyone thought he would just back me in and dunk the ball every point. Well, nobody is going to back me in. I told myself before the game that I would not let Tyrone come inside."

Tyrone didn't. Though Speedy was a good eight inches shorter than his opponent, he continually pushed the rail-thin Tyrone off the box. And when Speedy had the ball, Tyrone had no chance. As the rest of

New York would soon discover, no matter who he is playing against, Speedy simply cannot be guarded one-on-one. Speedy won in a laugher, 11–3. It was the easiest – and quickest – money he ever made. So began a career in hoops hustling.

Speedy explains his secret. "I play guys that are six-foot-six or six-seven all the time, and they always want to play because they think they can just back me under the basket and then use their height to score an easy bucket. But all I do is play basketball, all day, every day, and I've developed a strength and stamina that surprises guys. When ballplayers try to back me in, I'm strong enough to keep them outside, where they have to rely on a perimeter shot. That's my game.

"When I have the ball, I'm quicker than everyone I play and just run them from side to side, trying to wear them down. I'll drive, get close, then fake left with my left hand and shoot right, or I'll fake with my right hand and shoot left. I've been doing this for a long time, and I haven't found anyone who can stop me."

He's a prodigy without a program. Speedy never did play high school basketball. Friends of his like Rod Strickland, who earns millions of dollars a year playing in the NBA, got involved in organized basketball early on. Now they're financially secure. But Speedy doesn't regret his decision not to play – mostly because it wasn't a decision he had to make. Like so many multitalented players who never reach the NBA, Speedy loves to play basketball, but only on his terms. He doesn't follow orders well. He can't abide by someone else's philosophy. He doesn't want to pass the ball when he thinks he should shoot. And most of all, he doesn't like to be coached.

Early on, Speedy thought he would play high school ball. In both his sophomore and junior years, he attended the first two days of tryouts. He quickly wowed the coaches at Morris High – little surprise, given Speedy's abilities on the court. But both years he left the tryouts after the second day, never to return.

His explanation of why left comes in typical Speedy-speak, leaving you no more edified than before. "Don't know why," he replies, "I just do what I think is right."

Speedy worked at McDonald's during high school. He mopped floors and hauled boxes of food off the supply trucks and down into the basement. He earned $3.85 an hour, working there until he graduated in the spring of 1987.

In his first year after graduation, Speedy worked for UPS as a delivery driver. But one day in the summer of 1988, Nick Murphy saw Speedy play in a street game at 135th Street Park, behind Harlem High School. Like the Morris High coaches, Murphy quickly became enchanted with Speedy's game. What he remembered most vividly about that midsummer's night was Speedy's toughness. He recalls watching Speedy take some of the hardest fouls he can remember seeing, but every time Speedy was knocked down, he would jump back up and exact his revenge.

"I remember it was point-game for Speedy's team, and Speedy had the ball on a fast break," Murphy recalls. "It was one-on-two, but Speedy decided to drive the lane anyway. Speedy went straight at the first guy, on the left side of the lane, 100 miles per hour – then stopped on a dime and spun. The kid who was defending just fell down like a cripple. It was the funniest damn thing I ever saw. Against the other defender, a guy who was about six-foot-six, 250 pounds, Speedy jumped straight into him. Speedy actually went higher than this kid and got his shot off. The guy drilled him, but the ball went in. Point game. Just like that.

"When I saw that, I ran as fast as I could to my car to get a pen and paper to write this kid's name down. The kid is phenomenal."

Murphy told Speedy that if he came to Medgar Evers, he would do everything within his power to help him financially and academically. Murphy thought of Speedy as a rough jewel that just needed some polishing. If he could do that polishing – through coaching, and by placing Speedy in a stable situation where he could concentrate on basketball and books – Speedy could indeed become that rarest of players, a true star.

Despite Speedy's reservations – "I've never been the college type," he says – he attended Medgar Evers beginning in the fall of 1989. In his freshman year he averaged 24 points a game, second in the CUNY athletic conference. As a sophomore he averaged 20 points a game. But Speedy wasn't enjoying basketball. His teammates were mostly players from the Bronx and Brooklyn, and they feuded like the Hatfields and the McCoys. The infighting between players didn't leave them much energy for their opponents, and apathy was a problem. After Speedy's second season, Murphy quit. Without his coach's influence, faculty members stopped giving Speedy the breaks he had grown accustomed to. By the end of his sophomore year, Speedy was on the verge of flunking out. "I was going to have to bust my butt to make it after my sophomore season," says Speedy, "So I was outta there."

He then hooked on with a club team called Prime Time, known in street-ball circles as one of the finest nonprofessional teams in the country. James Ryan owns and coaches the team. A pharmacist who lives in Long Island, he is adept at recruiting top talent. NBA stars Anthony Mason and Kenny Anderson have played on Prime Time during the summer. The team – or, more accurately, the organization – has nearly 100 players on its roster, and it competes in tournaments around the world.

Ryan pays for his players' travel, supplies them with a hefty per diem, and always helps out when they're in a bind. Prime Time has won the open division in the national "Hoop It Up" tournament five of the last six years, taking home a purse of $20,000 each year they won.

After Speedy left Medgar Evers, Ryan personally recruited him to play for Prime Time, and Speedy spent three years on the organization's "A" team, but he quit in 1994. "Basically, I got tired of beating up on people so bad," says Speedy. "And people told me it was time for me to go away. They said I was too good not to be playing professionally. So I left."

Soon afterward, fate seemed to smile on Speedy. His performance at a tryout with the Continental Basketball Association's Scranton Minors left the coaching staff speechless. They signed him to a contract on the spot. Speedy delivered for the Minors: They were 8–12 when he arrived but were 12–3 with Speedy on the roster over the season's final fifteen games. Speedy averaged 19 points a game during the 1993–94 season, and his on-court tricks astounded Scranton coach Al Clocker. One particular basket is indelibly printed on Clocker's mind. In a single trip up the court, Speedy dribbled the ball through the legs of one opponent, bounced it *over* another defender, then wiggled into the lane, drove the basket and double-pumped, reversing the ball from his right to his left hand before laying it in. After seeing enough of such moves, Clocker called a friend to see if he could cut Speedy a break. The friend was Red Klotz, founder and owner of the Washington Generals, permanent opponents of the Harlem Globetrotters. Clocker told Klotz, "I got one hell of a Globetrotter for you."

"Speedy definitely has the skills of an NBA player," says Clocker. "When he plays under control, he's as good as there is anywhere. He creates shots for other players. He's the best ball-handler I've ever had on my team. He's a great streak shooter. I've seen him nail ten or fifteen in a row in a game. But the thing that really sticks out is that he knows how to get the crowd involved. Whatever it takes to get fans into a game – stealing the ball, waving them on, talking real loud, any type of gesture – Speedy will do it. He does it without having to try. That's why I thought he would be such a great Globetrotter."

When Scranton concluded its 1993–94 season, Clocker sent Speedy to work out for the Globetrotters, but no slots were available, However, Klotz and John Ferrari, the general manager of the Generals, adored his game, and they offered Speedy a job as a General. "We're very selective in who we take," says Klotz. "And Speedy was an easy choice."

Says Ferrari: "What sticks out in my mind about Speedy was that it took two months of me calling his apartment, leaving about a thousand messages on his answering machine, before we could even get him to come and try out. Most guys would jump at the chance, but Speedy just didn't seem all that interested.

"When we finally got him on the team, Speedy seemed out of step. On our tour, you have to be organized and on time. Unfortunately, that's not Speedy's strong point. You could say he was our Dennis Rodman. Speedy has a whole lot of game – no doubt about that – but in the end his free spirit got in the way of the tour."

Says Speedy: "I would have been a great Globetrotter, but I'm a head case. In my first season with the Generals I got in an argument with an official. A guy from the Trotters decked me as I was going to the rack, and the ref didn't make a call. I said, 'Why are you going to let me get hurt playing show basketball?' He ignored me, but I was on him for the rest of the game. He didn't appreciate it and told Red." Speedy pauses, lowers his eyes to the ground and mumbles, "Not the best career move."

The Globetrotters' job offer never came.

So now Speedy is his own boss. He has done some commercials for

Adidas, and he appeared in the movie *Above the Rim*. (Don't believe the hype about his game? Rent the movie.) More than anything, though, Speedy is a professional street basketball player. That's his craft, his trade. As the summer of 1995 was giving way to fall, it became clear that Speedy was born to work for himself, to play one-on-one for a living.

The scene was the last big-money game of the summer. Speedy had been playing in the Rucker Tournament, and early on he had actually lost a bet – "one the few times ever," he says – after boasting that he would score 40 points in one game. He put down 35, but a loss is a loss, and Speedy was determined to make his money back. So when Speedy was challenged to a one-on-one by another player – a guy who thought Speedy's game was a little too cute – Speedy's immediate reaction was, "When?"

The stakes would be $1,500. Speedy, of course, never fronts his own money. He borrows from those who can afford to carry around that kind of cash. In return, Speedy gives them a cut of the winnings, usually 50 percent. If Speedy loses, he owes nothing to whoever fronted him. Such are the rules of the street. That game went down at Rosedale Park in the Bronx. Of the roughly 150 spectators on hand, only 8 or 9 were supporting Speedy. He doesn't like to put himself in such situations, but he thought it would be easy money. As Speedy walked onto the court, he took solace in the fact that he'd been in a more dangerous situation at Hoffman Park earlier in the summer. His opponent was six-foot-five, but giving up height is hardly new to Speedy. As usual, he was talking smack as the game began. The game didn't last long.

"In all of my years of playing, nothing like that has ever happened," says Speedy. "The game was going to sixteen, and I was winning seven–two. After I scored my seventh basket the guy quit. I couldn't believe it. He said I was fouling him by boxing him out too hard.

"Listen: When you play for money, you have to play aggressive. He threw me down twice. I only made two calls. He made seven calls. I didn't call him when he threw me on the floor. But you could see that the guy was nervous. He went into the game thinking he was just going to back me down. He didn't realize how strong I was. I wore him down. And ain't no one man who can play me straight up."

No surprise, Speedy won the $1,500.

Speedy has not lacked for chances with the pros. Since his stint with Scranton, he has had at least a half-dozen offers for tryouts from CBA teams. "I screwed up my last tryout with the Harrisburg Hammerheads because I missed the ride that was going to take me there. Once I knew I was going to be late, I figured they would think I have an attitude problem, and I'd be in the doghouse. So I didn't even go to the tryout."

There have also been about a dozen offers to play in Europe, and even offers from as far away as the Philippines. He has turned them all down. "I don't want to leave my family," he says. "Plus, I need people I know around me."

So Speedy is stranded in Crown Heights. But don't pity him. True, he may have better served himself had he been able to take orders from refs, coaches and owners, had he stuck it out at Medgar Evers or with Prime Time. But as he gets older and his life gets complicated, Speedy finds sanctuary on the basketball court. That's his Shangri-la, his Eden.

Players like Speedy keep basketball – real, vibrant, street basketball – alive. And Speedy loves his life. He loves playing one-on-one for money. He loves being the best player on the court, and he loves being "the Man." His life may have its perils but he is happy. Speedy isn't making millions in the NBA, but when he's on the court – calling his shots on you, dribbling between your legs, or just making you look like a fool – he flashes a million-dollar smile.

◆ ◆ ◆

In the corner of the basketball court at Howard Park in Brownsville, Brooklyn, lies a mix of glass and plastic that shimmers with the reflection of the late-afternoon sun. Next to the pile is an empty brown vial with a black plastic topper. A 40-ounce bottle of malt liquor, its contents long gone, rolls back and forth over a crack in the pavement that emanates from an intersection with the iron fence that surrounds the playground, widens as it snakes its way towards the free throw line, and spider-webs from there into a dozen smaller fissures reaching beyond a faded three-point line. The pile in the corner is stuff strewn together in a way that resembles a Pollock abstract, but it is somehow too neat to be there randomly. Someone swept up the shards of glass and the garbage and left it there. Perhaps it was the two kids playing ball on the court. They shoot at rims bent awkwardly toward the ground, and at backboards tilted to the right. As they play, the boys are oblivious to the destruction that serves as their backdrop.

Just weeks earlier, in a Brownsville park like this, a sniper's bullet nearly killed a police officer who was making a phone call to his precinct, and days earlier a stray gunshot from a botched robbery attempt down the block almost killed a teenager walking nearby. Some months before, a woman's body had turned up behind Public School 183 – bound, gagged and burned beyond recognition. "This place is shot," says a New York City cop who has been walking the beat in Brownsville for four years but refuses to give his name. "Kids here start out dead."

Ramel Williams, fourteen years old, differs. "It's not that bad," he says. Immediately he is goaded by his friends standing nearby to "tell the truth." "OK," he admits. "It's not easy." Perhaps that is why the two boys continue to shoot as if they were playing in the middle of Madison Square Garden: Maybe they are too hardened to care.

Greg "Jacko" Jackson surveys the scene as he drives from Howard Park to the Hole. He grew up here, went on to play with the Knicks and the Phoenix Suns, and then returned to run the Brownsville Recreation Center. Oddly, he feels safe here. There's not a cop in sight, but, says Jackson, "That's because we don't need police around here. It's safe enough." He knows things aren't perfect. Last summer someone stole the copper wiring from the million-dollar air-conditioning system at his rec center, rendering the machine useless. But touring the parks reminds him that more good than evil dwells here. Seeing the kids on the courts gives him hope.

This part of Brownsville is the birthplace of modern basketball. Bob Cousy, Oscar Robertson, Julius Erving, Larry Bird, Magic Johnson, Michael Jordan – all are direct descendants of the playground style that was forged on the asphalt in Brownsville, Williamsburg, the Lower East Side, Harlem and the Bronx. Forget the peach baskets, the YMCA and Springfield, Mass. Lose the image of burly young Christian men in matching outfits playing basketball as a wholesome winter alternative to summertime sports. The game of power and finesse we watch today was born in a time and place of quiet desperation, the same desperation that swept that pile of junk into the corner of Howard Park. Visit the playground, and you'll see that Naismith's original concept has as much to do with today's graceful, fluid game of hoops as Ford's Model T has to do with the Ferrari.

For all its problems – crime, unemployment, high dropout rates – the Brownsville of today is not much different from the Brownsville of the early 1900s. The people of Brownsville struggled to survive back then, just as they do now. "We were poor," says Sammy Kaplan, who grew up in Brownsville between 1912 and 1930. "We didn't know about steak and shrimp. We just wanted to eat. When I went to a restaurant, I ordered soup and fifteen pieces of bread. I get upset today when I read about the ghetto kids saying they're poor, they can't do anything. We never missed a damn thing. We just went outside and played."

Brownsville today is 81 percent African American. The Brownsville of 1910–1930 was also a ghetto – a Jewish ghetto. The first Jew settled in Brownsville in 1886, and was soon followed by thousands of others. In the 1910s and 1920s, the little village of Brownsville, Brooklyn, developed into a sanctuary for Jews newly arrived from Eastern Europe. A two-mile square bounded by Livonia Avenue, Junius Street, Pitkin Avenue and Stone Avenue, Brownsville resembled the *Shtetls* (small towns) where many such immigrants grew up. Signs were printed in Yiddish, as were newspapers. The streets in Brownsville were named for Jewish personalities – Herzl Street, Strauss Street. So self-contained was the community that a resident of Brownsville could go his entire adult life without speaking a word of English. By 1925, there were 400,000 people living in Brownsville, 75 percent of whom were Jewish.

Jews dominatated basketball in its early development. The Young Men's Hebrew Association was formed in 1874 with an eye toward teaching Jewish immigrants how to be good Americans. Promoting the notion that athletics and morality were intertwined, the Y encouraged young men to be as active as possible in athletics. Basketball became especially popular, and with the Jews' burgeoning success in sports an old stereotype was shed and a new image formed.

In 1917 *The American Hebrew*, a Jewish newspaper based in New York, captured the new spirit generated in the Jewish community as

Jewish boys from the settlement houses of New York City dominated high school basketball in the city:

> The evolution of the Jew in this country from a shrunken, wizened creature afraid of its own shadow into a being unafraid, buoyant and erect ... how splendidly resilient the Jews ... two generations ago he cowered timidly in the ghettos of the dark countries: now he leaps toward the light like a young god of the sun.

Like young African Americans today, Jews in the early part of the century saw basketball as a way out, as a means of achieving equal social footing. "We were living in a ghetto," says Kaplan. "We used basketball as an escape from the conditions we were living in and the way people treated us. We were a new generation who didn't want to be punished for the ethnic backgrounds of our parents." Such was the attitude of young Jewish men throughout the country – for example, at the Kaufman Settlement House in Indianapolis and among the "Fighting Rabbis" of the 1920s, a team that dominated the basketball tournaments at the Emanuel Cohen settlement house in Minneapolis.

In Philadelphia in 1918, young Eddie Gottlieb hoodwinked the South Philadelphia Hebrew Association (SPHA) into buying uniforms for him and his friends so that they could organize their own club team. What began as a group of guys filling time mushroomed into a professional team that rivaled any in the nation. "It wasn't hard," Gottlieb said in a 1979 interview. "At the time, Jewish players dominated the game the way blacks do today. It was their big game." Max Patkin, who would gain fame as "the Clown Prince of Baseball," was a SPHA. So was Red Klotz, who went on to coach the Washington Generals. Harry Litwack, who coached basketball at Temple for forty-one years, began his career as a SPHA.

"South Philadelphia was known for basketball," says Litwack. "That was *the* sport there. It was inhabited by a lot of people of the Jewish faith. All around the poles there would be like a peach basket, and that's how we learned how to throw the ball in the basket. From there, as you grew up, every neighborhood had a team. You would go around places in South Philly – pretty near all over Philly – to play other teams."

Like New York City, Philadelphia, especially South Philadelphia, was a basketball nest. "Nobody had what we had, in terms of talent and

passion for the game," says Sid Gurschkov, who grew up in South
Philly in the 1930s. "Some people in New York might fight you on that,
but it's true." Sid and his friends played the game in an alley near Fifth
and Wolf, behind the local grocery store. Each day they would steal a
ladder from the store's shed, climb ten feet up a nearby telephone pole,
and nail a metal hoop to the pole. And each day the cops would come
and make them tear it down. "They always gave it back to us in one
piece," Gurschkov recalls. "In those days we didn't have too many
places to play unless you wanted to play."

Gurschkov's mother and father were Jews who, shortly after emi-
grating from Russia, settled in South Philadelphia because it looked
and sounded like home. In the tightly packed ghetto of South Philly, as
in Brownsville and other large Jewish communities, there was no room
for tennis courts, golf courses, expansive baseball diamonds or football
fields. But tucked in between the tenements and settlement houses
were concrete lots, and attached to every schoolhouse was a blacktop.
In a neighborhood full of rambunctious boys with little else to do,
these were everything.

"The kid with the wire cutter – who could cut through the fence of
the schoolyard and get us in on a Sunday – was always the most popular kid in the neighborhood," says Abe Gerchik, who grew up in
Brownsville in the 1920s and 1930s.

"Children of Jewish immigrants always took to sports because it was
an easier way to join the American mainstream," says Sammy Kaplan.
"And in our case it was basketball, because of the crowded conditions
in the ghetto. Other than the candy store on Pitkin Avenue, there
wasn't anywhere else for us to hang out. The game gave us a purpose
and an interest. The courts were near our home, and all we needed was
a ball."

Sometimes not even that. Gerchik remembers playing in the alley
with a small rubber ball from the Spalding Company and using the
bottom rung of a fire escape ladder as the "hoop." At other times
balled-knit hats or socks would suffice as balls, and garbage cans as
baskets. "We would draw a chalk line around the circumference of the
can, two paces away from its bottom," says Gerchik. "The guy on offense could not shoot from within that circle."

In 1910, seventy-five of New York City's ninety-two public schools had schoolyards with basketball hoops. The next year, William Lee, a New York City recreation center director, created the first playground basketball league, aiming at indoctrinating as many kids as possible into the game. The league would play outside, on playground courts, and thus promote mass participation. Lee organized the league tournament into brackets, with elite teams from each playground competing against one another. The showdowns drew fans, and the sport's popularity grew. Playground basketball became a spectator sport.

By the late 1930s basketball had come to be defined as "the Jewish game" – the meaning of which sometimes came filtered through the prism of the era's stereotypes and prejudices. In 1937 Paul Gallico, the sports editor at the *New York Daily News* in the late 1920s and early 1930s, wrote:

> Curiously, above all others, the game appeals to the temperament of Jews ... [While] a good Jewish basketball player is a rarity ... Jews flock to basketball by the thousands ... It places a premium on the alert, scheming mind ... flashy trickiness, artful dodging, and general smart aleckness, [traits naturally appealing] to the Hebrew with his Oriental background.

Stanley Frank, a campus sports editor at City College of New York (CCNY) in 1936, employed what would today be referred to as more politically correct language when he wrote that the Jewish affinity for basketball stemmed from "the characteristics inherent in the Jew ... mental agility, perception...imagination and subtlety ... If the Jew had set out to invent a game which incorporated traits indigenous to him ... he could not have had a happier inspiration than basketball ... Ever since Dr. James Naismith came up with a soccer ball, two peach baskets and a bright idea ... basketball players have been chasing Jewish athletes and never quite catching up with them."

One of those they were chasing was Nat Holman.

You push the button and grainy images begin to flicker on a dusty television screen: A 93-year-old man, his eyes watery and his skin sallow, is speaking eloquently and softly about basketball at the dawn of the twentieth century. But this is not just any home movie, not just any elderly, gray-eyed, gray-haired man talking about the way it used to be. On the television screen, speaking via low-quality videotape, is Nat

Holman, the first playground basketball player to be known around the world. He *was* the way it used to be.

"They used to call me the Babe Ruth of playground basketball," says the crackling voice on the videotape, just one artifact in the rich collection of material that Holman's family has saved and that documents his life and times. "When I played basketball, there was no stuffing – it was all ball-handling, movement, and shooting. Boy, did I love to shoot. But today there's no room for the little fella, so I guess I'm lucky I played in the early part of the century."

Hardly. Born in 1896 during Grover Cleveland's second presidential term and five years after Naismith first hung his peach baskets, Holman was billed as "the world's greatest basketball player" when he toured as one of the Original Celtics as they barnstormed across the country in the early 1920s. But he was more than just a star. Holman shaped the sport in much the same way Beethoven shaped the evolution of music: He routinely did the unthinkable, making the impossible suddenly seem possible. Holman used guile and finesse to improvise moves that, years later, are the foundation of contemporary basketball. Indeed, the family tree of basketball players begins with Holman. The five-foot-eleven, 165-pound guard is, in short, the progenitor of the playgrounds.

"He was simply great," says Red Holzman, who was coached by Holman at City College during the 1940s. "And when I see teams today that play smart, that play with a lot of movement, that play unselfishly, I see the legacy of Nat Holman."

Holman grew up on Manhattan's Lower East Side in a neighborhood of predominantly Jewish immigrants from Eastern Europe. Holman's parents, like Kaplan's in Brownsville and Gurschkov's in South Philly, were confused as to why sports were so important to their children raised in America. They would much preferred their kids to have studied to become doctors or lawyers. Sports generally were frowned upon by the older generations, but to many of the younger generation athletics were everything. And, at the Henry Street Settlement and the Educational Alliance in the early 1900s, everything was basketball.

Holman once succinctly explained why basketball flourished in his neighborhood, as it did in other impoverished areas throughout New York City. "Jewish athletes," he said, "excelled in the sports which required little space, because there was none on the crowded Lower East Side." Basketball also appealed to these kids because money was scarce and basketball required little capital. Holman, in fact, was so poor that when he was seven he couldn't afford a ball. He and his nine siblings would crumple up paper, wrap it with cord and go to the playground to shoot baskets.

Before Holman was even a teenager, he would gather as many of his friends as he could and lead them off in search of a basketball game. By this time he had his own ball, which he would dribble the entire way, past the pickle barrels and vendors, past the horses and pushcarts, until he and his friends arrived at the Seward Park playground on Hester Street. This is where it began. "I learned how to play at Seward Park," Holman said a few years before his death in 1995. "I got my first taste of anti-Semitism when I was playing there and someone in the stands said, 'Get the Jew.'"

Anti-Semitism did not deter the young Holman. He spent so much time at the Seward Park playground that in essence he became a piece of the landscape. From dawn to dusk, Holman could be seen hoisting two-handed set shots from all corners of the court. Sometimes he would play one-on-one for a nickel or a dime; other times he would play for an ice-cream cone. But he always played, always refining his shot and his skills. In those rare moments when he wasn't involved in a game, he was carefully watching the older guys, picking up the moves that constituted the perfect rhythm for playground basketball.

"The playground players knew how to move the ball and move the body," Holman once said. "These men played in small gymnasiums where you had to move fast. You couldn't stand around. Everything was free, voluntary movement."

The first person to take notice of Holman's talent was James Ginnerty, the playground director at Seward Park. He met Holman when Nat was ten, and together they sculpted Holman's game from raw clay into something exquisite. Like most great talents that eventually reach full bloom, Holman had the benefit of good coaching during his formative years.

When Holman was fourteen, Ginnerty asked Nat if he would play for the "Roosevelt Big Five," a playground team that often traveled to towns in the Appalachians, Catskills and Berkshires for games. Holman joined the team and immediately became the most dynamic basketball player in New York City.

The Roosevelt Big Five split their time between playgrounds and in dance halls, where they would play a game, preceded and followed by dancing, an entire package of evening entertainment. The games were black-and-blue affairs, with players looking like they were about to engage in gladitorial combat, wearing hip pads, knee guards and aluminum cups. Cut eyebrows and loose teeth were as common then as floor burns are today.

The pugilistic mentality that pervaded the game during those early years was heightened by the fact that many courts were enclosed by nets or chicken-wire screens as high as ten feet. The cage effect was necessary because boisterous fans often charged the court to get at players and referees. The protective cages were just as dangerous: Players often suffered infections from cutting themselves on rusty chicken-wire.

For his work with the Roosevelt Big Five, Holman earned $6 a night.

When Holman graduated from high school, he turned down an offer to pitch for the Cincinnati Reds, opting instead to stay with his basketball team. Holman was indeed an otherworldly athlete: He remains the only person in the history of New York City high schools to be named All-City in four sports – basketball, baseball, soccer and football.

At age twenty-three, Holman became a player-coach at City College, and there his brilliance flowered. Waving to his players with his trademark curled-up scorecard, Holman would preach a revolutionary brand of basketball that is still in practice today. He taught his players to pass rather than dribble. He showed them the pick-and-roll, the give-and-go, the fast break – plays that transformed the pace of the game from classical symphony to swing. But when he slowed things down, Holman proved to be one of the most astute tacticians the sport has seen. He would move his players around the floor as if they were chess pieces, positioning them precisely where he wanted them to be.

In 1921, while he was still coaching at City College, Holman joined the Original Celtics, the team that pioneered the concept of professional basketball. For six years, the Original Celtics criss-crossed the country, playing 150 games a year, sleeping in buses, washing uniforms in hotel sinks and drying them on radiators – and showing off their remarkable skills. As Joe Lapchick, one of Holman's teammates, said, "Holman could pass the ball through a keyhole."

The stories from Holman's days as a Celtic are legion. One time, playing in front of a hostile and mostly drunk crowd, Holman was fouled as he attempted a shot. He walked to the foul line as the hoots and catcalls cascaded from the crowd, the decibels reaching a deafening level. Holman turned to the opponents' bench, gave them an icy stare, paused for a moment to let the noise reach a crescendo, then, still staring at the bench, unleashed a free throw that hit nothing but net. It is the stuff of legend.

"When I played with the Celtics, we also had this thing called audience participation," Holman once said. "In Scranton one night, Johnny Beckman, one of the greatest Celtics, was hit by a chunk of tobacco while he was at the foul line. Old Johnny rubbed his hand over the side of his face and hollered, 'My god, I'm bleeding.' That was one of the funnier incidents, but often we didn't know what the coal miners were going to throw at us. Many of them came to the games wearing their mining caps with carbide lamps attached and were pretty rough-looking fellows.

"The Celtics were a great team. We had speed, could shoot clean from the outside and knew we were the best ball-handling outfit in the country. We were also showmen. Always during the last five minutes of the game we would 'pass the button.' Something like the Globetrotters. People in the stands would never know who had the ball. But we played to win, and we only lost about ten games a year."

After he retired from the Original Celtics in 1927, Holman coached City College full-time until 1960, retiring after thirty-seven years with a 421–190 record. The high point of his coaching career came in 1950, when City College pulled the unprecedented double (impossible now) of winning both the NIT and NCAA tournaments. But his career was not without pitfalls. Just one year after winning the NCAA title, Holman was suspended by the New York City Board of Higher Education for "conduct unbecoming to a teacher" when it was discovered that several of his players had shaved points from a basketball game. It would turn into the biggest scandal in college basketball history. Holman always contended that he had no knowledge of his players' deceit,

and two years after he was suspended he was reinstated and fully vindi-
cated. But the basketball program at CCNY, which during the 1940s
was one of the tops in the nation, was de-emphasized, and it has never
returned to Division I status. Some scars never heal.

In the videotape, and among all the yellowed press clippings Holman's family clings to like gold, no mention arises of that ugly incident.
It's for the best, because ultimately Holman will be remembered for
what he did for the game of basketball: He gave it form, texture and
substance. He gave it a standard for all who followed, someone to
measure themselves against.

It was Holman who inspired the Dux basketball club of Brownsville. In
August of 1925, ten fourteen-year-old boys from Brownsville won the
City Championship Tournament of Summer, an event sponsored by
New York's playground department. After their victory, the players began worrying about how they would maintain their rhythm until the
next summer. None of them were on the school basketball team,
which offered the only options for indoor play once the weather turned
cold, and the teens had grown tired of sweeping snow from the playgrounds of P. S. 184 and Nanny Goat Park every winter. So Sammy
Kaplan, one of the boys, came up with a solution: The boys would
organize as a club. Kaplan had learned that so organized, they would
have use of the neighborhood recreation center in the evenings. What's
more, by competing against teams from around the city the kids might
make a few bucks on the side. They called themselves the Dux (Latin
for "leaders" and pronounced Dukes) because, says Kaplan, "by having
only three letters, it was cheap to sew our team names onto our
shorts." The minutes of the club's first meeting tell the story of its
humble origin:

> The summer of 1925 witnessed the organization of four or five new clubs
> in the Brownsville section of Brooklyn. Among them – in fact obscured
> among them – was the DUX A.C.
> The first meeting was held on August 25, 1925, under the largest open-air
> club room in the world. To be specific, it was held under the blue August sky
> with a lumber pile serving as the seats for the ten organizers.
> Scarcely had the officers been inducted into their new offices when the
> meeting was suddenly adjourned without any such motion on the floor. At that

particular moment, the irate owner of the lumber pile appeared uninvited to our meeting with a two-by-four and he succeeded in hitting our dignified president right in the constitution. Immediately, an idea sprang spontaneously to the hearts of the new club members and the result was two broken window panes. This gave the treasurer the first opportunity to exercise his constitutional powers of "making such expenditures as sanctioned by the club."

In the beginning the games were more sideshow than main event. Often, the Dux were hired by a New Jersey team, from Paterson or Newark or Passaic, as predance entertainment. One night in the Bronx, at a gym off Kingsbridge Road, they played a team made up of deaf mutes representing the Bronx Silent Club, the event's sponsor. Whistles being useless in such circumstances, the referees used white flags to call a foul, which is exactly what the Dux were crying by the game's end. Incredibly, the Dux were soundly beaten.

But their successes outnumbered their failures. These sons of immigrants, like today's children of the inner city, learned to love the game of basketball, and to master it. By 1926 the Dux had captured the title at the local rec center; in 1927 they won the citywide boys club championship. "Our style was to move the ball and have everyone handle it, try to get free for a shot or to get loose and receive a pass for a layup," recalls Kaplan. "We did not find the game rough or too physical. Our effort was finesse – moving and cutting to the basket."

The Dux eventually grew from a mere playground team into a touring company. Once, in upstate New York, they shared a vaudeville stage with Red Skelton. They played exhibitions in Wilkes-Barre, Pennsylvania, and in Albany and Boston, traveling on rented buses, accompanied by dates whom they brought along for the dances afterwards.

The more they played, the more they developed a team synchronicism, and the more other teams wanted to challenge them. By 1929, the eighteen-year-old boys were brazen enough to take on all comers. That was a necessity on the eve of the Depresssion, because their families were simply too poor to let an able body leave for college. That summer of 1929 the boys scraped together whatever earnings hadn't gone towards feeding their families and bought a locker space at Washington Bath on Coney Island. Every Sunday, they had their chance to prove how good they were at the playground on 24th Street and Surf Avenue.

Word traveled quickly throughout the city that the Dux reigned. And so players who had left the slums to play college ball eventually drifted back and started showing up at the Washington Bath on the weekends to test their games. Those Sunday afternoon games between the college players, all-stars every one, and the Dux were pure battles between the haves and have-nots. The games were a microcosm of a class struggle being waged across America, and to the locals they were as vital to the collective community spirit as synagogue. In a letter to Kaplan, former Dux Dave Lindenbaum, wrote, "These were rough times for us because none of us had a college education. On those Sundays it was a chance to shine and prove we could have made it if not for the Depression."

Because they cared so much more, the Dux more often than not would win those epic affairs. In 1934, after Kaplan and his teammates had established themselves as the best club team in the city, if not on the entire East Coast, an exhibition was arranged between the Dux and CCNY. Basketball was just gaining recognition as a spectator sport around this time, and such staged games were popular promotions. If Holman and the college could make some money by taking on some fluky club team at a local Jewish community center, the CCNY coach wasn't above it. And the Dux were certainly not going to turn down Holman, their inspiration and the best-known personality in all of basketball. Previewing the game, the *Staten Island Advance*, on March 3, 1934, wrote:

> Very few sport events have ever struck the public's fancy as has this unusual contest. Wherever you go the game is on everyone's lips with the "Monday morning quarterbacks" discussing it vehemently pro and con.
>
> There is no question that the Dux are the cream of the crop of the city's amateur teams, and they will match basket with basket and pass with pass with the City College outfit with the result that the contest, which has raised plenty of excitement around these parts, will turn out to be a classic.

The game was all the more significant because the biggest college basketball game the city had yet seen was played the previous night. In that game, CCNY's bid for its first undefeated season was thwarted by an undefeated NYU. By the time Holman's team dressed for the game against the Dux at the Staten Island JCC, they were looking to redeem themselves against anyone who had the chutzpah to step on the court with them.

For the Dux, whose players were now in their early twenties, this game was the basketball equivalent of a Bar Mitzvah. It had been almost ten years since a group of Jewish teenagers founded their little club in a lumber yard under an August sky. Now they were facing Holman, the man after whose play they had patterned their games, and whom they had inducted into their Hall of Fame as its charter member. Those games on the vaudeville stages, at the park on Coney Island, and at countless rec centers up and down the eastern seaboard – all had been in preparation for such a match as this. As the *Advance* reported the day after the game, the Dux did not disappoint:

> While approximately 600 spectators watched in stupefied amazement, a brilliant JCC Dux quintet scored one of the greatest upsets in metropolitan basketball as they administered a staggering defeat to CCNY by the score of 32–26 last night at the Jewish Community Center court. Hailed as the greatest team in the country, beaten but once this season, City College met its Waterloo at the hands of the Dux, unknown and unheralded in college circles.
>
> Despite the extra seating capacity, the fans virtually stood on one another's heads and crammed every available inch of the gym to welcome a hectic thrilling encounter that left them gasping for breath and physically exhausted as the two teams put on the greatest basketball exhibition ever seen on any [Staten] Island court.

Those were the Dux at their peak. By the time of their historic victory over Holman's CCNY team, the boys from Brownsville's playgrounds were the greatest package of playground talent in the world. But they were considered renegades, partly because they refused to adhere to the usual progression other basketball players in the area made, and also because they were making money off their talents without ever really declaring themselves professionals.

When the Dux beat CCNY, New York City was the capital of college basketball. The toughest games in the country had always been on the playgrounds in Brooklyn, the Bronx and the lower East Side, and the products of these afternoon dramas in the ghetto went on to play for CCNY, Long Island University, St. Johns and New York University. Clair Bee's Long Island University team of 1935–36, which went 25–0, consisted of guys like Leo Merson and Jules Bender, both from the playground. The 1936 U.S. Olympic basketball team included so many former schoolyard players from New York's Jewish ghettos that the team voted to boycott the Berlin Games rather than play under the gaze of Hitler.

With newer players from Brownsville getting the shot at college basketball that Sammy Kaplan and his teammates never had, the Dux's reign as the greatest playground and barnstorming team in the nation came to an end less than five years after its win over CCNY. The team simply could not replenish its roster with enough talent. But there were other reasons for the downfall of the Dux. The game itself was undergoing its most drastic overhaul to date. In the early and mid-1930s, new rules were introduced, such as the 10-second backcourt rule and the 3-second violation, and outdated practices like jumping ball at center court after every basket were eliminated. Innovations were also being made in shooting techniques, like the one-handed jump shot first tried by Stanford's Hank Luisetti in 1936. The effect of these changes was to increase the pace from the slow, deliberate game the Dux had grown up playing in Brownsville. Certain teams, like the all-black Harlem Renaissance, that had been on the playground circuit as long as the Dux were quicker to pick up players schooled in the new style of basketball.

"When the Depression first hit, most of the guys who played for the Dux couldn't afford to go to college," says William "Pop" Gates, who played for the Rens in the late 1930s and early 1940s. "Later in the decade the young kids from Brownsville were going to college instead of the Dux. Since we were an all-black team, none of us were allowed to go to college for basketball, so we were always getting the best boys from the schoolyard."

Gates was born in Alabama, but when he was seven years old, his family moved to Harlem, seeking a better life in the North. Almost immediately, the young Gates learned of basketball's importance in the area. He began playing at the YMCA on 135th Street, between Seventh and Lenox, emulating older players like Willie Smith and Puggy Bell, both of whom would later team with Gates on the Rens. Once in school, Gates took his game to the playground at P. S. 139 at 139th and Lenox. The game there, Gates found, had a different feel than it did on the playgrounds in the South. The new rules fostered a quicker tempo, a game of give-and-gos, dribble-drives and long-range jump shots. "It was a learning process on the playground, picking up different things you didn't learn being coached in the YMCA," says Gates, now eighty-three and still living in Harlem. "The older guys let loose and had fun. From the beginning of every day to the end, you always learned something."

Gates learned enough at P. S. 139 that when he entered Benjamin Franklin High School as a freshman he was already one of the best players in the school. He was a starter each of his four years, although his playground days were numbered. "My coach wouldn't let me play because he thought the concrete was bad for my knees," Gates says. As a senior, Gates led Ben Franklin to the city championship, after which – long before the Kevin Garnetts and Kobe Bryants made it fashionable – he signed on as a pro, joining the Rens straight out of school.

In his first season, Gates averaged 15 points a game, and along with his playground idols Smith and Bell, helped the Rens to a 68-game winning streak. In 1939, at a tournament held in Chicago, the Rens defeated the Oshkosh All-Stars of Wisconsin for the first world championship of professional basketball. John Wooden, the legendary UCLA coach, once called Gates's Rens "the greatest team I ever saw."

The game thrived in impoverished, overcrowded Harlem just as it had in the Jewish ghettos in Manhattan, Brooklyn and the Bronx. But these city kids also played the game for reasons that were, literally, beyond the confines of space. Like players today, they shot baskets all day long, swept snow from the courts, played with deflated balls filled with newspaper. For love of the game, yes, but also for opportunity, escape and, most important, acceptance.

"We once played a team called the Cuffs, another club team, and they mimicked our Jewishness, calling us 'Sammy,' 'Ikey' and 'Abey,'" says Kaplan. "Then a fight broke out. Eventually we played the game, and we kicked their ass on the court. After that, they didn't mimic us anymore."

"Negro people at that time didn't have much to brag about, so we were the idols to many," recalls Gates. "We had to uphold our name and make them proud. Anytime we stepped on the floor we had to have an ego and show the other guys how good we were. It was a

2

The Fundamentalists

The Snug Harbor restaurant on 108th Street in Rockaway, Queens, doesn't look like the kind of place that has played a seminal role in the history of street basketball. On the outside, the restaurant's tan, cement facade and nondescript green awnings blend seamlessly with the beach bungalows that line the street two blocks down to the ocean. Inside, a long oak bar leads into an expansive dining room of varnished wood walls and dim lights. It is, by all appearances, an unremarkable place. Talk to a few of the gray-haired patrons there, though, and you'll soon discover that you've stumbled upon the onetime home of Dick McGuire, the greatest playground basketball player of the 1940s.

Dick, his parents, and his younger brothers Al and John lived in the attic above the restaurant, which at the time was a neighborhood tavern called McGuire's owned by the boys' parents. The exterior was covered in flaky white shingles, the inside walls were white-washed stucco, and the wood-plank floors were always dusty – a place that resembled an old western saloon where the only thing that flowed better than the conversation was the booze. "Really, it was a pit," says Snug Harbor's owner, Frank Gallagher, who bought the building from Dick and his brothers in 1996 but had been renting from the McGuires since 1960. "But all that has changed now."

Indeed, much has changed in Rockaway since Dick grew up here. As he drives down 108th Street, he notices that the old neighborhood appears to be brand new. The bungalows across the street from the bar have been replaced by high-rise apartment buildings. The neigborhood as he knew it is gone: Only an archaelogical dig could uncover the remnants of McGuire's past. Perhaps the most distressing of the changes is that the basketball court on the Boardwalk at the end of the block has been transformed into an in-line skating rink. But Dick still remembers. All he has to do is close his eyes and suddenly before him, before us, are the halcyon summers of his youth.

The endless summer began in 1939. As part of a cleanup effort in conjunction with the 1939 World's Fair, the city of New York built public parks and playgrounds in Rockaway over what had been vacant lots where winos slept off their hangovers. The empty space where 108th Street ended at the Boardwalk in Rockaway was perfectly suited for a blacktop and a couple of hoops. The court stretched for two blocks, from the foot of 108th to 110th Street, with one basket at each end. "They were really small blocks, not like real city ones, but like small alleyways," recalls Norm Ochs, who grew up in the area. The court was amorphous rather than rectangular and was surrounded by a cyclone fence with swinging gates at the 108th and 110th Street entrances. The gates were locked every night, but, as Ochs says, "That didn't matter because we just climbed over the fence." The court was the perfect refuge for Dick, Al, John and their friends – boys who had previously spent their days hanging out at the candy store.

"We would just sit there sipping soda fountain drinks," says Ochs. "There was a court, but it was pretty far from where we lived. Too far to walk. Besides, none of us had a basketball. The only person we knew that did have one was Pam Wilkes. She would ride by on her bicycle with a ball in her front basket. If we wanted to play we had to be nice to her and convince her to let us use her ball. Things changed with the new playground. The parks department actually gave us a ball."

The games at 108th Street were three-on-three, make-it-take-it, the ball going back to the free throw line on every change of possession. The wind off the ocean would play havoc with long-range shots, so the closer you got to the basket, the better your chance of scoring would be. That placed a premium on motion within a half-court space, which meant setting picks and passing rather than dribbling, and playing defense with more bite than the nearby junkyard dogs. Court time depended on it. First one to 7 stays. Winners take the ball out.

The savviest players had an intimate knowledge of the wind patterns off the Atlantic and of the dead spots on the tin backboard. But those games on the blacktop weren't about who had the prettiest two-hand set shot or who scored the most in one afternoon. The tone of the games was set by Dick McGuire, which meant a no-look pass outranked a long-range basket, humility drew more attention than bravado, and a turnover – no matter who committed it – was always followed up with Dick mumbling, "My fault." McGuire outshone every player on the court, yet he was quicker to pass along the praise than he was the ball – something that has never changed. At a Christmas party in 1991, Dave Checketts, the New York Knicks' president at the time, told McGuire, who spent eight seasons with the Knicks from 1949 to 1957 and ended his career there as the team's all-time assists leader, that his number would be retired the following season. "Thank you very much," Dick replied, "but I am going to try to find a way not to be there."

"He'll never tell you," says Al, who coached Marquette to the 1977 NCAA championship and is now a commentator for CBS, "but he is the greatest passer who ever lived. What the kids do now started with Dick."

"I don't know if that is so true," says Dick. "Al's always been a good talker." Al's praise would sound like just a bit of brotherly love splashed with hyperbole if not for all the others who reiterate the point. By the early 1940s, after Dick had proven himself to players throughout the city during his first two years of high school, the ultimate compliment was paid to the gang at 108th and the Boardwalk: Players from Brooklyn, Manhattan and New Jersey began leaving the sanctity of their home courts to come play with Dick and his boys in Queens. "Dick was the best at passing the ball [while] moving toward the basket, curling it around people in front of him," says Carl Braun, who came from Garden City, New Jersey, to play against McGuire on the beach and who later was McGuire's teammate on the Knicks. "He wouldn't take the easy shot. He'd rather pass it off."

"Everyone wanted to come and play Dick, saying they were gonna do this to him or that to him," says Ochs. "When they left all they could say was, 'That guy is good.'"

Rockaway was a quiet place for three seasons of the year, a place where, Al says, "The Jews owned the deli, the Irish owned the bar, and the Italians owned the shoemaker's shop. Everybody knew everybody." People called it Irish Town because so many Irish servants to the wealthy of Brooklyn and Manhattan spent their off days in the pubs and bars in Rockaway. In the summer, though, Rockaway overflowed with beach bums and basketball players. Dolph Schayes used to come in from the Bronx. Chuck Connors, who would play in the NBA and the major leagues before starring in *The Rifleman* television series, shot himself over from Brooklyn. Tommy Heinsohn trekked all the way from Union City, New Jersey. A kid a few years younger than Dick, from the St. Albans section of Queens, came to learn a few things as well: Bob Cousy. Fans would line the Boardwalk, which rose eight feet above the court, and lean over the railing, watching these soon-to-be legends strut their stuff.

"It was a melting pot at the time," says Al. "An event every weekend. The pride and the competition between us from Rockaway and the guys who came in was the biggest thrill. The summer would end, and you would immediately be looking forward to next year and taking on new guys. That's what it was about then."

The best games were always played on Sunday afternoons. "That's when the blue-chippers came out," recalls Al. In the predominantly Irish Catholic Rockaway of the time, most of the boys in the neighborhood had to go to mass. Norm Ochs, who is Jewish, used to walk over to his friend Jackie Craven's house ten minutes before mass every Sunday and ask if Jackie wanted to go play, knowing Jackie would have to go to church. Feigning disappointment that Jackie couldn't join him, Norm would then ask Jackie for his ball and tell him to meet him at the court. By the time Jackie got to the game, twenty-five guys would be waiting ahead of him.

Status on the court was measured by when a kid went to Sunday mass. If you were awful but wanted to get in some games, you attended the 8 a.m. mass and arrived at the court by 10:30. By going early, you could at least play for an hour or two before the better players kicked you off. If you were decent, you went to mass from 10 to 12 and got to the court a little after noon – about the time the non-Catholic kids and guys from out of town started playing. They would need more guys, and the best players wouldn't be out there yet. Those guys all slept late, caught the noon mass, and then stepped onto the court whenever they felt like it. "What hurt was when you realized your skills were getting worse," says Al. "All of a sudden you had to start going to mass at 10 a.m. again if you wanted to play."

When parents couldn't afford to buy their kids new shoes, the players would buy rubber soles from the local five-and-dime and tape them onto their worn-out sneaker bottoms. If the ball was flat, they'd fill it with newspaper. If that didn't work, they'd roll their knit hats together into a big ball. In winter the kids shoveled snow from the court. During the summer they would pop epsom salts to keep from getting dehydrated – nobody dared leave the court and miss some action for a measly sip of water. In short, players did whatever it took to get on the blacktop and stay there. "We didn't aspire to greatness," says Dick. "We just wanted to play."

More precisely, they just wanted to play with Dick McGuire. If he showed up on the court barefoot – having just come over from his parent's bar down the street or walked up from the beach – invariably someone would offer up his kicks to McGuire. Size 9, size 6 – it didn't matter. Dick always played. After mass one afternoon, he played in a suit and dress shoes against some showoffs from Andrew Jackson High. Dick's play at the beach court was always divine, something people talk about to this day. He was a whirling dervish of no-look passes, bounce passes, and pick-and-rolls.

"We didn't know it, but he was the original point guard," says Cousy. "He didn't have anyone to emulate, but the things he did are the things I tried to do. And, eventually, did."

Dick was named New York City's college player of the year in 1948 and 1949. By the time he finished college the infant NBA was ready for him. Selected by the Knicks in the 1949 draft, he became New York's marquee player. As a rookie in 1948–49, McGuire led the NBA with 386 assists. His pinpoint passes and ball-handling lured fans through the gates the way a rookie named Magic Johnson would three decades later. McGuire played eight seasons for the Knicks, leading them to three NBA championship series. (They fell to George Mikan and the Minneapolis Lakers all three times.) After his playing days, McGuire coached the Knicks for two seasons; he now is their top scout. He has never had a day's work that didn't involve the game he spent his childhood summers on the playground perfecting. Even in the winter of his life, McGuire's summer hasn't ended.

When Dick was finally elected to the Basketball Hall of Fame, it was the constant lobbying of Cousy, his Rockaway protegé, that opened the door. McGuire's paltry statistics – he had a career scoring average of 8.0 – caused him to be overlooked for years. But his contributions could never be measured by his stats, by his coaching career or how many great players he scouted. The proof of his ability lay in the accomplishments of others: the dozens of future hall-of-famers who at one time or another played with him. Or Cousy's six NBA championships with the Celtics. Or Al's momentous upset of North Carolina in the 1977 NCAA championship game. How many titles would Boston have won if McGuire hadn't shown Cousy the best way to throw a bounce pass? Would Al have reached the pinnacle of college hoops if he hadn't preached the fundamentals he learned watching Dick play on the Boardwalk in Rockaway? Dick McGuire's play on the blacktop defined a position in modern-day basketball. The prototypical point guard is best admired for what he has passed on, not what he has left behind.

◆ ◆ ◆

Boonie Vaught lives in a small white two-story house with a white picket fence on John Street in Bloomfield, Indiana. An alley runs by the side of his house, connecting John Street to Spring Street one block away. The alley expands every 20 feet to accommodate the driveways and garages of those folks who, like Boonie, live on either side of it. In one driveway a car is jacked up on its rear wheels for some kind of overhaul. In another, three bicycles are strewn haphazardly underneath the carport, making it impossible to park a car there. The other driveways along the alley are similarly undistinguished – except for Boonie's.

Behind Boonie's house, the driveway / alleyway is smaller because a basketball court has encroached on its space. Not just the lone hoop cemented into the ground that comes standard with almost every house in Indiana. There are two hoops here, one at each end of a smooth, gray slab of concrete. And there are basketballs waiting, ready to be plucked from the court and shot through the basket, like daisies that scream out for a vase. One ball sits beneath a basket. Another lies on a weathered and splintered gray wooden bench. A third rests in the still-dewy morning grass. From end to end, the court is about half the size of an NBA court.

Mike Sherrard, a 27-year-old guy from Bloomfield, strolls onto the court on a sleepy Sunday afternoon. He looks no more than sixteen and is slight of build, with a perpetual lump in his bottom lip where he has stuffed some Skoal fine-cut chewing tobacco. Mike grew up down the street from Boonie and has been playing on this court since he could dribble – from his mouth, that is. On this court he developed the rhythm in his jump shot that once made him one of the most feared high school players in the state. Ten years later, that rhythm hasn't deserted him, and with it over the years he has built a reputation as a deadly shooter, not only on the Indiana playgrounds but also in the state's AAU program.

The way basketball is played in Indiana today seems like a carbon copy of the Rockaway Beach game in the 1940s. The pickup games are clinics in how to play help defense, how to set downscreens, and how to use the pick-and-roll. It is a game that is virtually extinct in big cities like New York, Chicago and Los Angeles. Yet it is just as beautiful to watch. This is the game Mike plays.

Just now Mike is feeling good. Though an all-night softball tourna-ment sapped his strength, a late morning meal of chicken fingers, white bread and white gravy from the Dairy Queen brazier has reinvig-orated him. He spots the ball sitting on the bench in Boonie's yard and spins it in his hands. It whirs as the night's dust floats off. Mike takes a step onto the court and, with a squint that causes wrinkles to form on his soft young face, focuses on the wooden backboard and its brightly painted red square. From half-court, or just inside the three-point line on a regulation NBA court, he lofts the ball into the air. His shot is pure artistry: arm cocked at a 90-degree angle, release at the top of his jump, rotation so complete off his fingertips that the ball's seams disappear, and a follow-through that would make fellow Hoosier Larry Bird check his form. The ball sails through the hoop so softly that the net barely rustles from its slumber. "Boy, I can shoot, can't I?" Mike says to himself, as if he had forgotten.

Nowadays, the guys Mike's age don't play around Boonie's so much. In the summer they hang out at Bloomfield Park, where the court is more their size. In the winter they play at the Health and Physical Education Recreation (HPER – pronounced "hyper") Center at Indiana University in Bloomington, a half-hour east of Bloomfield. The HPER is a monument to basketball, a mammoth building with ten full-size basketball courts that are always in use, with two or three teams always waiting. Court 1 is where the best pickup games are played and where the Indiana style of basketball is best exhibited. In Indiana, as in Rockaway Beach in the 1940s, the game is more pick-and-roll than alley-oop; more in-your-face defense than in-your-face taunts; going left on your defender is as cherished as going over him. Pickup games here are toned-down affairs. No dunking is allowed at the HPER, and a premium is placed on guys who can shoot the rock.

"Styles evolve from the environment," says Bobby Plump, a state basketball legend. "In the inner city there are lots of players, so you need to make yourself stand out. In Indiana, there are so many small towns, and players on the high school basketball teams are taught fundamentals. The talent pool at these places isn't big enough to rely on a great player coming around to save the day."

Bloomfield is a little burg where you can count the number of stoplights on one hand. Big-city prices have yet to cross the town's borders: Parking at a meter for two hours will cost you only a dime, a newspaper is just a quarter and a burger, fries and a Coke at the Cardinal Cafe will run you two dollars. The town is small enough that a stranger walking around City Hall would cause enough of a stir to throw off the town's delicate equilibrium.

Bloomfield lies in the heart of the Bible Belt, but although religion is important, God has never hit a game-winning jump shot. Hoosiers pay homage to the Lord for creating the world and all that is in it, but basketball is their true religion. Depending on which Hoosier you talk to, Indiana has either the five largest, seven of the ten largest or twelve of the fifteen largest high school gyms in the country. In this case, the facts are irrelevant. The proof is in the passion.

Only 2,200 people live in Bloomfield, yet the high school gym there holds 2,400. John Wooden, who grew up in Martinsville, Indiana, and played at Purdue, recruited guys from Indiana when he was coaching at UCLA. Though they played in a sprawling city two thousand miles from home, the farm boys were never nervous playing, because in those days the gym at UCLA was smaller than most of the gyms they grew up playing in. "People from the cities play basketball to get away from something or get out of where they are," says Bobby Crane, a Bloomfield resident. "Here they play just because."

Basketball survives in the wide-open, amber spaces of Indiana despite all the reasons everyone says it shouldn't. Doesn't the game thrive in the city mainly because there is no room to play anything else? With all that open space, shouldn't kids be playing baseball or football? True, there is all the space in the world in Indiana, where miles can separate one neighbor from another. But that latter point is the problem: There aren't very many people. It's hard to get a baseball game going when there are only seventeen kids in your high school class. Says Everett Gates, the coach at Randolph High (237 students) and former coach at Daleville High (206 students), "All the open fields don't amount to much if you haven't got enough people to play on them. Basketball was popular because that's about the only sport a lot of schools could put together."

In rural Indiana on winter Friday nights, the local gym becomes the surrogate town hall. Parents discuss issues concerning the school, farmers discuss the crops, and small-town politics play themselves out on the bleachers rather than in the office of a moonlighting mayor who is also the local barber.

If you really want to understand basketball in Bloomfield, though, you must go to Roger's Spot Lounge. That's where you go for a stiff drink and honest conversation in the heart of the nation's heartland. The proprietor, Roger Sherrard, took over the bar when his father died in 1987. He will invite you in, buy you a Budweiser, introduce you to his golfing buddies, light up a cigarette, and let the opinions flow, just like they did at McGuire's.

As Roger throws down two dollars on the bar for another beer – he always pays for his drinks, even though he owns the place – Mike, his son, saunters in through the back door. Mike's face is sunburned from a season of summer softball games, and he wears a backward baseball cap, with his blondish red hair tucked underneath, showing off the fiery color on his forehead. His bottom lip bulges from a wad of Skoal thin-cut. He sits down at the bar and, just like his father, pays two dollars for a beer. He can already tell the topic of conversation by his father's facial expression, and he begins to shake his head. Mike immediately knows they are talking about the time in the late 1980s when he gave them a ride they will never forget.

In 1986 Bloomfield made it to the state's Sweet 16, or sem-i-states, as the locals call it. People talk about that magical year like it was the Second Coming. Bloomfield eventually lost to Evansville Memorial, but it didn't really matter. Before 1996, when legislation was passed dividing high school athletic teams into four separate classes based on size, the state had always used a one-class system. On any given day, the Davids had a chance to slay the Goliaths. By leading Bloomfield as far as he did, Mike and his small-town school had proven its point. If every boy in Indiana is born with a basketball beating in his chest, then those in the small towns are inflated the most.

Mike was a wispy five-foot-seven sophomore who looked too short and slight to cause any trouble. But he could come off a pick like oil sliding off a rock, and when he rose in the air, with his formidable 36-inch vertical leap, the crowd would wait with baited breath for his smooth stroke to unleash the perfect jump shot. "I always felt I could score on anyone at anytime," Sherrard says. And he could. That year would be the first of three straight in which he led Greene County in scoring.

"Everyone always knew the play would start with Mike," says Ron McBride, the current head coach at Bloomfield, who was an assistant when Mike played from 1984 to 1988. "The players were to get the ball in his hands, and he would do something with it – either make the shot or get it to someone who could."

Like every good Indiana schoolboy, Mike was trained in the fundamentals: reading, writing, arithmetic, planting your pivot foot, playing defense with your feet, using the two-handed chest pass. But at five-seven, he had to be flawless. Big guys can get away with clumsy play; little guys can't. Mike would do fingertip pushups each morning to strengthen his hands. He'd loft jumpers into the sky on a court illuminated only by the moon. Mike inherited a passion for the game from his father and grandfather. Until Mike was thirteen, Roger, who is six-foot-one, defeated him every time they played one-on-one. Because of his relationship with his father, which is strengthened by their shared love for basketball, at age sixteen Mike chose to live with his father when his parents divorced. So close is Mike to his dad that his favorite song is Conway Twitty's "It's My Job," a sappy little number about a father making sacrifices for his son. "If you are at all close with your father," Mike says, "it will make you cry."

Mike divulges his character in snappy, matter-of-fact revelations like that. No need to pontificate when one well-crafted phrase will suffice. "I haven't been eating well this week. A little heartsick, I guess," he'd say after he and his girlfriend of three years broke up. Or, his sensibilities offended after he reads in the paper that an NBA rookie has just signed for millions of dollars, he'll opine, "It's absurd a player should make more than a coach. It doesn't happen in high school. It doesn't even happen in college," adding dryly, "except at Michigan." Bobby Knight would love this no-nonsense approach. And Mike says he would have "given my left nut to play for him." He came damn close.

The summer after Mike's sophomore year he was the starting point guard on an AAU team that won the sixteen-and-under national championship in Orlando. Tony McGee of Terre Haute South, now the starting tight end with the Cincinnati Bengals, was one forward. Pat Graham, an eventual Indiana Mr. Basketball, was another. Matt Nover, a three-year starter for Knight in the early 1990s, was the center. Sherrard's backcourt mate was Damon Bailey, who would eventually become the state's all-time leading scorer and be named the nation's high school player of the 1980s. When Bailey was an eighth-grader in 1985, Knight claimed the kid was better than anyone on his IU team but Steve Alford.

Knight noticed Mike, too. When his AAU team was scheduled to play in a tournament in St. Louis, Mike mistakenly went to the airport in Bloomington instead of Indianapolis, where the flight was departing. He missed the flight, but within ten minutes of walking through his front door, the phone rang. "Be at the Bloomington airport in ten minutes," the baritone voice on the other end ordered. It was Knight. "The airport is half an hour away, but I tried like hell to get there.

When I did, a friend of Knight's had a private plane waiting to take off and get me to St. Louis. I'll never forget that."

As a junior, Mike was named Greene County's Mr. Basketball, averaging a county-high 23.6 points a game. In his senior season the rest of the Bloomfield team finally caught up to his wonderous talents. Upsets and minor miracles were the norm. One week, Bloomfield upset big Bloomington South, which was led by six-foot-ten IU recruit Chris Lawson. The game, played in Bloomington, was a back-and-forth affair, and over its course the crowd slowly shifted allegiances to the visitors. As Mike came out for warmups before the second half, he noticed Knight leaning against a doorway. Now was his time, and Mike wouldn't disappoint. He poured in 39 points as Bloomfield won.

But the victory would be forgotten, and so would Mike's final tally. Only one shot would be remembered. The *Bloomington Herald-Times* wrote:

> The game's most memorable play featured Lawson and Sherrard. With Bloomfield trailing by three and only 1:30 left in regulation, Sherrard got the ball on the right wing about 25 feet from the basket. Lawson stepped out to defend, saw that Sherrard was behind the three-point line, and stepped back to the arc to protect against the drive. Sherrard stole a glance at the Bloomfield bench and got the green light from [coach] Steve Brett. Standing flat-footed, he launched a perfect bullseye over the astounded Lawson.

Equally astounded was Knight, who showed up in Bloomfield the next week when Sherrard's team hosted Damon Bailey and Bedford North Lawrence, ranked third in the state at the time. Some kids from Bloomfield bought forty or fifty tickets each, according to Mike, and scalped them, making upwards of $2,000. The game started at 7:30, but fans began lining up three hours before that, jockeying for good seats. "Even the junior varsity game was tough to get into," McBride remembers. For the main event, the stands were packed, and fans spilled onto the edges of the court, where they sat cross-legged.

Terre Haute South and Bloomington South had fallen to Bloomfield. But Bloomfield wanted this win the most. Beating Damon Bailey, Knight's favorite son, would keep the patrons at the Spot partying until May.

The game went badly for Bloomfield from the opening tip. The six-foot-four Bailey dominated Bloomfield's smaller lineup, scoring at will in the post. In the fourth quarter, the local boys were down by 13. That's when they started chipping away. Bailey and Sherrard traded baskets, but Bailey's shots were layups while Mike was stroking from long range, scoring 3 points for every 2 points by Bedford North Lawrence. With less than a minute left, Bloomfield trailed 64–60. Mike cut the lead to 1 with a three. After a BNL miss, Mike had the ball with the chance to win.

He might as well have been shooting in Boonie Vaught's backyard. Standing beyond the arc, with just seconds left, he hoisted the ball softly, as if he were tossing a feather into the air. There was no doubt: Bloomfield won 66–64. Mike finished with 29 points to Bailey's 24. In the next week's polls, Bloomfield was eighth in the state. "That put us on the verge that year," says Mike.

Sherrard had received a baseball offer from Indiana State – he was also an All-State centerfielder – and a hoops offer from Ball State in Muncie, but was holding out in hopes of an offer from Knight. It never came. Knight called toward the end of the season, telling Mike he had all the skills but was simply too short for Big 10 basketball. In the sectional finals that year, Bloomfield was upset at home by Shakamak High on a last-second shot. After the season Mike was named one of the state's top forty players and Indiana's mini-Mr. Basketball, awarded to the best players six feet or under. The accolades did little to soothe his disappointment in being passed over by Knight and Indiana. "I was crushed," says Mike. "I thought he was wrong. I knew I could play there."

Mike turned down the offers from ISU and Ball State, instead opting for Wabash Valley Junior College. Two starting years at a junior college, he believed, would attract Knight's attention. But Mike had a falling out with the coach at Wabash Valley and transferred, ending, for all intents and purposes, his college basketball career. Mike left another school, Vincennes Junior College, one class shy of a degree in mortuary science. (He can still recite the proper way to embalm a body and how long it should take.) He came back to Bloomfield and took a job as a computer programmer at the nearby army base. "If I had to do it over again," says Mike. "I would have walked on at Indiana. It was a mistake."

The regret doesn't come from the belief that playing at Indiana could have improved his life. For Mike, things could not be much better. In a few years he will take over the Spot from his father. The days will be filled with golf, softball, meeting up with friends at the bar, and, of course, pickup hoops. He harbors no illusions that his basketball career would have lasted beyond college. "My life is pretty much set for me," Mike says. "But I don't mind that." What he does regret is that he never got the chance to prove himself in the heartland's highest court – Knight's court.

Mike still gets his shot at the Indiana guys every once in a while, at the HPER and in AAU tournaments. And, in what amounted to a subtle jab at Knight, in 1993 Mike's AAU team won the state title, beating a group of former IU players now living in Bloomington. Mike was named MVP of the tournament.

The kid from the small town could play with the big boys. After all these years of coaching in Indiana, Knight should have known.

Only in Indiana could a restaurant like Bobby Plump's Last Shot exist. From the neon sign burning brightly above the restaurant's patio and beer garden to the basketball hoop cemented in the back parking lot, this is an homage to the most endearing legend in the history of high school sports. Bobby Plump epitomizes Indiana basketball. For it was Plump and his team that inspired the movie *Hoosiers*.

In 1954 Plump made the game-winning shot against Muncie Central to give tiny Milan High the state championship. With no time left on the clock, Plump hit a picture-perfect jump shot that sailed through the net and lifted little Milan into the ranks of legend. The tale is recounted on the walls of the Indianapolis restaurant. There is a picture of Plump out-rebounding Oscar Robertson of prep powerhouse Crispus Attucks in the 1954 state semifinals, which Milan won 65—52. There is a poster-size Bobby wearing his Indiana All-Stars jacket. In the corner above the jukebox hangs a blowup of the headlines in the *Indianapolis Star* from the day after Milan won the title, signed by everyone from the Milan team. This is the power of Indiana basketball: More than forty years later, Plump is second only to Larry Bird as the state's most famous athlete.

"Sometimes people tell me to stop living in the fifties," Plump says as he sits underneath his Milan letterman's jacket encased in plastic on the wall. "But if they had been there to see …" He leaves the image hanging, like a ball balancing on the rim in the final moments of a game.

He is an older man now, working as an insurance agent in Indianapolis and running his restaurant. He had open-heart surgery in 1994 and still suffers occasional spells of fatigue. On this afternoon, he is wearing a bright, multicolored shirt, opened to the middle of his sternum, revealing about three inches of the scar left when the doctors cracked open his chest. A gold medallion, perfectly placed at the top of the dark scar, hangs from a chain. It looks as if someone has taped a fancy miniature walking stick with a solid-gold handle onto his chest. For a man who embodies the identity of an entire state, he appears quite ordinary.

Plump is also successful beyond his wildest dreams. Like many businessmen his age, he sports a healthy glow. Some say it's ego. Some say he truly *believes* in the legend of Bobby Plump. Yet no one can blame him if he is indeed still living in the 1950s. If Plump's critics had been there, they would have seen 40,000 people show up in Milan for the victory parade. They would know that when the team played away games, the town had to enlist a volunteer fire department from more than thirty miles away to cover the town, because all the local firefighters would be at the game. They would have heard that a letter marked only PLUMP, INDIANA, found its way to Bobby's mailbox. "Basketball meant everything to *this* town," Plump says. "When they raised a banner to commemorate our championship, it didn't say 'Milan High School, Basketball State Champions.' It just said 'State Champions.' No one questioned what sport it was, because there was only one sport that mattered."

Even though the single-class state basketball tournament had been abolished, Plump is still defiant. Nailed to a column that rises through the middle of Plump's restaurant is a wooden plaque. It is painted white and outlined in red. Written in red stenciling are the words: MILAN, 1954 STATE CHAMPION, IT COULD HAPPEN AGAIN, ONLY IN INDIANA. Plump won't take the plaque down, although it no longer rings true.

♦ ♦ ♦

Pull into the circular driveway at Kutsher's Resort in New York's Cat-
skill Mountains, and the grounds are still as bucolic as the day the place
opened in 1907. It is the beginning of August, and a haze lingers over
the rich green grass. The thickly wooded forest a mile beyond the hotel's manmade lakes shimmers in the intense heat. In a field behind the
main hotel, a couple walks hand-in-hand. Another rides a tandem bike
around the lake.

The hotel's first floor, decorated in pink and green, hosts a day-long
game of bingo, with a pot of $600 to the winner. Adults, looking mid-
dle-aged and worn, pull at the arms of their elderly parents, pleading
with them to take a walk outside, just as those parents must have done
with their children forty years ago.

Today the lobby is a hive of activity, and not just because of the
bingo. One by one, large black men, most of them six feet or taller,
stroll through the double glass doors toward the check-in desk. Each
carries a bag inscribed with the name of an NBA team – CHARLOTTE
HORNETS, NEW JERSEY NETS, NEW YORK KNICKS – and is trailed to
the check-in desk by a cluster of prepubscent boys. The kids from Coleman Day Camp in Merrimac, Long Island, on a three-day visit to Kutsher's, wave pens and paper high above their heads, in search of autographs.

In the 1940s heydey of the Catskills, the resorts of the region averaged one million visitors in the summer. Three activities dominated
the summer calendar back then. Eating ranked first – not for nothing
did the area become known as the Sour Cream Sierras and the Borscht
Belt. The two other main attractions were the young comedians like
Sid Caesar, Jerry Lewis and Milton Berle, who tested their material on
the vacationing crowd, and the country's best basketball players, who
came to the mountains to play in the Catskills' summer basketball
pickup leagues.

The pickup action in the Catskills was as formidable as any in New
York City, Chicago or Philadelphia, because at some point during the
summer, the best playground players in those cities would find their
way into the mountains. Like the games Dick McGuire played in Rockaway, these were games that stressed fundamentals. High school sen-

iors and college freshman could compete with pros and semi-pros because the games relied on the basics – setting screens and playing tight defense. This is the style that epitomized the playground basketball of the era. The players walking in today, guys like Jayson Williams and Anthony Mason, are here to pay tribute to that legacy.

Each year since 1959, NBA players have gathered at Kutsher's to play in the Maurice Stokes game, a benefit that raises money for former NBA players who need financial assistance due to illness or physical disability. Stokes himself had a brilliant but tragically brief NBA career with the Rochester and Cincinnati Royals in the late 1950s. He was an NBA rookie of the year in 1955–56, led the league in rebounding in 1956–57 with 17.4, and was avergaging 16.9 points and 18.1 rebounds in 1957–58 when tragedy struck. In Detroit on March 15, 1958, in the final game of the year, Stokes fell to the floor and banged his head on the hardwood. He finished the game, but later that night on the plane home, he slipped into a coma. When Stokes stirred from the coma one of the NBA's most promising stars had been stricken with irreversible brain damage, which left him immobile and speechless until his death in 1970. In 1959, and every summer since then, NBA players have paid their own way to Monticello to play in a game that serves as a memorial to the fallen Stokes.

The Stokes game is played at the Clair Bee Field House – named for Long Island University's first great coach – on the grounds of Kutsher's. With its musty odor, humidity levels approaching liquid, and exposed beams, the fieldhouse is a monument to the way gymnasiums looked when the Catskills were a basketball hotbed. The stands hold close to 500 people. Unfortunately, the Stokes game is the only time this gym is filled for a basketball game. It was built in the 1960s, long after the basketball boom in the area had passed. Now it serves mainly as the alternative when rain drives kids from Kutsher's Sports Academy summer camp indoors.

As the current NBA stars make their grand entrance, there are old-time hall-of-famers everywhere you turn. The kids looking for autographs don't know it, though. They pass by the grandfatherly men without a second glance, unaware they are the pioneers of the game. Dick McGuire sits poolside as the Merrimac kids invade, peeling off their green Coleman Camp T-shirts, diving in and sending a splash his way. McGuire, shirtless and shoeless, talks and laughs with friends about the old days, occasionally slapping his knee when he hears a really good story. Although his belly is large and round and his hair is gray, the seventy-year-old McGuire still has a boyish look. His voice purrs, and he speaks so fast it takes a moment to adjust to the pace.

Jack "Dutch" Garfinkel approaches Dick, walking so briskly that no one seems to have told him he is approaching eighty. Though they are nearly a decade apart in age, McGuire and Garfinkel share a bond that transcends time: They are New York City basketball players. Like Dick in the late 1940s, Dutch starred at St. Johns in the late 1930s, although he hit his prime before there was an NBA to showcase his talents. After earning a pittance playing with some barnstorming teams, Dutch got married. His mother-in-law told him it was time to stop being a kid, time to quit playing games. Summer can't last forever, after all. Become a *mensch*, she would say, invoking the Yiddish word for "man." Dutch agreed with her. He became a teacher.

But he never forgot the early days, on the playgrounds and in the parks and in the Catskills. Dutch, like Dick, can relate to the carefree kids floating like butterflies around their circle. Summers in the Catskills were their idea of perfect bliss, too.

In the early 1900s a group of Jewish farmers settled in the mountainous region hoping to till the land. When the earth proved too unyielding, they began cobbling together a living by renting out their spare rooms to relatives from the city. Hotels soon began cropping up.

Initially, the guests were primarily poor Jews from New York City who ventured north to escape, if only briefly, the squalor of the tenements. As they did in many of the *shtetls* in Brooklyn and Manhattan, guests spoke freely in Yiddish, as if they had never left the Old World. By the 1930s the affluent had reached the mountains. Luxurious bungalows housed families for weeks at a time. The clientele remained mostly Jewish, and hotels offered Friday night Sabbath services and kosher meals.

Basketball had become a predominantly Jewish game in the 1920s and 1930s and Jews took pride in their dominance. Even when that began to wane in the 1940s, the guests at resorts throughout the Borscht Belt still knew who the best players were and hotel owners were eager to capitalize. At that time, the best all played in the Catskills: Mountain Ball. From Brownsville to the Bronx and Syracuse to Union, New Jersey, every great ballplayer along the eastern seaboard made his rite of passage in the resorts of upstate New York.

The owners of the resorts knew the guests were coming up to watch basketball, and they spent their time and money making their basketball venues bigger and better. The more attractive the site, the more popular the hotel. The outdoor stands at the President's Hotel held close to 500 fans. Laurels Hotel staged its games at an indoor theater that held 200. The White Rose accommodated 400. Others, like the Nevele, created a makeshift court from two side-by-side tennis courts encircled by a set of bleachers.

"At night we all piled into two or three cars with the hotel owners," recalls Garfinkel. "They loved it. They would drive us to the ballgame, and after the game they always took us to a Chinese restaurant for dinner."

They also stockpiled their staffs with basketball stars. Sometimes the talent wouldn't come cheap, but no expense was spared to lure the top players for the summer. One year, Ben Fishman, who owned Klein's Hillside, invited Minneapolis Lakers center George Mikan up for the summer. Mikan played three games a week; in exchange, he and his wife, their three kids and their nanny had room and board for the summer. Eddie Gottlieb and the Philadelphia SPHAs were frequent guests at the Flaglers Hotel. The Nevele had Dolph Schayes. The basketball games in the Catskills were so competitive and so fierce that players from Nat Holman's CCNY team of the early 1940s would give up lucrative summer jobs in the city to practice in the mountains for two months.

"We played for Stevensville Lake Hotel," recalls Sonny Herzberg, who was on that CCNY team and later played for the New York Knicks. "Our freshman team from City College wanted to stay together and get better, and this was a great opportunity for us to learn all our moves. We couldn't afford to have a coach up there, so we developed a togetherness and cooperation that prospered during the season." Herzberg's teams from the 1940–41 and 1941–42 seasons were the first CCNY teams to go to consecutive NIT tournaments.

The best teams in the Catskills weren't always the ones the pros played on. In the early 1940s, the Nevele Resort had Garfinkel, who went to St. John's, and Ralph and Danny Kaplowitz, who grew up in the Bronx and went to NYU and LIU, respectively. The Nevele team consistently beat teams with professionals, a fact that sometimes didn't sit well with the pros. Ralph Kaplowitz recalls one game against the Flagler team, which boasted pros Sheky Gotthoffer and Davey Bass.

"We were young, and we ran like mad," says Kaplowitz. "They had not lost a game all summer, but we got hot and jumped out to an early lead. We made them crazy. Near the end of the game all they could do was push us and hold us and grab us. At the end of the game, I cut close to Davey Bass to pick him off.

"He is a big strong guy, and he stuck his hands out and grabbed my pants. My pants came off, and as I ran to the basket I was in my jockstrap. I didn't stop running until I got outside and could put on a new pair of pants."

Bob Cousy was seventeen years old when he spent his first summer in the Catskills. The athletic director at the Tamarak Resort, Artie Muzicart, was also the head basketball coach at Brooklyn College. Cousy had earned All-City honors his senior year at Andrew Jackson High in St. Albans and was headed to Holy Cross for college. Muzicart knew who Cousy was, of course – everybody who followed basketball did – and invited him up to the mountains. In the late 1940s, Cousy's Tamarak team dominated the Catskills circuit. "My first summer up there, before I got into college, we had four high school guys, and we beat the hell out of some college all-stars," Cousy recalls. Once he was in college, Cousy teamed with Dartmouth players Ed Leede and West Field to beat Dolph Schayes' team twice during the summer of 1948, and George Mikan's team once.

"The Catskills were a melting pot in those days," says Norm Drucker, a New Yorker who spent summers playing and refereeing in the mountains before a twenty-year career officiating in the NBA. "The players all migrated there. The hotel owner thought it would be great to get well-known kids from the city because most of the people visiting came from the city and knew of the players. They'd see Bob Cousy and Sonny Herzberg, and that would be the night's entertainment."

"You know how women are with rock stars now," says Lillian Garfinkel, Jack's wife. "In those days they all followed the basketball team. When the basketball team walked into the dining room, the girls went nuts. They were like rock stars. Seriously."

The guests may have treated the players like rock stars, but their working conditions were less than ideal. Sometimes the players would serve the morning and the midday meals, play ball in the scorching sun all afternoon and then serve more than 1,000 meals at night. Leede remembers sharing a room with twelve other waiters and a bathroom with the entire hotel staff of thirty-seven.

There would be two or three games a week, and Cousy spent his days working as a busboy in Tamarak's dining room. Other players taught old Jewish women who had emigrated from Eastern Europe how to swim, or organized softball and volleyball leagues for the kids. The real money, though, was made in the dining hall, busing tables and serving the patrons. The guests knew which waiters were the city's great basketball players, and those were the ones who got the biggest tips. It definitely paid to work the dining room. "We weren't really supposed to talk to the guests," recalls Leede, who later played alongside Cousy on the Celtics. "But usually they wanted to talk so much basketball that you didn't have a choice."

"They were kind of like hero-worshippers," says Chai Gotkin, who played for the President's Hotel. "People used to come and greet us at the door."

Cousy hadn't even seen a basketball until he was thirteen, but following in the footsteps of Dick McGuire, he learned to play at 108th Street in Rockaway. In just a few years he had made a name for himself as a crafty passer and gifted ballhandler. At Tamarak he prepared for college basketball by playing against the likes of Mikan and Schayes. But what impressed this poor kid from Queens most was the money he earned. At the end of his first summer in the Catskills, Cousy returned home and emptied a brown paper bag filled with $1,400 in singles onto the kitchen table.

"My father had never seen so much money," Cousy says. "My mom started to call the police because she thought I had knocked off a bank."

"You could really make good money in those days," says Dutch Garfinkel, who witnessed the action when he would come up from East New York in the early 1940s to referee games. "As a busboy, you could make a thousand dollars for the summer. But the money didn't mean much to us. We were coming up here to play ball."

As alluring as the games were to the guests was the easy money to be had by betting on them. These were heady days for vacationers in the Catskills. Many families had disposable income for the first time in their lives . Immigrants who had arrived as part of the great migration of the 1920s and who had spent years laboring for pennies, nickels and dimes were suddenly prospering in the wartime economy. Gambling proved to be an affordable leisure activity. "Usually there would be four or five hundred people betting on a game," says Garfinkel. "Just a game between two hotel teams."

The players were hardly immune to the gambling bug. They wanted a piece of the action, too. It was commonplace for the players to have a pool based on the outcome or the total number of points scored in a game. If a player bet that more than 70 points would be scored in the game, and 71 or more were scored, he won his bet. At first the action was harmless. The players would collect a quarter or a dollar from each of the fans as they entered the stands, and then the winner of the bet would get the money.

"Some of the ballplayers were doing business," says Garfinkel. "And they would lose games on purpose."

"We were college kids running a pool," says Gotkin. "Just trying to make some extra money."

Not surprisingly, though, the scheme spiraled out of control. The players were easy targets for vacationing bookies out to make contacts for the upcoming basketball season, and for fellow players looking for the big score. Eddie Gard, who played for Long Island University in the late 1940s, was working in the Catskills in 1949. That year he had inherited a lucrative point-shaving operation. For two years before that, a quintet of LIU players, including Gard, had been fixing games with a local gambler and former LIU Blackbird named Jack Goldsmith. He would front the five players as much as $5,000, to be split among the five of them, and in exchange they would guarantee that LIU would not exceed the point spread.

By the summer of 1949 Goldsmith had tired of his small-time gig with the players and branched off into a larger operation. He left the business to Gard. Two of the five players with whom Gard had been fixing games graduated in 1949, but Gard and two others remained at

LIU. Once things were in his hands, however, Gard wanted to expand his reach to other teams in the city. He wanted a piece not only of LIU games, but of all the games involving New York City teams taking place at Madison Square Garden. Eventually he hoped to take control of the NIT and NCAA championships.

One day while swimming by the pool he noticed a beautiful brunette named Jeanne Sollazzo lounging nearby. He walked over to introduce himself, but instead became acquainted with her husband, Salvatore. The chance encounter was more beneficial than Gard expected.

Salvatore Sollazzo was an ex-con who had spent time in jail for selling stolen jewelry. When he got out of prison he went to work for his brother, this time selling jewelry legitimately. Over time he saved enough to start his own ring-making business and to buy a load of platinum, which he stored in a warehouse. Shortly after he bought the platinum, the material was declared a scarce war metal. Suddenly, Sollazzo was rich.

He partied hard and gambled harder. He bought season tickets for the New York Yankees and New York Giants games, as well as club passes for all the local racetracks. Through his gambling habit, which sometimes exceeded $5,000 for a baseball game, he became acquainted with a cadre of racketeers and bookies. Sollazzo, despite his wealth and good-time attitude, was insecure and yearned for acceptance. Under the guise of friendship, bookmakers would take advantage of Sollazzo by tipping him off to weak horses. The eager Sollazzo would make his loser bet, and the bookies would reap the rewards.

Although his jewelry business was thriving, Sollazzo's gambling debts were mounting. When he and Gard met that day in the Catskills, each found the perfect partner: Gard needed someone to bankroll his point-shaving scheme, and Sollazzo needed a sure-fire way to make some quick cash.

That first season, 1949–50, Gard and Sollazzo confined their fixing to LIU games – games that Gard could control. Meanwhile, many members of the CCNY team, which would go on that season to unprecedented victories in both the NIT and NCAA championships, were taking money from another bookie to shave points. If Gard wanted control of the city, he needed that CCNY team.

In the summer of 1950, after his eligibility at LIU had expired, Gard

put on the full-court press to secure the services of several CCNY players. On trips to the Catskills, Gard approached CCNY player Ed Warner,
who was working at Klein's Hillside. Gard explained to Warner that a
good number of his teammates were making money with gamblers off
Warner's efforts, and that Warner should start doing the same with
Gard and Sollazzo. Gard and Warner then approached CCNY player
Floyd Lane who, after resisting for months, acquiesced to their de-
mands on the eve of the 1950–51 basketball season. Shortly after the
season began, Gard recruited CCNY's Eddie Roman and Al Roth.

Even with the influence they now exerted, Sollazzo and Gard found
it difficult to get a straight fix. In the stands and on the court, fixers
were ubiquitous. Almost everybody, it seemed, was working for somebody. Bookies began ignoring games at the Garden because they knew
the fix was in. In their stories, reporters intimated illicit behavior on the
part of the players. Clair Bee and Nat Holman had heard the rumors
and been given tips by anonymous sources about their players' gambling. When the coaches confronted them, however, the players denied
involvement.

In the meantime, by the late 1940s Catskills hotel owners were
growing weary of gambling's effect on their guests. Arthur Winarick,
who owned the Concord Hotel, confronted his team about the impro-
prieties. He said it reflected badly on his resort and affected the enjoy-
ment of his guests. Winarick eventually eliminated the sport from his
hotel's entertainment schedule, and many resorts followed his lead.

"There was so much gambling going on," says Cousy. "It was too
easy for shady types to get access to players. So the game in the mountains really kind of died down."

But elsewhere, the damage had been done. In February 1951, as his
team's train pulled into the station after returning from a game against
Temple in Philadelphia, Holman was approached by an investigator
from the Manhattan district attorney's office. "I've got bad news," he
said to Holman. "I've got orders to pick up your boys." Norman Mager,
Ed Roman, Ed Warner, Al Roth, Floyd Lane, Herb Cohen and Irwin
Dambrot – the MVP of the 1950 NCAA tournament – were arrested.
All pleaded guilty to misdemeanor charges of point-shaving. In a probe
that extended from 1947 to 1950, investigators discovered fixes in
eighty-six games in twenty-three cities and seventeen states. The guilty

included thirty-two players from seven colleges: CCNY, LIU, New York University, Manhattan College, Kentucky, Bradley and Toledo. For their roles in the scandal, Sollazzo was sentenced to eight to sixteen years in prison, and Gard received three years.

The convictions were a death blow to the basketball scene in the Catskills. The blame fell on Madison Square Garden, where New York City colleges like NYU, LIU and CCNY played many of their games, and on the Borscht Belt. Columnists called the resort teams "subterfuges for professionalism" and claimed that the softening of the moral fiber of these boys began in the Catskills. "The seeds are planted [in the Catskills] by the wily fixers for the future harvest," wrote one newspaperman.

"In the East," said Phog Allen, the coach at Kansas, "the boys, particularly those who participate in those resort hotel leagues during the summer months, are thrown into an environment which cannot help but breed evil."

Holman was distraught over the scandal. "The hotel teams are schools of crime," he said, "and since playing for these hotel teams may have a bad influence on the boys, we at CCNY have decided not to allow their participation."

After that, summers in the Catskills cooled considerably. Back in the city, though, the blacktop was heating up.

3

Escape

The undiscovered talent is among the greatest gems in sports. The glory of winning isn't the only prize. For a coach, such a discovery proves his eye for talent, for spotting a diamond in the rough where others merely saw a lump of coal. At the very least, it proves to a coach that his network of scouts is more loyal and more sophisticated than those of other coaches.

Such networks are the lifelines for modern coaches. Without the scout – the guy who sees 500 pickup games a year and tens of thousands of young players – the number of undernourished talents would be much higher. Someone has to know where to find the players, what their home phone numbers are, how to smooth things over with their parents and tell these future stars the things they want to hear.

Today those kinds of guys come to town handing out shoes like penny candy, trading sweet kicks for a little loyalty. Guys like Nate Cebrun, a small-time hustler from Florida who arranged for college basketball recruits at the University of Nevada-Las Vegas and other schools to take their college entrance exams in school districts where Cebrun could control the grading. But others are more harmless vagabonds, like Rodney Parker – part coach, part college counselor, part placement office and part ticket scalper. In the 1970s, no player came out of Brooklyn whom Rodney hadn't fostered through the recruiting process. He still knows everyone and sees everything. Characters like these began surfacing in the 1950s, and back then they were called street agents. They knew the shortcut to anybody and everybody who was somebody on the playground, and they left no tracks. Fred "Spook" Stegman was the the original.

These freelancing scouts, or bird dogs, as they are still called, were a byproduct of college basketball's emerging popularity in the late 1940s. Until that time, the best players almost always went to a local college. Dick McGuire, from Queens, went to St. John's. Chicago's Mickey Rottner attended Loyola. Philadelphia high school star Tom Gola played at LaSalle. San Franscisco kid Hank Luisetti enrolled at Stanford. But as the game grew into a money-maker for colleges, those schools wanted the best talent available, no matter where they had to go to find it. In those days, of course, recruiting budgets didn't exist, nor were summer camps or shoe company–sponsored prep all-star games around to showcase the best talent – only the local summer leagues and the playgrounds did that. Lacking the money to travel the playground circuit, coaches needed eyes and ears in every town, people to tell them who was worth seeing. In New York it was Spook whom the coaches called at feeding time.

"I was a single guy with no family who loved basketball," says Stegman, now sixty-nine. "I was like a stringer for the AP newswire. I'd find a kid playing on some playground and think, 'Hey, he would be perfect for this school.' Then I'd call and set something up."

Asthma prevented Stegman, who came from the Astoria section of Queens, from playing basketball himself; even today his words are interrupted by an occasional wheeze, like wind blowing through a whirring fan. If you were from Queens you spent every summer you could on the beach, which meant trekking to the sands in Rockaway. That's where Spook learned the game. Unable to play, he'd marvel from the sidelines at the fluid action unfolding in front of him. At first no one knew who this stranger was, this kid who showed up religiously every weekend but never played. He was awkward-looking. When he had his shirt off on those summer days, you could see a sort of indentation in the middle of his chest, as if someone had punched him there and it had just caved in. Normally he dressed in a coat and tie of the most outrageous color combinations: yellow and orange, plaid and pinstripes – whatever it took to get a second look. "We used to say he looked like he came out of a Dick Tracy comic strip, he was that much of a character," says Norm Ochs. Spook seemed to weigh no more than 110 pounds, and with his black hair slicked back, he had the appearance of a rocket ready to be launched.

As so many great players developed before Stegman's appreciative eyes – guys like Dick and Al McGuire, Bob Cousy, and Ray Lumpp – Spook started taking notes on who and what he saw. He recorded his observations with the diligence of a coach, jotting a player's best qualities in a little black book that he could stick in his back pocket. *Cousy's got some control of the ball. McGuire can thread the needle. Dolph Schayes is unstoppable inside.* Pretty soon Spook was everywhere there was a game. He'd travel to Harlem, Brooklyn, the Bronx or the Lower East Side. Always with his notebook, scribbling down quick assessments of the players he saw, making snap judgments about who could play and who had no game. The McGuire brothers started calling him Spook because, like a ghost, Stegman would magically materialize without your ever knowing it.

Over time Spook developed a relationship with Honey Russell, the coach at Seton Hall. Russell always wondered about this guy who was showing up in the same places he was to watch these kids play basketball. Who did he work for? Where did his players end up? One afternoon, at a game so far into Brooklyn only scouts and parents would ever show up for it, Russell approached Stegman, and they started talking. Stegman, it turned out, was neither a parent nor a professional scout, just a basketball junkie. Like a peacock spreading his plume, Stegman proudly showed Russell his notebook. Shortly thereafter, Spook was tipping off Russell to the best talent in the city.

In the streets, a reputation can grow like wildfire, and that's what happened to Spook. *He sent a player to Seton Hall* was the word around town. He could help guys out of the ghetto and, more important, he could provide coaches with an in. "We were the basketball capital of the world," Stegman says. "Word gets around when someone's done good or found a great player." Santa Clara, in California, asked him to keep in touch; the University of Seattle employed him like an East Coast correspondent. Spook's network was vast, spreading over New York City's playgrounds and, by extension, the country. He did his business out of the Nedix food stand in the old Madison Square Garden. Coaches called a nearby payphone so often that the Nedix owner, who answered the phone in a strong Asian accent, began taking messages. Some coaches thought it was Spook's secretary.

"He had one book with the telephone numbers of every Division I coach in the country," says Ochs. "He had another with the names of high school seniors. He went everywhere, so he knew everyone. If you had a cousin playing at Brooklyn Tech on the third string and asked Spook where could he play, he'd have an answer."

Al McGuire got his first head coaching job at Belmont-Abbey, a small Catholic college in North Carolina, late in the recruiting season of 1957. McGuire had no prior head coaching experience, although he had worked as an assistant at Dartmouth after retiring from the Knicks. After that, he worked in his parents' bar in Queens. The head coach at North Carolina, Frank McGuire (no relation to Al), then called him, offering to help him get the head coaching job at Belmont-Abbey or to hire Al as an assistant with the Tar Heels. Al took the Belmont-Abbey job. Frank eventually hired Dean Smith as his assistant.

Working at Dartmouth and then at his parents' bar, Al hadn't kept in touch with what was happening on the streets. He needed players – good players – and he needed them fast. The first person he called was Spook. "I knew he could help me," says McGuire. "No one else would know what good players were still hanging around [so late in the re-cruiting season]." Al offered to pay for some dental work for Spook in exchange for stockpiling Al's Belmont-Abbey team.

The best playground players were long gone. But up in Mt. Vernon, New York, a basketball hotbed about fifteen miles north of the city, was a six-foot-seven kid named Johnny von Bargen. He had gone to Santa Clara to start the season but had gotten homesick six weeks into the school year. A lot of people were still after him, and chances were slim that he'd consider a tiny school like Belmont-Abbey with an un-proven coach like Al McGuire. "My parents were immigrants, and they didn't know a lot about sports," says von Bargen. "They just wanted me to get an education. Spook came in and supported me and made me comfortable with going away again to play ball. Of course, then Al came in and charmed my mother." After von Bargen signed on, Spook convinced a six-foot-nine kid from Queens named Danny Doyle, who had already committed to Iona, to head south instead. Pretty soon Al's first team was filled out, and it featured four guys from New York, all of whom had cut their teeth on the playgrounds.

Spook had a way with people. He'd meet them on their terms. Doyle liked to gamble when he was in high school, so when it was time for their appointment Spook walked onto the schoolyard where Doyle was shooting craps. But he worked especially well with the parents, who usually had the final say. The parents who lived in cloistered neighborhoods within New York City – blacks, Jews, Catholics – believed Spook when he said the coach coming to visit from California would not take their boy away forever. His voice oozed conviction. He'd take a kid out for a hamburger or sleep over at his parents' house if he had to. Before "whatever it takes" trickled into the sports vernacular, Spook did whatever it took.

Because of his credibility as a street scout/agent, Spook became something of dignitary throughout the city. He saw 400 games a year, and by the late 1950s he had established pipelines to Frank McGuire at North Carolina and Honey Russell at Seton Hall, among others. At a time when basketball was changing rapidly, Spook's reverence for the game and for those who played it – no matter who they were or what color their skin – made him invaluable to coaches everywhere. In doing so, Spook made the playground a more important place.

The postwar era offered Americans unprecedented prosperity. World War II had brought an end to the Depression, and as the US emerged unscathed from the war's devastation its economy hummed like a finely tuned Chevy engine and churned out money by the bucketful. The American Dream was becoming reality. A steady, well-paying job, two-car garage, house in the 'burbs and happy kids seemed as easy to come by as a drink of water – at least for some.

It is no coincidence that the period in which playground basketball began to be dominated by African Americans coincides with the dawn of postwar prosperity. When the soldiers returned home, white families abandoned the cities for the sanctity of the suburbs, essentially leaving the cities to African Americans migrating from the South. By 1950, 62 percent of blacks lived in cities.

Postwar prosperity didn't necessarily trickle down to the black urban population, nor did it suddenly transform prejudices. In many of the suburbs to which newly affluent whites were moving, blacks were, for all intents and purposes, forbidden from buying property. "Let's just say it was not a golden era for blacks," says Tee Parham, a black man who grew up playing ball in North Philadelphia during this era. "We still struggled, especially in the first few years after the war. We thought we may have gained some respect because so many blacks fought bravely in the war. That wasn't the case."

"It seemed like the only people moving out of the ghetto were whites, and the only people moving in were blacks," says Mack Irvin, a black playground star from Chicago's South Side projects. "All of a sudden, an area that was once full of Jews, Italians, Irish and blacks was all black. That didn't seem fair."

As the nation's economics and demographics changed, so too did the makeup of the playground. Catholics and Jews, for so long inhabitants of the inner city, moved to the suburbs, where their children discovered the automobile, backyard recreation and summer camp. These kids played basketball, but only as an afterthought. The best ball could now be found in the black ghettos.

Inner-city basketball, though, still offered the same things: escape, respect, acceptance. And when Jackie Robinson broke baseball's color barrier with the Brooklyn Dodgers in 1947, urban blacks all across the country began believing in the power of sport to change people's opinions. The next year one momentous game between the Harlem Globetrotters and George Mikan's Minneapolis Lakers would serve as the pick that unlocked the door to college and pro basketball for African American players.

In the 1940s the Globetrotters had picked up where the Harlem Renaissance left off as the nation's premier all-black team. But they were not the team of tricksters and showmen they are today. In the years after the war, with the NBA still in its infancy, the Globetrotters were consistently the nation's best-known basketball team, a dynasty. They expanded on the Rens' barnstorming approach, wreaking havoc on opponents from New York to Cuba. During the 1947–48 schedule the Globetrotters won fifty-two straight games – including one over the Lakers.

At that time the lily-white Lakers, featuring the massive Mikan, were one of the NBA's best teams; they would win five NBA titles between 1948 and 1954. The exhibition with the Globetrotters was scheduled as the undercard to a February 19, 1948, game at Chicago Stadium between the New York Knickerbockers and the Chicago Stags. But while the nightcap played to less than capacity, the 'Trotters and the Lakers squared off in front of a full house of 17,823 fans who showed up to see basketball's most successful independent professional team take on the powerhouse of the fledgling NBA. It was black against white, cagey veterans versus upstarts from a new league.

The score reflected the game's physical nature. The lead changed with almost every possession, including the last. The February 20 *Chicago Tribune* recounted that last basket: "The final two points were scored on a long shot by Ermer Robinson as the gun ending the game went off while the ball was arching its way to the basket." Final score: Globetrotters 61, Lakers 59.

As in baseball, African American basketball players could no longer be ignored. "Remember one thing about coaches," says Ray Meyer, who ran the show at DePaul for forty-two years. "They are more interested in winning than in excluding." Much to the dismay of Globetrotters owner Abe Saperstein, the NBA integrated for the 1950–51 season: No longer would Saperstein have a monopoly on the country's best black players. Almost immediately, the Globetrotters degenerated from champions to a decent team of ballplayers with some fancy footwork and deft dribbling. "Abe wasn't very happy when the NBA first started to integrate," Wilt Chamberlain once said. "Walter Brown, one of the founders of the NBA, was owner of the Boston Celtics, and he was going to sign Chuck Cooper as the first black man in the league. Abe went crazy. He threatened to boycott Boston Garden." Brown did sign Cooper to the Celtics. Then Earl Lloyd of West Virginia State joined the Washington Capitols and Nat "Sweetwater" Clifton from Xavier, Louisiana, ended up with the Knicks. While none of them dominated that season, the door had been opened.

And it wasn't just the pros putting out the welcome mat. Although a number of schools had begun integrating in the 1930s and 1940s, colleges all over the country began admitting blacks en masse in the 1950s. Walter Dukes entered Seton Hall in 1949, and in his first season as a varsity player, 1950–51, he averaged 13 points. Dukes graduated in

1953 with averages of 19.9 points and 18.9 rebounds per game. Jackie Moore entered LaSalle in 1951 and proved to be the best player in the school's history after Tom Gola. Joe Bertrand averaged almost 15 points a game in 1951–52, his first year at Notre Dame. Cleo Littleton, who began his career at Wichita State in 1951–52, remains the school's all-time leading scorer. These men were pioneers: Each was the first black to play basketball at these schools. Their success laid the groundwork for the recruitment of other black players by major programs later in the decade: Wilt Chamberlain by Kansas, Oscar Robertson by Cincinnati, Bill Russell by San Francisco. "Blacks dominated the game and changed the way it was played – for the better – from this point," says Al McGuire.

Success on the basketball court empowered African Americans in ways that baseball and Jackie Robinson had nothing to do with. This was the one game inner-city black kids could play right outside their homes. "In the thirties and forties, you're talking about a lot of ballplayers with no direction, and therefore no passion for the game," says Mack Irvin. "But in the fifties, you're talking about hoops as an opportunity. The times were changing, and there were more people playing. Basketball became the game around the city, every city. The odds might have been a thousand to one that you'd make it [to the pros], but even then, everyone was sure they would be that one."

"In the fifties we were really able to see a lot of black stars, much more than before," says Bob McCullough, who grew up in Harlem, played for the Cincinnati Royals in the early 1960s, and returned to Harlem after his playing career to become a guidance counselor and social worker. "There was Charlie Hoaxie on a great Niagara team, and Sihugo Green at Duquense. Maurice Stokes won the MVP of the NIT at Madison Square Garden when he was at St. Francis. Blacks were being showcased on television, and we took inspiration."

Now basketball offered opportunity, and that opportunity sparked a competitiveness that changed the pace, the tone and the style of the game from the ghetto on up. Earlier generations of inner-city kids played the game for acceptance, but there was no organized pro league to shoot for, to lift them up from their surroundings. In contrast, the ghetto kids of the 1950s strove for the NBA, and as they pushed the skill level of the game up from its roots, it blossomed. Even if only 1 out of every 1,000 kids made it, all 1,000 would do their damnedest to be noticed. "The hot dogging all started out on the playgrounds at this time," says Irvin. "This is when we had to show our skills, our chance to impress each other and anyone else who was watching." Thus was born what Nelson George, a columnist for the *Village Voice* in the late 1980s, termed the "Black Athletic Aesthetic." In 1989 George described that aesthetic:

> Simply put, it is the unmistakable way brothers and quite a few sisters play ball, and it is particularly a force in b-ball, a sport once populated by slow-footed East Coast ethnics (Jews, the Irish, and Italians) and midwestern WASPs for whom an elevated hoop represented welcome relief from the relentless flat horizon. It was a game that fitted players to the rigid patterns of the great white fathers, like Phog Allen, Hank Iba, and Adolph Rupp. What began as a waltz-time game and picked up to big-band swing during World War II, evolved glacially through the era of Perry Como and Sandra Dee ... BAA didn't begin to manifest itself until the '50s and '60s, when blacks in numbers finally entered the NCAA and NBA. Their speed changed the tempo from Sinatra to Motown ...

Nowhere was this new style and pace more in evidence than in the Rucker League in Harlem. The league – actually a two-month tournament – was the brainchild of Holcombe Rucker, a high school dropout and a decorated World War II veteran who, despite his experiences in the war, didn't feel much like a hero or a conqueror. Instead, Rucker felt slighted, mistreated. Like so many others, he had served his country and laid his life on the line, but as a black man Rucker had been treated as a second-class citizen in the still-segregated armed forces. "It was full-steam ahead for apartheid in the US military back then," says James Rucker, Holcombe's brother, who served in the military from 1946 to 1975.

The Rucker family had a long history of military heroism and loyalty. Holcombe's great-great grandfather fought for the Union in the Civil War. When the war ended, he was so impressed by the courage and honor of his white commanding officer, a man named Rucker, that he dropped his surname and adopted the name Rucker as his own. When Holcombe returned from overseas after World War II, his feelings for the men who led him were just as strong, though not nearly so positive. After unpacking his bags, he promptly burned his uniform, medals and ribbons. The memories went up in smoke.

Back home, where he worked as an attendant for the New York City Parks Department, he was pained to find things no better in civilian life. Rucker ached to make a difference for the generations that followed him. Quickly he recognized the grip that basketball, and those who played it, had on the kids in his neighborhood. In 1946 he organized a league to give local boys something to do on summer weekends. By the 1950s the Rucker League had grown into the premier exhibition of playground basketball in the country. The greatest players in the world congregated at 130th Street and Seventh Avenue in Harlem at the behest of Rucker. As always, the wispy Rucker would be chain-smoking in a corner of the park, preaching his stay-in-school message. Players called him "Ruck" or "Mr. Rucker," but most important to Rucker was that they called at all. He would be there to counsel some wayward soul in the local police precinct at two in the morning or in the park at three in the afternoon. "He saw that youngsters were going to jail and having problems," says his son Phil. "He also knew they loved playing ball. He was able to tap into the idea that if you could get them interested in something they liked you could teach about things they needed to do."

"He was a lovely man," McCullough says, sitting in his office at the El Faro Beacon Community Center. "It always seemed like your biggest problem immediately became his biggest problem. He was not a disciplinarian." McCullough retired from his job as a social worker at Manhattan's Hunter College in 1996, but he still runs the youth programs at this center on 120th and First Avenue in Harlem. Rucker's life has been the model by which he lives. "He had unconditional regard for you," McCullough says. "He was not a social worker or guidance counselor – he was a community counselor. There is a difference. He was a mentor."

McCullough knows first-hand. It was Rucker who bailed a twelve-year-old McCullough out of jail after the youth had been in a gang fight. It was Rucker who got McCullough into college and, after McCullough screwed that up, got him into another one. Rucker, it seemed, would find redemption for Satan. He always preached education – ironically, since he himself never finished high school. Rucker, though, saw the problem in not practicing what he preached, and so he went back to school to earn his high school diploma and then received his B.A. from City College at age thirty-five. Rucker was working on his Masters in education when he died of cancer in 1965. The cigarette he had always held in his hand while he cajoled, taught and lectured his playground pupils had done him in. Those he mentored recall the dramatic sight of the miasma of smoke surrounding Rucker's head as he animatedly proffered a lesson on life or basketball, or both. Those lessons would be missed.

"I felt abandoned," says Phil Rucker, who helped found Brooklyn's Jackie Robinson Center for Physical Culture. "We all felt abandoned. I was heading towards adulthood, and his death shaped the way I lived my life. But, most certainly, the man's work was done."

Rucker had succeeded in making his point. Just as the Jewish ghettos were the focal point of basketball in the 1920s, the black ghettos of Harlem had ushered in a new era in the game. Rucker's playground was a haven for the style. He brought in superstars from the NBA and college to show the younger kids how they, too, could make it. Eventually he dubbed the league the "college express," because more than 700 of his kids went on to play basketball at a higher level after playing in his tournament. Rucker also opened the tourney to playground players whose shot had long passed – just so they could take on the pros and, maybe, beat them and rebuild their self-esteem. Rucker realized that basketball and his tournament offered an escape, not just physically, but – though it might be only for the duration of a pickup game – for the psyche as well.

These were games of attitude, of freelancing on the court, and of showing up your opponent at every opportunity. They called it "get back" competition, as in instant retaliation. If one guy made his defender look bad on a drive to the hoop, the fans gathered around the court would begin screaming at the victim to "get back, get back." The next time down the man who just took would usually get taken himself. "It wasn't about who you were, it was about what you did," says Phil Rucker. "Guys go out there dueling and showing off for the crowd."

Isaac "Rabbitt" Walthou had that attitude. The summer he graduated from Franklin High School, he went up to Kutsher's Resort in the

Catskills and scored 25 points on Dick McGuire in a summer league game. After a tryout with the Celtics, Rabbitt was cocky enough to tap Bob Cousy on the butt as they walked off the court and say, "Nice game, kid." He may have been too cocky. Celtics coach Red Auerbach cut Walthau the next day.

Rabbitt played the Rucker. He played his opponents – stars like Calvin Ramsey and Ray Felix – for chumps. He played for his fans and he played for himself, because that's who most appreciated him. "There was a game later in the afternoon, and it was close to getting dark out," McCullough remembers. "Rabbitt was dribbling around, and Rucker shouted out 'Ten seconds left.' Rabbitt kept dribbling, and Rucker was down to five seconds. Rabbitt pulled up from the key, shouted out, 'String music,' even though the rims had no nets, and then everyone got up and walked away.

"I couldn't see what happened because it was dark. I didn't know if he made the shot, but everyone was leaving. I asked Rucker how they knew what happened, and he just looked at me and said, 'Because that is Rabbitt Walthau.'"

Rabbitt never showed his wares outside the confines of the ghetto, but that didn't matter. He had the admiration of anyone who played, watched, or knew the game. "With people in the ghetto comes a higher reverence for what happens inside their boundaries than out-side," says Richard "Pee Wee" Kirkland, who grew up in Harlem and is considered one of the best guards ever to grace a New York City play-ground. "We knew about the NBA and college, that they could all of a sudden be an option for us, but in the ghetto the street ball players, not the pros, had all the respect."

That's what made the Rucker so important: Guys made their repu-tations playing on that sun-baked playground. They earned their nick-names. Other people's respect for their skills was an elixir that kept them hanging around the rim far beyond their usefulness, just like pro athletes who stick around after their skills have faded.

Three thousand miles away, in the state of Washington and throughout the Northwest, Native Americans were undergoing similar struggles to define themselves. Public Law 83-280, enacted in 1953, began what was known as the "termination" era in federal and tribal regulations regarding the Native American population. The legislation was designed to assimilate Indians into the white culture and reduce the federal government's assistance to Indians. Essentially, this translated into an attempt by the federal government to terminate the tribes and lessen the load on the federal budget. Many tribes were disbanded, taking money from the government in exchange for their land, name and heritage.

In Yakima, Washington, the Yakima tribe was feeling increased pressure to sell out. Richard Isaac, Bill Yop and Ed Sampson, all tribal members, were looking for a way to unite all Indian nations, to save their culture from being laid waste. All three played basketball, and so they traveled throughout the state to various Indian tournaments. In March 1955, the three decided to bring these tournaments together and establish an event that was open to players from tribes all over the country. Such a gathering, they thought, would foster support for imperiled tribes and embolden young Native Americans. "It started out as an idea and became a movement," says Joe Sampson, Ed's brother, who has been running the Yakima Tournament since 1964. "As a nation, our boys liked basketball. They were good at it. It was a common bond to bring us together."

Public Law 83-280 was repealed in 1968, but the tournament continues to thrive. Unlike African Americans, however, Native Americans are a minority that has yet to find mainstream basketball success.

◆ ◆ ◆

The great American Indian prophet Smohalla once said, "Life is a drum" – a circle with no beginning or end, just a cycle of life, death, and life. The drum's beat echoes the pulse of the human heart. The same could easily be said about a basketball. It, too, is a perfect circle, and the rhythm of leather on hardwood is the syncopated sound of the heart in an excited state. If basketball has always been the great equalizer, placing those with less on equal footing with those who are privileged, then in no culture is the basketball-as-life analogy more apt than on an Indian reservation. That's been true for David Cunningham, and he's found the circle of life to be particularly vicious.

It is late autumn of 1996, and David, a starter on the North Idaho College basketball team in Coeur d'Alene, is returning home to the

Nez Perce Indian Reservation in Lapwai, Idaho, for one last weekend before the season begins. Driving out of the Lewiston Hills in central Idaho, David begins shaking his head in disgust. He can see the smoke forming heavy, silhouetted clouds just above the ridge, and he knows what lurks around the bend. "Careful now," he warns. "It may begin to stink." As the putrid exhaust from a factory wafts through the car's heating vents, the Potlatch paper mill comes into view. It is the bane of David's existence. "That mill is using all our resources," he says. "The company has already cut everything down on one side of the mountain. Now it's creeping closer and closer to home."

Past meets present at every turn in the road from the mountains, and the present is winning out. At the top of one hill is a pattern carved by weather and time that resembles the Nez Perce warrior Chief Joseph lying down in his headdress, still clutching an ax. At the base of the hill is a historic landmark commemorating the site of a former Nez Perce village called Coyote's Fishing Net, which overlooks the Clearwater River. The landmark's lot is empty of cars, and the salmon in the Clearwater that the Nez Perce used to snatch from the river with spears are now poisoned. But across the highway, a casino – looking as out of place as a minimall in the desert – is packed with cars. Reverend Henry Spalding, one of the first white men to act as teacher to the Nez Perce people, said 160 years ago, "What is done for the poor Indians of this Western world must be done soon. The only thing that can save these people from annihilation is the introduction of civilization." Driving towards Lapwai, it seems the good Reverend was mistaken.

Lapwai is, other than Lewiston, the only city in the valley of the Lewiston Hills. It's easy to find. Follow the stink from the paper mill, which funnels through the valley along the path of the Clearwater River until it reaches a clearing in Lapwai, where it spreads out and covers the town in a blanket of sickly sweet stench. Lapwai is home to the Nez Perce Indians, who inhabited most of southeastern Washington, northeastern Oregon, and central Idaho before the Europeans moved westward. Confined to Lapwai since the treaty of 1863, the Nez Perce are reminded by the encroaching smell of the Potlatch that even the little space they've kept for themselves is not really their own.

"There is an inherent conflict between Indian nations and the US government that goes beyond whatever wars there were a hundred years ago," David says. "We are a sovereign nation trying to exist within a sovereign nation. And what is good for our nation is not always, or even likely to be, good for the nation in which we're based."

Unemployment in Lapwai is 36 percent in the summer, when people find work fighting forest fires. In the winter, the jobless rate climbs to 79 percent. Less than 30 percent of Lapwai's high school students go on to college. The reservation is no different from other impoverished areas: Sports, basketball in particular, are the ticket out of town for many Nez Perce boys and girls. The kids who make it, though, are not only saving themselves, but improving the chances of the next Indian player with potential. Right now David, considered the best player on the Nez Perce reservation and winner of the last three MVP titles in the Yakima nation tournament, carries that burden.

Unlike the inner cities, where scouts scour the asphalt looking for that next million-dollar prodigy, great players from the reservations often go overlooked or are flat-out ignored. Indian kids, the coaches say, never last at college. They get homesick, give up, and leave in the middle of the season. The Indians, however, believe that college recruiters are prejudiced and lazy, buying into the stereotype of Indians as quitters and drinkers. "Most Indians already feel like they've been defeated before they get there, so they don't bother trying at all," says David's father, David Cunningham, Sr., who is white. Says his son, "It's hard for people to believe in anything that doesn't come from the reservation, even a college degree, because of our history with the government. A lot of people just give up on getting an education because they don't believe in what a diploma stands for."

For those who do believe in higher education, college life can be prickly. Every moment off the reservation is spent trying to erase a stereotype, while every moment on it is measured in caution. "There are two worlds around here – inside the reservation and outside the reservation," says David Sr. "Once you thrive on the outside, people on the inside try to bring you back down. A lot of people here want to be the same. But they would rather you come down to their level than them rising up to yours."

David, because of his life off the reservation, is called an "apple": red-skinned on the outside, white on the inside. The more time he spends away from home, the more people believe he's turning his back on them. "Opportunities are there, and it's just a question of Indians taking them. Some people just don't want any more than what they have on the reservation. And they don't want anyone else to have it either." David speaks from experience, and he knows that he himself has come close to languishing forever on the reservation. Either way, it's basketball that is pushing him out or pulling him in.

"I was talking to an assistant of mine who coached on a reservation in Arizona," says Bruce Crossfield, who coached Lapwai High School to three consecutive state titles in the late 1980s. "We were talking about a warrior mentality, which is something I found the kids in Lapwai really brought to defense. They all had this goal for keeping opponents under 35 percent shooting for the game. I was amazed. They bought into this idea with such enthusiasm without an extrinsic reward. It was all internal motivation.

"When the game was out of hand and I brought in the second string and we gave up an easy basket or two, the first string would be on their feet screaming at their teammates to stop the other team and at me to put them back in the game. They got so upset if we came close to allowing 35 percent. It wasn't phony. It was genuine. When these guys would come back to visit after they graduated, they still asked if we were holding opponents below 35 percent.

"This assistant was telling me about what he learned on the reservation in Arizona. The Sioux had a tradition in which they would sneak up on their enemy, and instead of killing them, they'd just touch them, like they were playing tag. It was a proof of your manhood early on, a kind of one-upsmanship. The principle was the same with my players. It was a question of their manhood, that warrior mentality, the need to prove something to their opponents because they are Indians, that made these kids buy into keeping the other team under 35 percent."

Crossfield led the Lapwai High School Wildcats during its most illustrious period. In his first season, 1986, the varsity team went 26–0 and won the state tournament. The next season, Lapwai finished 24–0, again winning the state title. So deep was the tiny town's pool of talent that the junior varsity was considered the second best team in the Central Idaho League.

As Crossfield's third year rolled around, the team had two state titles and had yet to lose under him, riding a 50-game winning streak. Lapwai could break the Idaho record for consecutive wins, 75, if it continued unbeaten to the state finals again. As the season wore on, national media latched on to the story of the little school that could. The CBS Evening News did a feature on the basketball team, which was averaging close to 85 points a game during Crossfield's tenure. The other networks followed. Lapwai tied the record in the state semifinals, and by the night of the championship game in Rigby, Idaho, about 300 miles from Lapwai, the mood in Lapwai, Crossfield recalls, was, "Last one out of town hit the lights when you leave." Everyone headed to Rigby for the title game.

Lapwai won and set the state record for wins. But it was more than just an Idaho state championship and a new state record that the people of Lapwai celebrated that night. Crossfield had learned earlier in the season what basketball success meant to those on the reservation. He had kicked a kid off the team for drinking, and the player's stepmother approached him and asked why the coach was picking on her boy when almost all the kids on the team were getting drunk most every night after practice. Crossfield recalls the exchange. "I said, 'Tell me who they are and I'll kick them off, too.' Then she said to me, 'I'm not doing that. I want to win.'

"Basketball there is bigger than life. The threat of losing is too great."

Despite Lapwai's phenomenal success over those three years – an unbeaten, three-time state champion – only two players garnered any interest from colleges. Compare that to high school powerhouse Dunbar in Baltimore, which won 83 straight from 1981 to 1983. All five of the starters from the 1983 team earned college scholarships; even the sixth man got a college ride. "There is a stigma that Indian kids won't last in college," says Bob Sobotta, who was on Lapwai's 1984 state championship basketball team and is now the coordinator of minority student services at Lewis and Clark State in Lewiston. "And many don't. Family is probably what draws a lot of people back to the reservation. Families on the reservation are pretty extended, but it's not like the typical American family that is spread throughout the country. When you leave the reservation, you don't have the support that you had when you were eighteen, and you get drawn back. It happens no matter how good you are at basketball."

"They say we're slackers," says Ted Strom, the head coach at Wapato High on the Yakima reservation in Washington. "But part of it is that there is still a lot of prejudice. We don't get the coverage in the papers that we should. It's changed for some minority groups. For Indians, it's still the same."

Coaches in states with strong Native American populations – states like Montana, the Dakotas and New Mexico – are making efforts to change that. Admittedly, they are motivated not by righting a wrong but by the prospect of winning more basketball games. Dave Bliss, coach at the University of New Mexico since 1988, started running basketball camps at the Pojuaque reservation thirty miles northwest of Santa Fe in 1994. He began with 70 campers; in three years the number swelled to 200. "There are incredible talents on the reservations," Bliss says, "because the Native Americans love basketball. And it's a lot easier for me to find a guy here and convince him to come to my school than find some kid from the inner city of Chicago.

"The problem for these kids is exposure. None of them wants to play in summer leagues against the top players, and their high school competition is not a good barometer of their talent. It's tough to find them if you're not looking off the beaten path."

University of Montana basketball coach Blaine Taylor adds, "Saying there is still some prejudice against Indians is not an overstatement, nor is it wrong to say fewer Indians get recruited. But first you want to look at the requisite abilities. Sometimes there may be a question about whether or not a player can play at the next level, and when the talent of an Indian player is questioned it immediately becomes innuendo on the reservation."

Taylor, who actively recruits on reservations throughout Montana, knows the competing forces at work on an Indian player who goes off to college. His starting point guard is six-foot-two J. R. Camel, who as a sophomore in 1996–97 made the All-Big Sky Conference team. Camel, whose family lives on the Flathead reservation just north of Missoula, is one of the few Native Americans thriving in Division I basketball. Every day Taylor sees Camel balancing his life on and off the reservation with skills as graceful as any he exhibits on the basketball court. "If a kid from the inner city gets a scholarship and plays Division I ball,

that is an accomplishment," says Taylor. "He has achieved something.
On the reservation there is a pull and allure to stay there. The guys
who leave for college and college sports don't get the validation that
they are doing something good. There is a lot of distrust of life off the
reservation, and for good reason."

As a sixth-grader, David played for a team off the reservation. He
was the only Indian, the only player with a ponytail bouncing from his
neck. When a player or parent from an opposing team called him "sav-
age," "heathen," or "crazy injun," he had no one to laugh it off with
after the game. He can see why so many of his predecessors had a hard
time lasting at college and in the white man's world. At the end of the
1995–96 at North Idaho, a well-intentioned blonde girl came up to
David in the gym after a game and, with her flat palm stuck in his face,
said, "How."

"Sometimes the black players come up to me and complain that
there are no sisters up here," David says, "no one like them. I ask them,
'How do you think it is for me?'"

On the reservation, David is more than just another basketball
player. He's the latest savior, educator and vindicator. At a time when
he is just discovering his talents, he is being told that it is his responsibility to change the white man's view of the Indian. "At first I just
wanted to play basketball," says David. "When I got really good, people started looking up to me. All of a sudden I'm an example. Now
even if I don't want to play, I have to because if I quit people on the
reservation and off will think I'm just another lazy Indian who wasted
his potential."

As a boy, David would wander over to Cloud Court in Lapwai with
his older sisters Ruby and Kim and shoot until his sisters had beaten
him into submission. Ruby starred at Lapwai High School before blowing out both her knees, and Kim played at Loyola Marymount in Los
Angeles. David would run back home, crying all the way, and tell his
mother how much he hated them. Before she had dried the tears from
his cheeks, he'd turn around and head back outside. They taught David
well.

When he was twelve, David was featured in an article in *Sports Illustrated for Kids*. By the time he was fourteen he was starting for Lapwai
High as a freshman. As a sophomore he led an undefeated team into

the state tournament. As a senior he was a high school All-American, in the same class as the NBA's Jerry Stackhouse. "David was the smartest player I've ever had," says Crossfield. "You wished you knew more just so you could teach him more."

David earned his reputation as a great player at the Indian tournaments, of which there are hundreds every summer. Each nation fields a team and hosts a tournament. On an Indian reservation, basketball players carry the same cachet as the playgrounds legends do in the inner city. And David, like so many other players, is known for one shot that brought down the house.

The game occurred in the summer after David's senior year in high school. The Nez Perce were playing the Yakima Bucks in the Nez Perce Nation Tournament at the oven-baked Pin-Nee-Was, an un-air-conditioned gym where David still plays pickup ball on the weekends. David stands only five-foot-ten. His game is based on speed and strength, which he combined in one play for a stunning display. David stole the ball from his man at the three-point line. At midcourt he checked back to see if anyone was chasing him. No one was. At the top of the key, he bounced the ball high off the ground, and, taking just two steps, jammed it home with both hands on its way back to earth. Forget traveling, double-dribbling, palming or even flying without a license. On that play, there was no such thing as a moving violation. If it had happened in Harlem, someone would have made a movie about it.

"We once saw Chris Mullin do that, and David always said he would try it," says Sobotta, who was playing on David's team in the tournament that day. "But no one thought he could. Mullin is six-foot-seven. That he did that in a game situation – well, we had never seen anything like that."

Only one other Nez Perce player has earned such reverence: Willie Weeks, a six-foot-four shooter with a velvet touch who was once what David is today, the tribe's shining star and its hope. "He really just toyed with his competition," says Ted Strom of Weeks. "He could shoot. He was mobile, a good passer and relentless. The guy never got tired. It's a shame he never had the chance to play against really great competition."

Like David, Weeks was at his best at the Nez Perce tournament, once scoring 72 points in a single game. One particular shot from that game is remembered vividly by those who saw it. Weeks lined up for a shot from the corner, where the three-point line would be if it had existed back then, and began his shooting motion. A six-foot-five defender came at him while he was in mid-air, with a spot in the stands already picked out where he would swat Weeks' shot. In the middle of his shot and hanging in the air, Weeks transferred the ball from his right hand to his left and, in one motion, canned the jumper, lefthanded, in the dumbfounded defender's face.

"One of the things that is important about basketball, and one of the reasons the success of guys like David and Weeks is so relevant to the tribe, is the symbolism carried within the game," says Leroy Seth, a Nez Perce tribal elder who has lived in Lapwai for most of the last fifty years and was a member of Lapwai High's first state basketball championship team, in 1956. "It's the power of the circle to heal us. It's the sharing and a group – or team – acting as one that reminds us of days when the tribe acted in concert. The great players or teams remind us of the spirits that are around us."

In traditional Nez Perce beliefs, each person, if he or she chooses, has what is called a Wyakin, a guardian spirit. A Nez Perce could appeal to the Wyakin for assistance in times of trouble or could call on the Wyakin to warn and protect him on a harrowing journey. Each person would come to their Wyakin through a ritual performed between the ninth and fifteenth birthdays. After years of training from a grandparent already possessing a Wyakin – the Nez Perce call tribal elders grandparents, whether they are related by blood or not – the youth would set off by himself into the mountains, with no food or water. The child would seek out a lonely, desolate place in the hills and begin to fast and to search for his or her guardian.

Some returned, scared and hungry, before ever having the sacred encounter. Most, though, persevered. These visions may have been real or the result of delusions or hallucinations after going days without food or water. Whatever the case, once a Nez Perce had seen something, he was protected for life. "After that," David says, "everything in life supposedly tastes better, smells better, and your decisions are easier. They say people would come back glowing, like they had a secret." Though David has never sought out his Wyakin, his fellow Nez Perce swore there was something different about him beginning in his senior year in high school. He had that glow. He had a secret. He had discovered a guardian spirit.

David never lived with his real mother, an Indian. His father worked as a spike layer and engineer for the Burlington Railroad. His mother was unemployed, spending a lot of her time hopping from one bar to the next. They had a drunken encounter one night in 1975 and neither of them expected to see each other again. "Then one day, " David Sr. recalls, "she shows up at my door, drops off the kid and leaves."

A year and a half later, David's grandmother decided she and her daughter should have custody and sued David's father. On the day of the hearing, however, David's mother failed to show up and his father became the first man in Idaho to ever win custody over the birth-mother. "After that hearing, my Dad limited how often she could see me and how long I could stay with her at one time," David Jr. says.

David's father married the woman David now calls mom – he bristles if you refer to her as his stepmother – when David was six. Cheryl had Ruby and Kim from a previous marriage; David Sr. and Cheryl had two boys together, Pete and Ricky. As David grew older, and closer to Cheryl, his already tenuous relationship with his biological mother deteriorated further.

Though he would often go on fishing trips with his mother's family and his cousins in Oregon, he would spend as little time around his birth mother as possible, uncertain how to treat her. His cousins sensed his discomfort and incessantly picked on him. "They used to try and make me ask her for money," David says. "Even though they knew I couldn't do it. How could I ask her for money? I didn't even know her." That is why, when she died, David couldn't shed a tear.

He found out about her death by accident. David's Aunt Sherri called his house late one night during his freshman year of high school, expecting to speak with David Sr. She wanted the father to be the one who told the son that his mother had passed away. But David Jr. answered the phone. "David?" Sherri asked. "Yes," he responded, then heard what happened: She had had a heart attack, possibly brought on by drugs and alcohol. There was nothing the doctors could do to save her. As his aunt cried over the phone, David said thank you and hung up. Sherri never realized who she had really been talking to.

David didn't sleep that night. He still can't remember if he told his father the news the next morning at the breakfast table. He does remember his dad asking him how he was feeling, in that way parents do every morning, and responding that he was fine. He went to school that day as if nothing had happened. "At the funeral I tried so hard to cry, but I couldn't," says David. "I just didn't know her."

For David, the next four years were a morass of disappointment and emptiness. Lapwai went undefeated in his sophomore season, but in the first round of the playoffs three seniors decided they would win the title for Lapwai themselves and froze David out by not passing him the ball. That night, coming home from the loss, one of David's closest friends, who was driving behind him, hit a sheet of black ice, crashed and was pinned under a trailer. She died in David's arms.

He could feel himself slipping away. Frustrated with basketball, full of grief for his friend, he was on the verge of becoming the stereotype he had fought. A week later, David left Lapwai to get away from his problems, spending the next year living in the state of Washington with Ted Strom and his family. That summer, after his junior year, he worked in Washington, D.C., for the Department of Energy. He returned to Lapwai in the fall stubborn in his belief that as much as his tribe spurned the white man's education, that education offered him and his people their only means of protection. "Nobody wants to be taken advantage of," says David. "But nobody wants to learn the laws to keep that from happening." Life is like a circle.

That summer had been an awakening. As David was packing his bags to leave D.C., he noticed a small baby book tucked in the front pocket of his suitcase. His name was inside of it. He hadn't seen it for four years, since he put it in the suitcase to hide it from his father. Now he looked at it, and what he saw took his breath away.

Shortly after his mother died, David's maternal grandmother had given the book to him in the hope that it would help explain to David how much he had meant to his mother. The memories it held were bittersweet. There was a letter from David's father telling his mother she couldn't see David anymore. The pages that were intended to record a growing child's accomplishments – his first word, his first step – were virtually blank. All his mother could write was, "I don't know.

Your dad has those."

But there were also pages where his mother had chronicled in vivid detail other achievements, such as whether he was sitting up by himself at six months, and other notes, like his full name and at what hospital he was born. Written on the inside cover of the jacket, barely legible over the flowered paper, was a note to David from his mother. In it she explained how much she loved him and wished she could take care of him, and she apologized for the way their relationship, even years before she died, had developed. "Up until I was eighteen I didn't really think of her as my mom," David says. "But after everything that happened in high school, reading the book was like having her talk to me in a way we never had or could before. This is all I have until the next time we can talk."

Through reading his mother's diary, David had discovered his Wyakin.

In a special ceremony at a powwow during his senior year in high school, David was given the Indian name Hemene Ilppilp, which means Red Wolf. That was the name of a great Indian warrior who had been instrumental in treaty talks with the white man during the 1850s. No one had earned the name Red Wolf since he had died, and only his descendants were allowed to bestow the name on someone else. Even then, tradition held, the name had to stay in Red Wolf's immediate family. Yet Saucer Powauke, the eldest of Red Wolf's lineage, broke with tradition and gave the name to David. "David agonizes over accepting the praise for what he's done and accepting a leadership role on the reservation," Cheryl says. "But he feels that if he doesn't, no one will." Because of the weight of expectations, David constantly walks the line between setting a good example and becoming another bad one. "Sometimes the pressure is too much for him," says his father, "Every once in a while he loses it."

It happened in March 1996, after his first season at North Idaho College. For two months, he dropped out of school and lived in Lapwai, working for the reservation's Environmental Restoration and Waste Management Department. He played ball at nights with his friends, and spent time with his girlfriend, Janelle, and his brothers and sisters. No classes to attend, no practices. Life was good because life was easy – so easy that David started growing comfortable with the idea of being a failure in the eyes of himself and his people.

Then he became anxious. He felt the pain of responsibility digging at his gut, so he went back to school and stayed there for almost six months, with no vacation. "I felt like I was slipping into a pattern of being comfortable," says David. "I realized I was going against everything I believe in."

He had to make up the classes he missed when he skipped those two months. It wasn't any easier than it was before he left. In fact, it was harder: Janelle was pregnant. All of David's free time would be spent shuttling the 120 miles between Coeur d'Alene and Lapwai. In addition, a new basketball coach, David Watson, had taken over at North Idaho. Watson installed a new system that emphasized a half-court offense, which is less conducive to David's style of play. It didn't help matters that Watson's son played the same position as David.

Midway through the season Watson told David that the credits for the classes he had taken in the summer didn't transfer. He also told him that because he was getting money from the government for school, he wouldn't be getting a scholarship. By December, David was back in Lapwai, taking classes at Lewis and Clark State and working part-time for the Environmental Waste and Restoration Management facility on the reservation. "The coach told David about the scholarship right before Christmas," says David's father. "I don't really know what happened. Everyone at the school blames each other for not making sure he could be eligible and then for losing his scholarship. I think the new coach just wanted to go with his own guys."

Yet David's spirit remains unbroken. He still has eligibility and hopes a Division II or NAIA school will pick him up for the fall of 1998. "As long as I stay on line and keep playing well in Indian tournaments, it's going to be easier to achieve the dream," David says. "I've got to get that diploma. It's not my basketball that will help the reservation, but my education."

When he was still attending North Idaho, David always regretted leaving Lapwai after a weekend's visit. He had grown most comfortable in the one place where the most was expected of him. Driving over the Clearwater River and into the Lewiston Hills late on Sunday nights, with Lapwai at a distance and the Potlatch mill a faint light behind him, his head would shake from side to side, just as it did every time he spotted the paper mill on his way into town. David wasn't disgusted at what was in front of him, but grieved about what he was leaving behind. "It's getting harder and harder to leave," he would say. But now that he is home, he knows he cannot stay.

◆ ◆ ◆

In all his years as a street agent, Spook Stegman coveted one player above all others. And when Spook retired from his trade in 1972 – his new wife didn't appreciate his itinerant lifestyle or his sketchy associates – this guy was still the big quarry Spook wished he had hooked. Stegman could lay claim to having discovered thousands of players, but none was ever as good as the one he couldn't claim: Connie Hawkins.

"I saw this kid play for the first time at the Rucker tournament in the late fifties," Stegman says. "I was sitting on the fence that ran next to 130th Street. Everyone told me to watch for him. When the game ended I ran up to him, struck up a conversation. For the next two years I worked this kid, I had him and Roger Brown – the second best player in the city – all wrapped up for the University of Seattle, and then he slipped away from me. I still don't know how it happened."

Hawkins could do that to you – just slip away when you thought you had him, mystify you with moves generated from somewhere beyond the realm of normal men, entangle you in confusion with arms that stretched from blacktop to blue sky. "I remember going to a game when I was ten or eleven years old," says Pee Wee Kirkland. "Wilt Chamberlain is playing on one team. Connie and a guy named Jackie Jackson were on the other. Wilt is a seven-foot superstar supposed to be coming to the playground to teach all the ghetto boys a lesson. But he didn't know about Connie, who was around six-foot-eight or so. Connie gets the ball just outside the lane, takes off and dunks right on Wilt's head. On the other end he blocks one of Wilt's shots. He has Wilt so dumbfounded he can only shoot fadeaways. Then Jackie Jackson blocks him from behind. Then Wilt was pretty mad."

"People still talk about the time I went up and hook-dunked over Wilt Chamberlain in the Rucker," Hawkins told a group of reporters before his induction into Basketball Hall of Fame in 1992. "But that was only the start of the story. That hook dunk got Wilt mad, then Jackie Jackson really got Wilt mad. Jackie was one of the great leapers. I've seen him leap and snatch a quarter off the top of the backboard.

"After my hook dunk, Jackie told me to let Wilt take that fadeaway one-hander that banked high off the backboard, and when Wilt put the ball up there, Jackie leaped and trapped it, pinning the ball against the board.

"Everybody hollered and screamed, but Wilt called time out. He didn't say anything, but when we looked over we could see him glaring at us. The next ten times down the court, Wilt said, 'Gimme the ball' and he dunked it every time. Hard. One time he dunked the ball so hard it bounced up over a fifteen-foot fence. Wilt didn't like to be shown up."

Sitting in his office in Phoenix, where he has been director of community relations for the Suns since 1992, Connie admits that maybe the hook dunk had become part of his legend. So many shots, dunks and passes from that era have morphed from fact into fiction because fans and players want so much to believe in them, to say they had seen it. "To be honest," Hawkins says, "I don't really remember that play. But I've heard from so many people that they've seen it, I just figure it's true."

As a boy growing up in the Bedford-Stuyvesant section of Brooklyn, Connie was as unlikely to eventually show up Wilt Chamberlain as he was to show up for school. He was tall, lanky, shy and had no self-confidence. From his first day at P. S. 3 grammar school, Connie fell behind the rest of his class. Each year in school, he understood less and less of what the teachers were saying, and he was too afraid to ask them to explain. Because of his height, Connie was already wary of being picked on, and he didn't need the extra hassles of being called stupid. So he essentially stopped going when he reached junior high. On those rare occasions when he did show up, the teachers embarrassed him in front of his classmates, actually announcing that he was dumb. One time, he says, a teacher held up Connie's exam paper and told the class to turn around and look at the moron. "It was hard for me, and I regret it now," Connie says. "I didn't know what the teachers were talking about and what was written in the books. Every day, I was ashamed. I came to hate school, hate being dumb."

Connie spent some of his newly free time playing basketball, but he didn't enjoy the game very much. His hand-eye coordination had yet to catch up to his tall, wispy body, and he looked awkward on the court. More often than not someone would make fun of him there, too. So instead of playing hoops, he would pitch pennies for a bit of change or commit petty crimes – stealing comic books or candy bars.

Shortly after he turned twelve, things changed.

The summer of 1954 was too hot for Connie to spend in his mother's cramped, stuffy apartment. He began showing up more on the playground at nearby P. S. 45, shooting by himself while the other kids played, building confidence as his skills grew to match his body. Then, one sultry afternoon, he shed his protective shell. "I was six-foot-two," he says. "Everyone at the high school team could dunk, and I wanted to try. So I did. I kind of surprised myself."

Everything he had lacked during the first twelve years of his life, Connie received tenfold once his name and his game emerged on the playgrounds. "Before basketball," Connie recalls, "there wasn't anything I liked about myself." He started playing with Eddie Simmons, a cat-quick guard who as a sophomore was starring for Boys & Girls High, the best team in the New York City public leagues. The trio of Hawkins, Simmons and Jackie Jackson – another varsity player at Boys & Girls whom Hawkins has called, "the greatest schoolyard player I ever saw" – made up the best barnstorming playground team in Brooklyn.

The court to play at in those days was in Kingstone Park. Guys like Solly Walker of St. John's, Vinnie Cohen of Syracuse and Sihugo Green of the St. Louis Hawks spent their summers on that playground. When Connie was fifteen, Eddie and Jackie felt he was ready to play with the big boys. Connie could feel his game surge whenever he played the local stars. He jumped higher, passed better, played a smoother brand of ball than any of the All-Americans he was up against. "Connie was really in with the top people," Gene Smith, who coached Hawkins at Brooklyn's Carlton Y, said in *Foul*, Connie's biography. "You weren't a ballplayer unless you played at Kingstone Park. That's where the action was. Every game, somebody had a reputation to defend."

Connie, Eddie and Jackie succeeded in making names for themselves in Brooklyn. Now the challenge was to prove themselves away from home. If you were from Brooklyn, that meant hopping on the subway and taking the train to Harlem, to Rucker.

Just a few miles separate Harlem and Brooklyn. Both house poor neighborhoods, and both boast of their basketball greatness. Back in Connie's day, though, kids from Harlem acted as though Brooklyn was in another state, and Brooklyn guys thought of Harlem players as city punks. The Brooklyn style of play was wide-open and creative, highlighted by no-look passes and long-range jumpers. In Harlem, the game was physical, full of dribble-drives and stifling defense. In Brooklyn, every defensive rebound reset at the top of the key. In Harlem, no one ever took the ball back. When Brooklyn and Harlem players faced each other on the court, the games were steeped in hatred. Simmons, who died in the mid-1970s, recalled in *Foul* that when he, Connie and Jackie came uptown to play Cal Ramsey, Satch Sanders and Russ Cunningham, "the word would spread through the neighborhood that we were goin' after them. The park would start to crowd up. Games stopped on other courts. People would stand around and cheer and argue and bet six-packs. It was half-court, three-on-three. People would talk about those games for days."

"Here is the way it was with those three," says Bernie Parker, who grew up and played in Harlem at the time. "You talk about a point guard? No one could do it like Eddie. Jackie could grab the sun when he jumped. And then there was Connie. He had everything all in one. He had to be the greatest street player to come through. When they knew he was playing, you couldn't get a seat in the park."

The toughest gym in Harlem was at St. Phillips Church, where Holcombe Rucker worked. The baskets were flush against the brick wall, which meant three things: Driving for a layup was more dangerous than driving a car blindfolded, passing off the walls was legal, and diving for loose balls was a bad idea. It is also where Connie learned to steel himself against those who had tormented him when he was a gawky kid. Basketball did this for him. Connie's talent made him invincible, and he would rather die than be without it. When another teenager walked up to him with a gun pointed and said, "Give me your shoes or I'll shoot you," Connie didn't think twice. No shoes meant no ball. He couldn't afford to buy new ones. Those were all he had. "So shoot me," the once shy Connie said. The assailant ran away. A legend had been born.

Each year beginning in the 1950s, Holcombe Rucker took the best players from New York and pitted them against the best from Philly in an annual all-star game that achieved the status of de facto championship of East Coast playground basketball. The seminal matchup occurred in 1958, at 130th Street in Harlem. Connie, six-foot-five at the time, had just earned All-City for the first time as a sophomore at Boys & Girls High. The main attraction, though, was six-foot-ten center Wayne Hightower, a senior from Philadelphia's Overbrook High School, the country's top prep player, who on his way to the University of Kansas.

The rivalry was fierce, and the attention focused on Hightower only heightened the drama. Though the game would be held in New York, Hightower had been talking smack to his friends. The playground circuit was, and is, a small world of proud but highly sensitive adolescent boys. Insults travel quickly and are not easily forgotten. "The papers were always writing about how he never lost a game," recalls Bob McCullough, who played that day. "But he was on our turf now."

The talking continued into the game's opening minutes. Hightower was on the free throw line muttering, "There's no one who can stop me. None of you better get in my way."

McCullough asked Hawkins who Hightower was talking to. "I don't know, but he better not be talking to me," Hawkins said.

"I'm talking to you and everybody on your team," Hightower responded.

"I said, 'Connie, fuck him,'" McCullough recalls. "Then Connie stood up and I was stunned at how tall he looked. He always slouched, so you could never really see how big he was. The rest of the day, he didn't let Hightower get a shot off. The poor kid was embarrassed. Meanwhile, Connie put the world on notice of his talents."

"He started flying out there and he changed the game for us," Parker says. "We had never seen anything like that."

Basketball came of age in the 1950s because that is when it took flight. It developed an edge and a pace that hadn't been there before. This was a game, it became clear, that had to be played above the rim. And black athletes, for whatever reasons, came to dominate the game more than any other group. The burgeoning summer leagues in New

York served as backdrops for dramas that rivaled Shakespeare in the Park. Those who took part became the Picassos of the playground, discovering new possibilities and new forms of expression. They created an art form, something more akin to ballet than sport.

4

The Best There Never Was

The face is unchanged. The arms and hands – gouged as they are by needle marks and dotted with blotches of thick white keloid – appear rotted and elderly, but the face, even from behind a soft cloud of smoke that billows up from a burning cigarette, looks young and vibrant, with its perfectly articulated angles and hard, haunting features, as if unaffected by the passing of time. It's the kind of face you've seen on a Roman bust or Michaelangelo's *David* – strong, willful, resolute. How, after all these years of heroin and alcohol abuse, which have ravaged the body and withered the soul, does this face look so, so ... good?

"I've always had the face of a young man," he says, "but even though I'm fifty-two, I feel like I'm a hundred. I've had a long, hard life. The way I figure it, I'm just lucky to be alive, lucky to still be on the playground."

It would be folly to try to name the greatest player of the playground. Over the years so many players have quietly fallen prey to the vices of the street that pinpointing one person's story as the quintessential street-ball tragedy is impossible. That being the case, one man is mentioned more frequently than anyone else on the nation's playgrounds as the best, the one against whom everyone else must be measured. His myth has grown over the years. The publication of Pete Axthelm's *The City Game* in 1970 brought his story to light, and since then journalists have followed the tale. Though his ruination came at the callow age of twenty-two, he had more than enough time to create a legend. And though the story has been told often, in print and, most recently, in film, he belongs in these pages because in many ways he embodies the fate that befalls so many in the theater of the playground. If not the first to fall on his sword, he is the most famous. He is Earl "the Goat" Manigault, the man with the face of a king.

"It's hard for me to say if I was the best ever on the playground," says Manigault as he sits on a bench in a park on 99th and Amsterdam Avenue in Manhattan, where he now runs a summer tournament. "I do know this: No one could ever touch me when I was playing. I was kind of like a Jordan of the playground. But for every Jordan, there is an Earl Manigault. I didn't hurt anybody but myself."

With this thought his deep dark eyes, blemished and muddy as the bottom of the Hudson River, grow dewey. "I wasted my fuckin' life. Wasted it. But I'm trying to make up for it now."

This is the site of his attempt at redemption, this park on Manhattan's Upper West Side. A few empty beer bottles lie on the ground, and the smell of marijuana breezes through the sultry summer air, but for a Manhattan playground the park is in relatively good shape. Manigault tends to it as a gardener tends to his nursery, always cleaning it and making sure the landscape looks healthy. Friends help him keep the unsavory elements out of the park. Two of them are sitting on a bench watching the action unfold on the court. They have both known the Goat for more than thirty years.

"Earl was the only guy I've ever known who could walk through Harlem without a penny in his pocket and get whatever he wanted," says James Samuels. "He was the king of Harlem, even when he was strung out on heroin. People would do anything for him because he was such a low-key guy whose personality never changed."

"There's no doubt he's the best playground player ever," says Dave Evans as he squints under the dappled sunlight that streams though the tall trees encasing the park. "You might think this is bullshit, but it's true. It's something that Jordan couldn't even do. Earl was playing in a semipro game in 1965 in a little gym up in East Harlem. He was late for the game and the coach said he couldn't play. But Earl forced his way in, and he immediately took five jump shots from the same place and hit each one. On the sixth possession a guy they called Aubry grabbed the rebound and pitched the ball half-court to Earl. Everyone in the gym stood up. There was one guy back on defense, and he tried to draw a charge by stopping at the foul line. Earl took off a few feet in front of him and stepped on his forehead – his goddamn *forehead* – and catapulted over him and dunked the ball. Maybe Doctor J could do something like that, but Earl is only six-foot-one. I swear this is true. Ask anyone." Five people, asked in different places at different times, confirmed the story.

Manigault first felt a basketball when he was twelve. Earl was a loner as a young child – even today he is a figure trying to cloak itself in isolation – and the place to which he would escape was the basketball court. He was born in Charleston, South Carolina, as the ninth child to parents who didn't give a lick about him. Eventually he was given to a childless country woman named Mary Manigault. He spent his first six years of life with her, living in a one-room house in the backwoods of South Carolina, with no electricity, heat or running water. Young Earl had virtually no communication with the outside world. On the rare occasions when he ventured into town, people whispered about him, wondering if he was mute.

In 1951, when Earl was seven, Mary found a job through relatives at a laundromat on Manhattan's Upper West Side. Earl was placed in school, but with the interpersonal skills of a toddler, he fared no better around kids his age than he had as a lonely child in South Carolina. By the time he reached the fourth grade, Earl was living in a room by himself at the Hotel Pennington on 95th and Riverside Drive. Mary had landed a job managing the hotel, and as a benefit she and Earl each got their own rooms. Perpetuating Earl's isolation was the treatment he received from his classmates at school. They didn't take to him, Earl says, because he was viewed as an outsider, as a country boy who would never cut it in the big city.

Without friends or much of a family, Earl turned to basketball. "It was fifth or sixth grade that I realized I could be a real good ballplayer," he says. "I knew I had springs like no one else – I was outjumping guys who were nearly twice as tall as me when I was in the sixth grade. So I would wander all around Harlem, watching the older guys play and dreaming about someday getting on the court. It sounds strange, but I dreamed of being a playground player, not a professional player. I dreamed of adding things to the game that no one had ever thought of before, doing crazy things that people couldn't even imagine."

By the time Earl was thirteen he could dunk two volleyballs at once. In junior high he set a city record by scoring 52 points in one game. Soon he was one of the most sought-after players on the playground circuit. At the age of sixteen, he solidified his reputation as the city's top player during an unofficial citywide all-star tournament held at Riis Beach in Queens on the Fourth of July. At the tourney Manigault brought the crowd to its knees with a dunk that is still talked about, in Harlem and elsewhere. With one great leap he soared over Lew Alcindor *and* Connie Hawkins on his way to the rim. "I remember that one," says Manigault. "Lew came up to me afterwards and just shook his head and said, 'That was incredible.'"

"He had a lot of skills similar to Michael Jordan," says Kareem Abdul-Jabbar, the former Lew Alcindor, who played with and against Manigault as the two grew up in New York during the 1960s.

"Kareem called me a walking monument," says Manigault. "And I called him God. Because that's what he was on the basketball court."

On the playground, Manigault's moves came from the heart, from the place where passion and creativity begin. The fact that he was a loner, a dreamer, seemed to give the Goat a heightened sense of what it took to be beautiful on the basketball court, at the same time that his solitude made his life off the court, down to the way he expressed himself, sometimes less than beautiful. "I ate, I shit, and I fucked basketball," he says. "That was all that mattered." Even when he was sipping his cheap wine or shooting toxins into his veins, he was thinking the game, living the game. And so, just like Nat Holman at the turn of the century, he was inspired to come up with moves that could someday revolutionize the game, change the way people thought about it. One move he tried over and over – and he still regrets his failure to accomplish it – was dunking the ball and then sitting on the rim.

"I tried that so many times, and I came real close," says Manigault, "but I kept hurting my back. I got the idea because sometimes when I'd be dunking I noticed that my waist would be hovering near the rim. So I tried wiggling my way onto the rim, but I strained so many muscles trying that I had to give up. Damn."

Manigault attended Franklin High, and the stories of how he was treated there foreshadow his downfall. One time, after Manigault scored 43 points in the city championships, a faculty member smelled wine on his breath. Instead of chastising the star, the administrator suggested that Manigault drink before every game. When Earl was kicked out of school for smoking marijuana in the bathroom a month after his eligibility as a basketball player had run out, he was virtually illiterate. (Manigault still vehemently denies smoking dope that day.)

"If I had been better prepared in high school perhaps I would have made better decisions," says Manigault. "But all I ever wanted to do was play ball."

Even while he was in high school, Manigault lived in a world of parks and playground courts. He would travel to all five boroughs of New York during every season of the year, in search of a game. From the time he was twelve until he essentially quit playing at the age of twenty-two, Manigault haunted the parks. It took the Goat years of playing guys one-on-one and pulling off jaw-dropping moves for his reputation to develop, but once you have a rep on the playground, it's as good as a career's worth of NBA boxscores attesting to your greatness. It is because so many people saw the Goat as he traveled throughout the city, because so many witnessed the melodrama as it unfolded, that he became the city's tragic hero, a man who represented everything divine and disgusting about life on the playground.

"He's a legend because everyone saw him, and no one could believe what they were seeing," says Earl's friend James Samuels, as he sits on a bench at the park where Goat's tournament is played. "Even if he had made it to the NBA and became known around the world, he would still be a legend in Harlem for what he did on the playground. Though he was always by himself, he brought people together like no one ever has in Harlem. People would stop their lives just to get glimpse of this kid playing in the park. No one will ever be able to have that kind of effect on people again. He was the first, and he will be the only."

Samuels carries no particular expertise on the subject, other than that he has known Earl for most of his life, and that he is a lifelong Harlem resident. If anyone should know about the legend, it is someone like him.

Of course, a legend is always more intriguing when beset by a flaw, by a moral failing that prevents him from fulfilling his destiny. In the mid 1960s, after Earl had been kicked out of high school, Holcombe Rucker saved him from oblivion. Rucker had developed a relationship with Frank McDuffy at Laurington Academy in North Carolina, and he sent many of the kids who showed promise, as players and people, there for seasoning. Now he made such arrangements for Manigault. Earl seemed to straighten out his life in the academy's serene atmosphere and earned his diploma. Then he moved on to Johnson C. Smith, an all-black college in Charlotte. However, the coach at Smith, Bill McCullough, was cut from the same cloth as former Oklahoma State coach Henry Iba: He demanded controlled play and precision passing, a style Earl had never seen, much less played. Because McCullough didn't take to Earl's way – the way of the city where you beat your man one-on-one whenever you can – he sat Earl on the bench. Manigault started one game in 1966 and scored 27 points, leading his team to its first victory of the season, but he was quickly sent back to the bench. It was too much for the Goat. When he returned to Harlem for Christmas break in 1966, he stayed.

Earl says he had never even heard of heroin until returning to Harlem. One October afternoon, after a pickup game at Rucker Park, Earl found a plastic bag full of white powder under a bench. His innocence was forever lost. That afternoon marked the beginning of his journey into the heart of a heroin-induced darkness. "When some people look down on the street they find money and maybe something they could keep," says Earl. "But when I looked down that day in Rucker Park, my life was over. I just didn't see it then."

Imagine what could have been had he not looked down, not sampled the drug. A whole generation of players, the generation now in the NBA, could have been influenced by this man, who instead is still trying to figure out what went wrong. He now has a weak heart – his aortic valve is deteriorating. He has been on the transplant list since 1991, but, because of his past drug use, he is considered a poor candidate for a new heart. Did he ever think about not trying the drug?

"That never really crossed my mind," he says, shaking his head with a sad smile. "My friends were, like, 'Oh, the white lady – she'll rock us all night long. It's our lucky day.' So I tried it. The first time, I puked all over the place, but it was like I enjoyed throwing up. It's hard to explain, but it's a powerful drug, like it's Christmas every day and you got no worries. You're just living in this dreamlike world where everything seems perfect. Of course it wasn't perfect. It ruined me." A week after his twenty-second birthday, Earl Manigault became a junkie. His playing career ends right there, but the story does not.

Manigault spent fourteen empty years wandering the streets of Harlem in search of a fix. He stole to support his habit, and served a few stints in jail. Then, at the age of thirty-six, the Goat cleaned himself up. His talent was long gone by then, even though he never poked a needle in his legs – "never was I going to screw with my ups" – but his ability to enthrall and transform a community remained intact. Indeed, Manigault's true and lasting gift is not his basketball ability – evanescent in any case and fatefully so in his – but the indefinable power he holds over the people who saw him play. It's as if those who witnessed him play, even once, owe the Goat a debt of gratitude for being allowed to share in such greatness, such perfection.

In 1971, still nursing a heroin addiction, Earl approached a drug dealer who for all intents and purposes owned Morningside Park in South Harlem. The park sits at the base of a hill abutting property owned by Columbia University but lies in a world vastly different from that of the Ivy League. Today needles and vials litter its patchy grass, and drug deals go down as police stand not more than fifty feet off, aware but completely indifferent. Much the same was the case back in 1971, when the Goat decided to try to reclaim the park from a drug lord.

"I can't tell you his name, but he was one of the biggest dealers in Harlem at the time," says Manigault. "I asked him if he'd help me start a summer tournament, and he agreed. I'm pretty sure he would have killed somebody who didn't have the respect I did had they asked him the same thing. But I was different. It was basically the only good thing that has ever come out of my reputation."

Using $10,000 that was given to him by the dealer, Manigault began his tournament. He purchased jerseys and equipment and paid for time-keepers and referees. For the first year, the dealers and the junkies stayed away. The man who gave Earl the seed money and the park had issued a decree saying, in effect, that neither Earl nor anyone associated with the tournament was to be hassled.

During the second year, though, a side business began to build alongside the tournament, an industry that eventually grew into a cash-cow in the world of playground basketball in New York: Small-time drug dealers started betting on games. As far as Earl can tell, the summer of 1972 was the first instance of drug money playing a role in playground hoops. By the end of the tournament's second year, dealers had begun assembling their own teams and playing each other for money. These days, stakes have been rumored to be as high as $100,000 per game.

"I know it was the first time dealers started getting involved in the game," says Manigault. "They'd bet as much as a hundred thousand dollars on games where the players were barely teenagers. So I had to do something."

He did. In 1973 he moved the tournament to its current location. But what started in Morningside Heights park in 1972 has spawned an entire generation of players like James "Speedy" Williams who make a nice living playing in drug games.

"That's not my legacy," says Goat. "What you see before you, how I'm trying to help these kids stay away from drugs – that's my legacy." With that, he stands up, fixing a cold stare on a Jeep that pulls up, gangsta rap blaring from its sizable woofers. He takes a few steps forward, catching the attention of the driver.

"Sorry, Goat," says the driver, a teenager with what looks like panty hose on his head. "I'll turn it down. No disrespect, brother, no disrespect at all."

Yes, the Goat is a legend. Maybe he's not the best ever, but as long as he's alive, he will always be the king of Harlem.

The king's best days, he's quick to tell you, came when he was playing at the Rucker tournament. Holcombe Rucker had rescued the Goat when he was kicked out of high school, and had pulled the strings to get him into Laurington Academy. The Goat was always teetering on the brink of failure. He was fragile, and mentors like Rucker acted as props holding up the heavyweight talent with the featherweight psyche. But when the Goat returned home that winter after his first semester at Johnson C. Smith, distraught over his lack of playing time, he found the props kicked out from under him: Holcombe Rucker had died. You can only hold a person's hand for so long before that person must walk alone. Each time new responsibilities or expectations had the Goat's legs wobbling like a newborn calf's, Rucker had been there to stabilize him. But not this time. Who knows how differently the game would have evolved if he had lived?

Rucker's death retarded more than the maturity of one player, regardless of that player's talents. His premature death stunted the growth, economically and philosophically, of his program. No real chain of command had been established beneath Rucker. Though his minions believed in what he was doing and each year intensified their efforts to bring his ideals to the community, like any organization with a strong central figure and several equally influential advisors, the Rucker league splintered after its founder's death. Everyone thought they knew what was best for Rucker's legacy, and everyone wanted to lead it there. Bob McCullough felt the best way to teach neighborhood kids was to maintain the tradition of pitting pro players against local guys so the kids could have something to strive for. But to do that and also run the kids' league would cost more money than the Rucker program had. It required corporate sponsorships, and that would mean the Rucker would lose its status as a nonprofit with the Parks Department. Don Adams, another Rucker advisor, disagreed with continuing the pro tournaments. He was inclined to eliminate the celebrity aspect and focus only on developing programs for local kids. "Basically, we had to split," says Adams. "We wanted different things."

McCullough took his league up to 155th and Eighth Avenue to what is now known as Holcombe Rucker Park. In fact, the original Rucker league never played a single minute in this park. McCullough's league adopted the moniker Harlem Pro League, but because it had the stars who had been playing in the Rucker when Holcombe was alive, the Rucker name stuck. In the long run, the split did irreparable damage to both tournaments. McCullough had to disband his league in the mid-1980s for lack of funding, and the original Rucker league, which Adams fostered, hasn't been a force on the tournament scene since the mid-1960s. "They had the number one basketball tournament in the world," says Phil Rucker, Holcombe's son, "and now it's just another tournament."

At the same time as McCullough was taking the Rucker pro with corporate sponsorship from Mobil, other summer leagues catering to local hoops stars and professional-caliber players began springing up around the country. The Dust Bowl tournament in Lexington, Kentucky, drew former stars from the University of Kentucky and the ABA's Kentucky Colonels. But the biggest threat to the Rucker's dominance would come from just down I-95. Would Philadelphia stand idly by as its rival, New York City, solidified its reputation as the world's basketball capital? Of course not. In the 1960s Philadelphia's Baker League emerged as an alternative to the Rucker, and it had something McCullough's incarnation of the Rucker did not. The Rucker took place outside on concrete – a peril to any pro worried about his knees – while the Baker would be played indoors, and would be open only to professionals. None of those unpredictable playground types would be allowed.

"The Rucker was always fun to watch in the sixties, but it really was a tournament for the playground player and not the professional," says Bill Bradley, who starred for Princeton in the 1960s before moving on to the New York Knicks, with whom he won two NBA titles. "The real competition for the pros in the sixties was the Baker League in Philadelphia. It was a real competitive league for us, and it served as the precursor to the summer pro leagues in New Jersey and California."

For Bradley, the Baker league carries a special significance. Upon returning from England in 1967 after finishing his Rhodes scholarship, Bradley discovered that his basketball skills had eroded. "An abysmal failure," is how he describes his rookie season in the NBA. The following summer he was working as a volunteer for the Urban League in Harlem when Sonny Hill, the founder of the Baker League, called and invited Bradley down to Philly for a run in his tourney. "I took the train to Philly," says Bradley. "I was still trying to play guard at this point, and Sonny was very positive. He told me I could do it. That was an important summer for me because it restored my confidence and got back some of the skills I had lost. That's what happens when you go against guys like Earl Monroe."

The Baker League was created for that exact purpose: to help professional-caliber players hone their games in pickup contests against other top competition. The first tournament was organized in 1960 by Hill, who at that time was a five-foot-nine guard in the old semipro

Eastern Basketball League. Hill wanted to keep his skills sharp during the offseason, so he rounded up a group of local pro players – guys like Hal Greer, Guy Rogers, Ray Scott and Wilt Chamberlain – and started the league. The players traveled around Philly, from playground to YMCA, looking for open gyms and parks where locals weren't always trying to prove themselves against the pros. Charles Baker, Greer's uncle, who worked as the deputy commissioner of the city's Parks Department, procured permits for the players to use parks around the city at certain times. At first the league consisted of four teams, and the games were played on the hard, hot concrete outside places like the Moylan Rec Center at 25th and Diamond Streets in North Philly – not exactly a tony suburb. In the mid-1960s Hill moved the league to the basement of the Bright Hope Baptist Church at 12th and Oxford. That court would get so steamy that players would take salt tablets before the game to prevent dehydration. But they learned to play tired, and that helped during the winter. When the tournament moved it was rechristened the Baker League in honor of the man who had helped get it started.

In 1968 Hill founded the Sonny Hill League for local high school kids. During its first few years, five teams competed in the Hill League, one each from Northeast Philly, Germantown, South Philly, West Philly and North Philly, and they played their games as undercards to the Baker League. "One of the reasons I started the league was because there was so much gang warring going on at the time," says Hill. "But when we got to McGonicle Hall [the gym at Temple University], it was like a happy valley inside. All the troubles were still on the next block, but we were totally unaffected." Since its founding in 1968, only one Philadelphiia player who went on to play in the NBA – Phil Walker, who played for the Baltimore Bullets – hasn't participated in the Hill.

Unlike other playground tournaments, Philly's Baker has always had a strict code of defense. "If you didn't play defense," says Tony Samartino, one of the league's original coaches, "you didn't play. It was – and still is – that simple. The referees don't take a lot of guff, either. You have to keep your shirt tucked in and play fair. You can play hard, but you must play fair."

The Baker League proved that New York didn't hold a monopoly on high-profile pickup tournaments. And an event like the Dust Bowl loosened the East Coast's stranglehold on basketball in general. Detroit garnered some attention, too, with a slippery, sleek, high-scoring guard named George Gervin, who lit up the playgrounds during his high school and college years. But it was in Chicago that the Midwest's best basketball was being played.

On the city's South Side in the 1960s pro players from the NBA's Detroit, Cincinnati and Chicago franchises found they didn't have to travel all the way the New York to keep their games sharp.

"Seventy-first and King was one long court," says Mack Irvin. "Only guys with a reputation could play there. It was the premier court, the prestige court, and it was important to win. This is when Chicago got its reputation for some serious ballplayers."

Since it no longer held the patent on playground ball, New York was no longer the only place with playground legends. They say Chicago earned the nickname the Windy City not because of its weather but because of its blow-hard politicians. The name could just as easily have come from the sweet-talking players practicing their sermons on the blacktops. They were at 71st and King, at Washington Park or Cole Park. When it came to basketball, Chicago was no longer the Second City.

Neither did it take a back seat when it came to tragic heroes. Twenty years after the Goat first made his mark, a similarly talented athlete seemed to disappear into the clouds hovering above the playgrounds of Chicago.

◆ ◆ ◆

It was a disturbing ritual with haunting repercussions. But for Mary Space, that didn't matter. She'd rather have her ten-year-old son Steve endure the bad dreams than watch his life become a nightmare years later. Monthly, she would lay out articles on the kitchen table for Steve to read that depicted children who had been killed in gang-related activities. Then, having scanned the latest editions and listened to the radio, she'd lead Steve on harrowing walking tours of crime scenes around their neighborhood on the West Side of Chicago. Mary had plenty of tangible exhibits for her field trips. The family lived near the corner of of 16th Street and Kedzie Avenue, in a neighborhood that at the time had the highest murder rate in the country. One look at the blood-stained sidewalks framed neatly by yellow police tape proved more educational than any class excursion to the Art Institute.

The Space family was an anomaly on the decaying West Side, settling there in 1959. It was a two-parent household, and both mother and father were gainfully employed. The Spaces had a second home on six and a half acres in Monmouth, Illinois, 170 miles southwest of Chicago and about 20 miles from the Mississippi River. There Steve and his father, George, camped, hunted, fished and farmed on the weekends and during the summers. Steve's parents constantly tried to shield their son from the city's life-sucking, time-wasting enticements.

Mary Space despised basketball almost as much as any of the ghetto's other, more fatal attractions. When Steve's older brothers Darrell and Marty played in high school, she couldn't even bring herself to attend their games. She believed the playgrounds were forums for gangbangers to hot-dog, trash-talk, and recruit new members. The rhythm of the bouncing ball and the constant rattling of the chain net were, to her, ghoulish sounds.

For twelve years, George and Mary Space succeeded in keeping Steve away from the guns and gangs and hoops. Then one day in 1973, Steve's thirteenth year, his father left him with little else to do.

Sometimes a player makes a move that is so extraordinary people in the gym have the urge to stand up and leave, never to watch a basketball game again, convinced that it can't get any better. The folklore surrounding Steve Space began with such a move. In 1987 Space was playing in a pro-am league at Malcolm X College in Chicago. A lithe 26-year-old on the verge of latching on with a CBA team, Space was in his prime as a playground ballplayer. "He could do any dunk on anybody anywhere," says Tim Hardaway of the Miami Heat, who grew up in Chicago and still plays in summer leagues there. "It got to the point where guys on the playground were having fights to see who got Space on their team." Word of Space's ungodly hang time and mid-air creativity even reached Michael Jordan's atmosphere. In 1989 Jordan featured Space in two Nike promotional videos in which they played one-on-one. "A couple of times he went up and I said to him, 'I think I can block that,'" Space remembers. "Then he let me know pretty quickly

that I couldn't. I mean, he *is* Michael Jordan." Nevertheless, Space
played MJ close: Jordan won both games 12–8.

Space's opponents were as humbled as he had been by Jordan during
the pro-am tournament that day at Malcolm X. A right-handed player,
Space dribbled with his left down the left side of the floor. Overplaying
Space's left side was six-foot-six Byron Irvin, a future college All-American at Missouri and first-round draft choice of the Portland Trail Blaz-
ers. Guarding the basket was a six-foot-nine player who ended up so
embarrassed no one remembers his name – he was never seen at the
gym again. At the top of the key, Space cupped the ball in his left hand,
flipped it behind his back, over his right shoulder, stepped by Irvin as if
he wasn't there, climbed over the six-foot-nine paper enforcer, then
caught the ball with his right hand and dunked it.

"He could have played in the NBA," says Irvin. "He was such a great
leaper and scorer, one of those guys you have to come into the gym
ready to play your A game against, otherwise he will embarrass you.
He should have been playing somewhere, that's for sure."

Steve Space can't be mistaken for anything but a basketball player.
His palms are wide and flat, and his fingers seem infinitely long, like
five points on a star. His walk is so buoyant it seems as if he wouldn't
displace a grain of sand walking on the beach. His muscles are firm and
stretched taut over his six-foot-four, 200-pound frame. He glides when
he plays, like he's on rollerblades and everyone else is wearing snow-
shoes. And his deftness with the ball is something to behold. Ron Eskridge, his former freshman high school coach, swears Space can dribble
from hand to hand behind his back as fast as most people can cross over
in front of them. Even his surname embodies his style of play: wide-
open, uninhibited, existing in the ether above the rim, where few have
gone so gracefully. But every explosive first step or rim-rattling slam is
laced with anger toward his father – for not letting him play as a boy,
and then for not leaving him any other choice.

George Space had a drinking problem. Each night he would come
home after a twelve-hour day working construction and soothe his
aching body with alcohol. Often he drank so much his children would
hear a deep thud resonate through the house and would know their
father had just fallen down, passed out for the night.

The nine older Space children coddled Steve, their baby brother, as he grew up. When both parents worked late, a sibling made sure dinner was fixed and Steve was fed. One night when Steve was thirteen, his brothers George Jr. and Marty were home taking care of him while their mother worked overtime testing buttons at a Bell Telephone factory. George Sr. came home during dinner and, before long, the three boys heard the familiar sound of their father's body crashing to the floor. As violent as the falls always sounded, they never resulted in serious injury. George always rose with the sun and made his way to the construction site the next day.

After putting their father into bed and finishing dinner, Marty and George Jr. went out for the night. Steve climbed into his parents' bed, waiting for his mother to come home. When he awoke, his father was still lying next to him. "It was strange because dad was always up and out before we got up," Space says. "I shook him, pleading with him to wake up, but he didn't." George Space had died in the night from a blood clot lodged in his brain, the result of a massive blow to his head when he fell to the floor.

When George Space hit the ground for the last time, he brought down the shelter that he and Mary had so carefully constructed around Steve. Unable to maintain their style of living on her meager income, Mary sold the home in Monmouth. Her walks around the neighborhood with Steve became more infrequent and then stopped altogether because she had to take on extra work as a housekeeper. For lack of other options, Steve began playing basketball. "He kept to himself for a while," his brother Darrell says. "All he really did was play ball. He kind of grew up on the court after my father died."

The Space's home was forty yards from the courts at Dvorak Middle School, named for the nineteenth-century Bohemian composer Anton Dvorak. During the day Space would sit at courtside and watch guys like Lamar "Money" Mundane rain 25-foot jumpers as though they were layups. Or he'd listen to the trash-talking Billy Harris, who was cut by the Chicago Bulls reportedly because his mouth outplayed his game. Space would dribble on the sideline with his right hand stuffed in his pants, improving his left. At night he'd practice the moves he had seen all day, composing his own symphonies in the shadows of Dvorak. "I wanted to play, but I was always afraid to get out there," Space says. "When I finally did play with the big boys, it was like I had rehearsed everything to the point that the moves were second nature."

Space entered Farragut Academy, a southwest side public high school, with two reputations: as an incomparably talented teenage basketball player who enjoyed ripping players on defense as much as showcasing his hang-time; and as an apathetic student who was already a year behind in school and showed little interest in catching up to his classmates. "He could never gather that you have to spend as much time on academics as you do on basketball," says family friend Charlie Dortsch. Not until the second semester of his freshman year did Space join the basketball team. "I really didn't think I could be on the team," Space says. "My friends always asked me to be on it, and my response was always, 'How can I be on the school team? I don't even go to school that often.'"

By the end of his sophomore year, though, coaches at Farragut had given up completely on the player they all considered the most talented in his class. "Steve has always worshipped two gods," says Eskridge. "The first is basketball, and the second is women. If he had a girl and she told him to quit and spend more time with her, he'd do it." Space's habit of skipping school also pulled him down that year. Space, who was seventeen at the time, was caught cutting classes to hang out with friends in the school cafeteria. Illinois law allows school administrators to expel students for disciplinary reasons once they reach their seventeenth birthday. Farragut exercised its option regarding Steve.

After his expulsion, Space wandered the neighborhood, frightened by what he saw. Within four years he had shrunk from the privileged boy who summered on a farm into the kind of kid who could end up bloody and dead on the street corner. His nightmares were becoming reality. Frantic, Space began sneaking back into school. "The principal saw me in the hallway and asked, 'Didn't I kick you out?'" Space says. "I begged him to let me come back. I said, 'Man, what am I supposed to do? I'm gonna end up a gangbanger."

For his junior year, Space entered the Farragut Outpost, an arm of the high school that deals specifically with problem students. He tried out for Farragut varsity basketball and became the starting point guard on a team that featured the city's top two scorers in 1979. In his senior year, Space was named captain, and for the first three weeks of the season Farragut went undefeated. Space was an All-State candidate.

Former Bulls great Bob Love was working as an assistant coach at the University of Seattle that year, and he offered Space a scholarship. The marketing opportunities were too obvious to ignore. The Steve Space-Needle. Space soaring alongside a Boeing jet. He'd make Seattle home to the US (University of Seattle) Space Program. "It should have been great," Eskridge says. "But things didn't ever happen that way for Steve."

While Space was often apathetic when it came to academics, the Chicago Board of Education was, in general, just plain pathetic. In 1979–80, Steve Space's senior year, the public schools were in dire straits. The board ran out of cash in November 1979. For the final three weeks of the first semester, Chicago's teachers worked without pay. Before students returned from winter break, the teachers union went on strike despite a court order. For almost a month after the Christmas vacation, classes, and consequently athletic events, were canceled. The strike finally ended in February 1980 when the board borrowed more than $200 million to cover the teachers' back pay and pay their salaries for the rest of the school year. "The strike killed our momentum," Eskridge says. "With Steve and his friends, it was like they lost their focus, and when they came back we were starting from day one." Even worse, the University of Seattle dropped its basketball program from Division I to Division I-AA and eliminated basketball scholarships. The US Space Program would remain in Houston.

Space received no other scholarship offers during his senior year. "He was one of those kids who should have gone to college but never did," says his high school coach, Wardell Vaughn. "I remember getting a couple of letters, but I can't recall what went down or why he didn't go." Space and Vaughn had clashed a couple of times about Farragut's style of play. Because of their differences, Space claims, Vaughn hid the recruiting letters from him and deterred college coaches. "He told them I was too interested in girls to stay disciplined," Space says. "To a certain extent, he was right."

Ironically, it was because he ditched a date at a school picnic that Space eventually earned a college basketball scholarship. His brother Darrell, who played at the University of Wisconsin-Parkside, told Steve that a Parkside coach would be scouting a local pickup game. Space left the picnic to play in the game, and the coach signed him that afternoon. Midway through his freshman year at Parkside, however, Space became homesick, lost interest in school, and quit. "The coaches were pretty upset," says Darrell, who had a tryout with the Cleveland Cavaliers after college. "They threatened to take away *my* scholarship if I couldn't keep him there. He just needed to be home. He's the baby and kind of a mama's boy."

Following a brief stint at Sinclair Junior College in Dayton, Steve settled down in Chicago again, taking classes at Malcolm X College. "It really was my intention to get my degree," Space says. "But I never had a goal, a focus for my education, so if school got tough after basketball season or something better came along, I just did that." In the summer after his first year at Malcolm X, Space began coaching a team of preteens at the BBR, a local community center. The team, called Reaganomics, won the league title its first year. The local YMCA recruited Space to coach there as well, and his teams won two YMCA city championships. "I finally felt directed," Space says. "I tried telling these kids they could use basketball as a tool, that it would open doors for them and they could go to school."

Space did not follow his own advice. He dropped out of Malcolm X two years short of his degree to coach at the Y full-time, all the while harboring dreams of somehow making it in professional basketball. "The guy was NBA all the way," says Hardaway. "He just couldn't do the right thing and stay in school. Even at a small school, the scouts would have found him." One summer he played semipro in Dayton with Cedric Toney, formerly of the Phoenix Suns, and Ron Harper, an Ohioan who began his NBA career with the Cleveland Cavaliers. In 1987 Space made it to the final tryouts of the CBA's Rockford Lightning, only to get cut in what he calls a name game. "Basically, there were guys trying out for the same spots as me who were former college All-Americans," Space says. "The coaches needed name recognition to draw the crowds, which left me in the cold."

Space coped with getting struck from the Lightning by diving further into the lives of his young players. "I had no outside life," he says. "I saw single moms that didn't care what their kids were doing. I would go introduce myself to them and say, 'Hey, you need to know who I am! I coach your son and see him more than you do.'" Space preached staying in school and staying away from drugs before the NBA glamorized such slogans. Finally, he was acting like an NBA player; like Charles Barkley, Space told kids how important education was although he never earned his college degree.

Despite his "do as I say, not as I do" position on education, Space was a leader in the community. In 1991 he was earning $37,500 a year coaching at the Y. His former players looked to him for advice when they faced the decision of quitting the high school basketball team and joining a gang. Single mothers felt safer leaving their kids with Space than they did plopping them in front of the living room TV.

Space's own life, however, had begun to crumble.

Some of the advertisers he met while shooting the Nike videos with Jordan asked Space to do some sportswear modeling for them. He agreed, and at a party early in 1990 celebrating their partnership, Space tried his first line of cocaine. "I kept waiting for something to happen," Space says. "But I guess it already was, because I couldn't stop after that." At first he used coke every weekend for a year – snorting it and smoking it and running on high for forty hours straight, leaving himself just enough time to sleep off the buzz and be the sage for his kids at the Y on Monday. At the end of that year he took two weeks off over the Christmas holiday and never went back to work. "I told my boss I was a hypocrite," Space says. "I was losing my patience with the kids, and I could see myself changing because of the drugs. But instead of quitting cocaine, I quit my job."

Space became a basketball junkie. He was strung out on coke in the winter months, supporting himself and his habit by playing for pay in spring and summer pro-ams or semipro leagues. Playground players like Space come out like buds on a tree in the warm weather. "They can be somebody again," says Farragut coach William Nelson, who coached Kevin Garnett in his last year of high school before Garnett jumped to the NBA. "The rest of the year they are hibernating and practically don't exist." The number of players living this cyclical existence began growing with the construction of Chicago's housing projects in the mid-1950s. The blacktops were easy to lay down in the middle of these immense dwellings and cost less than baseball, football or soccer fields to maintain. From the moment school was out until it was too dark to even sense the ball coming their way, kids were playing hoops. The first generation of Chicago's playground legends grew out of this era. Families sat at picnic tables near the court, watching their sons play ball, at a time when death by stray gunfire happened only in gangster movies.

In the late 1970s the Chicago Housing Authority ran out of money to maintain its high-rise projects, and the CHA has since been taken over by the federal government's Department of Housing and Urban Development. It's been twenty years since many of the CHA's apartments had any wholesale repairs or improvements, and if there are any picnic tables remaining outside, they're more likely to be used as cover against bullets. The basketball courts are the last link to the promise these low-priced multifamily apartment blocks offered in the 1950s and 1960s. At the Stateway Gardens complex on the city's South Side, there are nine full courts between the blocks of 35th and 38th Streets. "Every area has its own courts, and always has," says Hank Clark of the CHA's Sports and Recreation program. "And if you put up basketball hoops, you get basketball players."

The style of play has always been dictated by the reigning local NBA star, which in the Chicago of Bob Love and Michael Jordan has meant creativity, speed and finesse. Clark, who grew up at the Stateway House, says those three characteristics have remained the core of basketball in the city, but adds that society – specifically the society of the inner city – has allowed style to prevail over substance. "I call it the Michael Jordan Syndrome," he says. "No one knows how to shoot anymore. They all want to showcase their skills in flashier ways."

While the MJ Syndrome is a citywide phenomena, it's not binding enough to hold together Chicago's basketball community, which has become as balkanized as the former Yugoslavia. Guys from the West Side play at LeClair Courts or at Malcolm X College. The North Siders stay at the Moody Bible Institute's gym, and the players on the South Side hang at De LaSalle High or at Kennedy-King College. The days of all-city legends like Billy Harris and Lamar Mundane are over. "Violence isn't that big of a deal when you're on the court," Clark says. "But the game itself has become more confined to the specific areas because of the gangs. You can't interchange anymore, or you're dead." Adds Hardaway, "The West Side is ruthless. Guys from the South Side won't go over there because they know they won't come back. I know guys over there, and I'm not going."

In 1989 the CHA's Gil Walker started Chicago's version of the Midnight Basketball Program, which helped erase the lines separating the city's gangbangers from its hoopsters. For a couple of hours at least, players from all over the city can come together at a neutral site, drop their weapons into a bin, and play the most scintillating basketball in the city outside of the United Center. For playing in the league, athletes earn a bus pass, haircuts, shoes, and job and drug counseling.

Midnight Basketball began at the Henry Horner Homes housing project on the West Side, blocks from where the Bulls would open the multimillion dollar United Center in 1994. While the area around the new stadium has blossomed with well-groomed lawns and new homes and businesses, the arena is still within a three-pointer of areas plagued by drive-by shootings. The proximity keeps the Bulls organization cognizant of basketball's positive effect, as long as the game is played on unclaimed territory. Every year the Bulls sponsor a three-on-three tournament called Shoot the Bull. The city's lakefront is lined with portable hoops and courts as more than 8,000 players compete in 100 divisions. Steve Space entered his first Shoot the Bull in 1992, playing with two friends in the bracket for participants with small-college experience.

By this time Space had been wasted for a year, living off of girlfriends and playing ball only occasionally. Days before the tournament began, his best friend entered a drug rehab facility. Space visited her and, amid the stench of withdrawal and recovery in the hospital ward, snapped out of his cocaine-induced haze. Space always felt that if he stayed away from gangs, he would do okay. He wouldn't be disgracing his family, specifically his mother. Suddenly he realized that though not a gangbanger, he was acting with the same disregard for his own life. "Admittedly, I was overwhelmed with coaching the kids and I got weak, turning to drugs to cope," Space says. "Every day I did drugs, I asked for forgiveness, thinking it wasn't really me doing them, until finally I came out of denial and realized it was time to stop." Space's team won the three-on-three tournament that year and the next as well. In 1995, playing in the tourney's 31-and-over corporate-sponsored division, Steve and his teammates won again.

From the living room of his house, Space can see the playground at Melodie Middle School. Except for a thin beam of light coming through the crack in the drawn curtains and a shadeless lamp burning dimly in the corner, the living room is dark. What light there is glimmers off the pile of trophies sitting on the coffee table, the majority of which are from Steve's coaching days. In October 1993, after his second Shoot the Bull tourney, Space stopped playing basketball. He was tired, he said. To make money, he did part-time factory work and other menial tasks. But in March 1995, a friend's daughter asked him for some basketball pointers, and his interest in coaching was rekindled.

Space has dropped off resumés at all the local schools, boys' clubs and YMCAs, searching for a teaching or coaching position. In the meantime, he makes ends meet as a driver for UPS. Even that proved nerve-racking for Space. He started working only four weeks before the fifteen-day strike in August 1997 and was not yet a member of the union. Given the choice by his boss of showing up for work or being fired, Space crossed the picket line, enduring taunts and threats each day. It never has been easy for him. The timing has never been right.

He insists that this time, if he gets another teaching or coaching position, he'll try to be less involved in his players' lives, focusing on teaching them basketball, letting that be his form of therapy and support. He thumps twice on the paperback bible he now takes with him every where he goes, as though he is drawing strength from the pages. Mary Space's baby boy is finally grown up, finally prepared to become as a man what he never was as a basketball player: a professional.

♦ ♦ ♦

It is approaching 9 p.m. and 65-year-old Ernie Lorch paces the sidelines of the gym at Bishop Loughlin High School in Brooklyn looking like he just stepped out of the boardroom of some white-shoe Park Avenue law firm. He wears a navy blue suit, a yellow tie that would make the brashest power broker envious, and a pin-stripe blue shirt as crisp-looking as when he put it on at 7:30 this morning. He is coaching his club team, the Riverside Hawks, as they put on a clinic against Bishop Loughlin. Rarely do his hands leave his pockets, never does he raise his voice. A play that produces a basket but is performed poorly is frowned upon, just as a well-executed play that results in a missed shot is applauded.

At halftime the Hawks are winning 36–18. In the corner of the gymnasium, away from the twenty people lounging in the bleachers, Lorch gathers his team around him. When they are in the huddle, he is visible only by the black dress shoes that stick out among the white leather hi-tops worn by his players. The gym is quiet, but he speaks even softer. It is hard to believe that this is one of the most influential men in youth basketball over the last thirty-five years.

A bachelor with a droopy, Mr. McGoo face, oversized glasses, and a serene countenance that is suggestive of a priest, Lorch is in fact a clergyman-like figure to thousands of playground players: He is both savior and last resort, a friend and a counselor, a doting father and a disciplinarian. Since 1961 Lorch – coach, creator, godfather and whatever else you want to call him of the Riverside Hawks youth basketball program in Manhattan – has compiled a staggering record. In the summer of 1997 alone, the twenty-five teams made up of players ranging in age from eight through nineteen years old that comprise the Riverside Hawks won 363 games, lost just 30, and won thirty-eight different championships at various tournaments throughout the country. The following fall, fifteen of his players went on to Division I college basketball programs, including Ron Artest at St. John's and Elton Brand at Duke.

"I've been coaching for thirty-six years and, in total, I would guess that more than ten thousand kids have passed through the program here," Lorch says in his soft voice. "I'd like to think that I've saved at least a few of the kids I've been in touch with. In fact, I know I have. A lot of them."

That's obvious during the game at Bishop Loughlin. Soon after benching a player for making two ill-advised passes, he's telling him to put his overshirt on before he gets a chill. Imagine Bobby Knight doing that. Lorch's tentacles extend so far that they touch every corner of the big city. Last fall, a member of Riverside's biddy team – its youngest – was the son of a former Hawk in the 1960s. Both the athletic director and the coach at Bishop Loughlin played for Lorch back in the 1960s, and both seem to worship Lorch as if he alone has the power to make the seas part. "Incredible man," says Bishop Loughlin's athletic director, Michael Williams, after the game. "Just incredible. Done more for basketball in this city than anyone in history." And this even after Lorch's

Hawks won the game 83—33.

Afterward, Lorch gathers his players into a tight huddle and implores them to visualize their roles in the 2-2-1 full court press that
Lorch had them run during the entire game. Lorch preaches an in-
your-face, pressing brand of basketball that resembles the system embraced by Boston Celtics coach Rick Pitino. It is a sophisticated system,
especially for kids who are not yet even in college.

Back in 1961, Lorch, a member of the Riverside Church on 120th
Street in Manhattan, was asked by the Riverside staff to start a youth
athletic program. The church, a hulking Gothic cathedral built by John
Rockefeller, Jr. in 1926, had always catered to the white upper and middle classes in fashionable Morningside Heights. But the neighborhood
was changing, new housing projects were being built in the shadow of
the church, and the Riverside staff was dumbfounded as to how it
could recruit new members. "Up until the late nineteen-fifties the
neighborhood around the church was mostly academic because of Columbia University and other cultural institutions close by," says Lorch.
"When new housing projects went up right around the corner in Harlem, the church had to decide how it would respond to the changing
constituency. It could either isolate itself or reach out to the community. Fortunately, it decided to reach out, and we knew the kids would
be particularly important."

Armed with a knowledge of basketball acquired from playing at
Division III Middlebury College in Vermont and from coaching as an
unpaid graduate assistant for two years at the University of Virginia
(where Lorch attended law school from 1954 to 1957), Lorch canvassed
the nearby Grant Housing Projects for potential players. "That's how
we started, with twelve T-shirts and twelve pairs of gym shorts," he
says. "I went out and rounded up the toughest twelve kids I could find
and brought them all back to the church."

The next year, more than seventy kids showed up for tryouts. By the
late 1960s, Lorch had added a junior team to his senior team and in the
early 1970s he expanded again, beginning teams for kids as young as
twelve. Around this time Lorch formed the traveling squad, which
trekked as far as the Soviet Union. Riverside's basketball program
would be copied all over New York City, and in time, the country as
community leaders became aware of both the changing environments

within the inner cities and the effect basketball could have on kids in these areas.

The Hawks' biggest rivals – indeed, the second most renowned summer boys team in the country – are the New York City Gauchos, a club that has nurtured such NBA players as Chris Mullin, Mark Jackson, John Salley, Rod Strickland, Kenny Anderson and Jamal Mashburn. The Gauchos were organized by Lou D'Almeida in 1967. D'Almeida, who never played the game, wasn't the slightest bit interested in basketball until he was asked by a friend to buy some T-shirts for a fourteen- to fifteen-year-old boys' YMCA team. When the team's coach unexpectedly quit, D'Almeida took over, and it was as if the hand of destiny had finally revealed to him his calling. D'Almeida fell in love with the game and eventually founded the Gauchos. Much like the Hawks, the Gauchos started small, just a local group providing an outlet for the community by organizing a team and summer tournaments. But over the years the Gauchos have grown in step with Lorch's Hawks. Tryouts for D'Almeida's team annually draw 2,000 boys and no one gets cut until they reach the thirteen and over division. The operating budget of the Gauchos has soared as high as $500,000 a year.

There are some – including former Gauchos players – who say that D'Almeida borders on the obsessive when it comes to competing with and beating Ernie Lorch. Although when Lorch is asked about D'Almeida, he chuckles and answers, "We don't have to compete with anybody. Kids around here know what it means to be a member of this program."

Lorch coaches his Junior and Senior teams, and a staff of eight coaches and assistants help him ensure that the program operates smoothly over eleven months of full-time activity. Over 2,000 kids will come in off the streets to try out for the Hawks each year, and Lorch seemingly knows almost everyone by his first name. A traveling team of New York City All Stars – eight of whom were first team high school All-Americans in 1997 – went 97–4 from April 1 to October 1 while traveling from France to Virginia to Dallas to Los Angeles.

But it is the teenagers in front of Lorch this evening in Brooklyn who are his favorite players in the the Riverside Church basketball program. These kids, eighteen and nineteen years old, have had behavioral and academic problems in the past and know Riverside is the last stop, the last chance, before they become full-time playground players. "I feel that I can have a big impact on these kids' lives. The kids on the traveling summer team know they are superstars and it's up to us to tell them they are not," says Lorch. "All of these kids, though, know that if they mess up once, just once, then their shot at college ball and a scholarship is gone."

Lorch leads the team out of Bishop Loughlin and into the cool night. They all pile into an eighteen-passenger van and by the time they are cruising over the Brooklyn Bridge it becomes apparent just how short some these kids' fuses are. "You say one more word to me and I'll kill you," says one player to another who is sitting behind him. "You been disrespecting me for weeks, and I ain't going take it no more. I'm serious, one more word and you're dead."

Lorch can't hear what's going on. Though he barely can see over the steering wheel, he's driving so aggressively that you can tell he's lived in Manhattan nearly all of his life. It's an odd scene, really, one that cannot be understood easily: Why does this man, who is white and on the threshold of being able to collect social security, spend *all* of his free time with young men, mostly black, who come from backgrounds that couldn't be more opposite from his own. "When do you have kids listen to any authority figure giving advice?" asks NBA player Ed Pinckney, who played for the Hawks. "And a white man in a black situation, it boggles my mind."

"That is a question I often get," says Lorch, sitting in the locker room back at Riverside Church. "And the answer is that I really feel like I make a difference in people's lives through basketball. That is a powerful thing, and it has enriched my life immensely."

About twenty feet from the basement locker room where Lorch sits is a basketball court, where you will find one of the nation's most fertile breeding grounds for hoops talent. The basement court has virtually no out-of-bounds and, to make matters worse, two huge pillars loom under one of the baskets. Nevertheless, to thousands of inner-city kids this little court, which resembles a squash court, has come to represent the dream of NBA riches. After all, since the Riverside Hawks were born in 1961, sixty-three players have made it out of that stuffy basement and into the NBA.

"We've never put padding on the pillars or around the walls because that way it doesn't become a problem," Lorch says. "The kids know exactly what kind of physical play we expect and when you have to tone it down. It's all about discipline, and it takes a lot of discipline to win. Winning is important here not for its own sake – although some rival coaches wouldn't believe that – but for the sake of using that as a lure. Once the winning tradition was established, kids began to respect the program here and were willing to meet some of our expectations just to play for Riverside. We don't think we have any competition when it comes to getting the best players in the city because we are the elite team, the best."

If you want testimony to attest to Riverside's nationwide domininance over the years, all you have to do is walk into the basketball closet in the church's basement. When you open the door, it's like seeing the inside of a massive treasure chest. Trophies, some as tall as 6 feet, line both sides of the room, which is 5 feet wide and 20 feet deep. There are banners hanging on the wall proclaiming the Hawks as Boys Class A Boys & Girls Club Champions for 1997. Though winning has been a constant over the years for Lorch, he has witnessed many changes in the city game since the early 1960s.

"The biggest change is that the playground game and even our games are much faster now," Lorch says. "In the sixties, if you went to a Harlem playground you would see guys who were more interested in passing than in shooting. I used to say that for every offense there was thirty passes to every turnover. Well, that's certainly not the case anymore. Because of the influence of the me-first attitude that almost every NBA player seems to have, kids today on the playground copy that. This means no passing, all shooting and no emphasis on fundamentals. But one thing hasn't changed. Most kids still want to play ball. And they will adhere to a system if the other option is not playing at all."

In 1977, Lorch had a kid on his team named Albert King. King – a playground star in his native Brooklyn by the time he was thirteen who eventually spent seven years in the NBA – was the most sought after high school player in the country. The constant phone calls and visits from college coaches during the recruiting process became too much for King and his family to handle, so he moved in with Lorch for a few weeks to get away. At that moment, Lorch realized for the first time

Far from the bright lights of Broadway and Madison Square Garden, you'll find the city game in its purest form at Harlem's fabled Holcombe Rucker Park. (Photo by John Huet)

James "Speedy" Williams, the most coveted street player in New York City, will beat you outside, inside or with a thunderous throwdown – and he'll be sure to let you and everyone else know it when he does.

Though he starred at Princeton and later with the Knicks, Bill Bradley (right) honed his game playing alongside Sonny Hill (left) in the less rarefied air of Philadelphia's gritty Baker League. (Photo courtesy *Sports Illustrated*)

Fred "Spook" Stegman, the first to scout the street game, has sent hundreds of kids to college.

David Cunningham, a once-in-a-generation Native American basketball talent, ponders his future on Cloud Court in Lapwai, Idaho.

Forget the artistry of the pass or the precision of the outside shot – on the court at West Fourth Street in lower Manhattan, you're only as good as your last flush. (Photo by John Huet)

As he awaits an appeal that may never be resolved, Derrick Curry finds basketball a salvation from the monotony of prison life. Curry is considered by many to be the top prison player in the US – for what it's worth.

The power to heal: Dr. David Lazerson (left) and Richard Green formed the Increase the Peace League to diffuse tensions between the Hasidic and African American communities in Brooklyn. In 1991 the two met with New York City mayor David Dinkins.

The mega-hype surrounding modern playground hoops creates new legends practically by the day. Worthy or not, Booger Smith – *Soul in the Hole* star and *Sports Illustrated* cover subject – has been pushed into the playground pantheon. (Photo by John Huet)

The Entertainers Classic at Rucker is a showcase for the highest quality street basketball in America – and for a widening array of sponsors tapping into the power of the
playground. (Photo by John Huet)

At its best, the street game – as Entertainers Classic announcer Thomas Hill likes to say – is about "showing some love." That isn't always the spirit when off-court rivals meet on the blacktop. (Photo by John Huet)

5

The Expansion Years

The story is about to begin. Our narrator, a skinny man with a sprinkle of gray in his neatly coifed hair and wrinkles that spread across his face like the lines on a map, sinks into his chair and looks outside at the gray, hard Harlem afternoon. He takes a deep breath. One second passes, then two, then three. Silence. He slowly shakes his head. Finally, he exhales. The dramatic pause now established, he is ready to spin one of the most celebrated tales in the saga of street basketball. After more than a quarter of a century, the story is still fresh in his mind, vividly lingering there as if it were the defining day, the defining moment, of Joe Hammond's life.

"It was the Rucker League finals in 1970," Hammond says, his voice rumbling in a manner that could only come from a twenty-year pack-a-day habit. He sits in a nondescript second-floor office of the nonprofit organization on 125th Street in Harlem where he sometimes volunteers. "I was late for the game, so I only got to play in the second half. But it really didn't matter. I was matched up against Doctor J, the great Julius Erving, and I put down fifty on him in one half. He only scored thirty-nine for the entire game. I whupped him, and everyone saw it. We lost, but afterwards Doc made his way through the crowd, came up to me and said, 'Damn, Joe, you're just as good as everyone says you are. Everything I heard about you is true.'"

Though it sounds apocryphal, the story is the unadulterated truth. That summer afternoon in 1970 – the day that Joe Hammond, one the best players Harlem's playgrounds has ever produced, scored 50 points on Doctor J – is real. Still talked about in every nook of Harlem, the day has become part of the local lore, much the same as the rise, fall and resurrection of Earl Manigault.

On a larger scale, players like Hammond transformed basketball in the 1970s. During that decade the playground game, the playground style, exploded on the national scene. As a growing number of players began to display skills once seen only in the NBA or the top college programs, advertisers and marketers began to take notice. As a result, ever more tournaments geared toward the playground player popped up around the country. It was a decade, in short, when the street game went from parochial sideshow to American phenomenon.

On that sunny day when he scorched the Doctor for 50, Hammond heralded the start of the revolution. His team, a neighborhood squad named Milbank comprising playground phenoms such as Pee Wee Kirkland and Eric Cobb, took on the Westsiders, a group of pros led by Julius Erving, the Roosevelt, New York, product who had starred at the University of Massachusetts, spurned the NBA for the upstart American Basketball Association, and signed with the Virginia Squires in 1971, becoming the first superstar of the high-flying ABA.

The game between Milbank and the Westsiders played out like a sociological experiment to determine what would happen when the playground went head-to-head with the pros. On a more visceral level, it offered a chance for all of Harlem to feel as if it were playing for an NBA championship. And so they came, thousands and thousands of people, to make some noise for the local boys. Because Rucker Park is a cramped place, many climbed to the top of the chain-link fence that encloses the park and watched from there. Some perched on tree limbs, others stood on car hoods. On this day, there was no hotter ticket in town.

At game time, Hammond was nowhere to be found. Milbank stalled as long as it could, but after ten minutes the referees ordered them to play. As chants of "We want Joe" rained down from the fence and the trees, the game began. Without Jumpin' Joe, however, Milbank foundered. Erving, with his glistening Afro the size of a medicine ball, took charge. At half-time the Westsiders held a double-digit lead.

"I was told that the game started at two o'clock, and it really started at one," Hammond explains, his hands outstretched as if pleading his case before God. "It was that simple. Really."

Then he arrived. Hammond climbed out of a limousine across Eighth Avenue and received a hero's welcome. Men, women and kids from the neighborhood – and journalists, too – all ran across the street to greet Hammond, to touch him, as if he wielded some magic power. After twisting his way through the mob, Hammond shed his street clothes and entered the game. The second half had just begun.

Charlie Scott, who played nine seasons in the NBA, was the first to guard Hammond. But in three trips down the court – boom, boom, boom – Hammond swished two jumpers and threw down a dunk that registered on the Richter scale. Then Brian Taylor, another NBA vet, took a turn at Hammond. He, too, failed, and then everyone got what they had come for: Doctor J switched over and matched up against Hammond.

"It was all offense," says Hammond today, his face aglow. "We slammed in each other's faces, we hit J's, we hit pull-ups – we were both just sizzling. But anybody will tell you I got the better of him."

"I remember that game," says Earl Manigault. "Joe was just terrific. And when he says he got the better of Doctor J, no one who saw the game would ever dispute that claim. It had to be the high point of Joe's career." Though Milbank lost the game, Hammond was named the tournament's MVP. It was, as Manigault says, Hammond's finest hour.

"Joe Hammond is the greatest playground player ever," says Bob McCullough, "Now, when I say 'playground,' I don't mean greatest player ever. But of the guys who didn't make it – because that is what a playground player is – he is the best. I can't say he is better than Doc or Connie, though."

"You could say that the Rucker Finals in 'seventy was as good as it got for me," says Hammond. "Looking back, I was pretty stupid with what I did with my talent."

This is a common refrain on the playground, but it's especially poignant for Hammond. Born in East Harlem, Hammond was a precocious talent who from the start failed to listen to the counsel of his elders. By the time Joe was twelve years old, Manigault and others saw that he had the talent to make it out of the ghetto. One day when Joe was not yet even a teenager, the Goat, in a rare fit of sobriety for that time, cornered Hammond at the Morris Park playground in East Harlem and told him if that he stayed clean, stayed focused, the good life would someday be his. "Stay in school, Joe," Manigault told Hammond. "Learn from me and my mistakes, and you'll make it out. You'll make me proud. Don't take the easy path like I did."

But that's just what Hammond did. By the time he was in junior high, Hammond was immersed in a lucrative drug trade. He dropped out of school in the eighth grade and took up a life on the streets, which for him meant drugs and basketball. He had grown into a six-foot-three shooter with a touch so true the ball seemed to ride a beam straight to the bottom of the net. He played at Morris Park, where on many occasions he swindled drug dealers out of their money. Here's how it worked: For $5,000, Hammond, backed by money generated from his own drug deal, would play guys one-on-one to 31 points. Hammond rarely lost, so the local players eventually quit accepting his challenge. To find players, Hammond's friends would travel up and down the East Coast, combing the playgrounds in search of guys with large attitudes and large wallets. They would offer to pay the player's transportation to New York as long as the sucker agreed to wager at least $5,000 on the game with Hammond. Hundreds fell for the scam, one of the best in the rich lore of the playground.

One day when Hammond was seventeen, Cazzie Russell, a star at Michigan at the time, walked up to him at Morris Park and said he was looking for a guy named Joe Hammond. He'd heard Hammond was pretty good, and he wanted to see for himself. Hammond said he didn't know who Russell was talking about, but hey, since Russell was already here, they might as well play. Hammond won in a laugher. Afterwards he said, "By the way, I didn't tell you my name. I'm Joe Hammond, and welcome to my court."

"I knew it," Russell replied.

He walked away, never to return.

That same year a scout for the Los Angeles Lakers appeared at the Morris playground on a summer morning. He told Hammond that the Lakers were interested and that if Hammond didn't mess up too egregiously, they would draft him when Hammond turned nineteen. Sure enough, in 1971 Los Angeles selected Hammond in the hardship draft. Lakers owner Jack Kent Cooke offered Hammond a one-year, $50,000 contract. Hammond turned it down.

"They thought they were offering the world to this poor kid from the ghetto, but I didn't need the money," says Hammond. "I was dealing drugs, playing ball and shooting dice from the age of ten, and by the time I was fifteen I had my father hiding fifty thousand dollars for me in his bank account. By the time the Lakers made their offer, I had over two hundred thousand stashed in my apartment. I was making thousands of dollars a year selling marijuana and heroin. What was I going to do with fifty thousand dollars?"

Soon after he rejected the contract, Hammond began using his own product. Not surprisingly, he began to get sloppy in his dealing and was eventually arrested for his involvement with drugs. Just like that, Hammond became a myth, a shadow, a lesson to learn from, another Earl Manigault. "The only reason I'm talking to you or anyone else that comes around asking questions is because of my message of telling people to avoid street life and stay in school," Hammond says.

Ironic, isn't it? That's the message Manigault delivered to Hammond so long ago. Is anyone listening now?

"I don't know," says Hammond, "I don't know. But it gives me a purpose, and I haven't had that for a good while."

Hammond twice served prison terms for his involvement with drugs. From 1985 to 1988, he spent time at both Camp Gabriels prison at Lake Placid and the Clinton Penitentiary at Dannemora, New York. In 1990 he served six months at Rikers Island. While incarcerated, his basketball reputation afforded him high status in the feudal hierarchy of the prison population. At Clinton, Hammond would challenge other inmates to a free-throw shooting contest: The first to connect on 23 of 25 would win a can of tuna from the other player. After a few months, Hammond had more than 100 cans of tuna stacked in his cell. "I would give them away to guys who were hungry," says Hammond. "That's why I had a whole lot friends."

Not only the inmates were his friends. Aware of Hammond's skills and laid-back demeanor, the chief parole officer at Clinton arranged for Hammond to teach his son a few moves. At night. During lockdown. In the prison.

"That parole officer liked me," says Hammond. "They all did. They said I turned a maximum security prison into a rec center. Imagine that."

In fact, the guards trusted Hammond and his reputation so much that a Clinton staffer asked Hammond to act as peacekeeper if any altercation erupted. One afternoon during a basketball game, Hammond was innocently tripped and broke his arm. The inmate who tripped Hammond so feared retaliation from guards and fellow inmates that he immediately cradled the fallen player in his arms and pushed his way past two guards to rush him to the infirmary. As he lay Hammond on a bed, four guards beat the inmate into a state of near unconsciousness with their nightsticks. Yes, it's safe to say that everyone liked Hammond. For whatever that's worth.

Hammond's fiercest rival on the New York playgrounds, at least in terms of reputation, was Herman "Helicopter" Knowings. Though similar in size – both stood around six-foot-five as adults – the two were opposites in style. Hammonds was smooth as ice cream; Helicopter exploded like popcorn. The myth has it that on more than one occasion, an opponent who faked Knowings into the air was whistled for a three-second violation as he waited for the 'Copter to land. His leaping ability was measured not so much by its height, which was phenomenal, but by hang time. "He would just sort of float around the rim, defying gravity," Bob McCullough says.

Knowings was born in South Carolina and moved to Harlem with his family as a boy. Though he never played high school basketball and played only briefly at a small college in Washington, D.C., he built enough of a reputation to earn a short stint in the Eastern League, a long-defunct pro outfit. His real proving ground, though, was the Rucker.

In 1968 Knowings played in a game that solidified his legend. The game pitted Knowings' Colonial All-Stars, a renegade group of playground guys, against a team made up of members of the New York Knicks, including Willis Reed. Knowings that day lived up to his reputation. "In one play," McCullough recalls, "the pros brought the ball down, and Herman blocked the shot. Someone shot it again, and he blocked it again. One more time, and he blocked it *again*. These were pros, yet they couldn't get a shot off against this guy."

The pros won that game, but the Colonials went on to win the tournament. Partially based on his performance that day, Knowings earned a spot on the Harlem Globetrotters for the 1970 season. It was the closest he would come to full-time, highly competitive professional basketball. Knowings was what is described today as a 'tweener – an inside player who, at just six-foot-five, was too short to consistently compete up front against pro-caliber talent, but lacked the outside shot to play guard. By the mid-1970s, bad knees – the result of too many landings on the unyielding concrete of playground courts – had permanently grounded the 'Copter. He was killed in a car accident while driving a taxi in 1980.

Travel some 3,000 miles across the United States, to a Los Angeles neighborhood that in the 1970s was ruled by a man named Raymond Lewis. Though Lewis never played against Hammond, they knew of each other, and each claimed he could beat the other in a game of one-on-one. It would have been quite a match, the two best street players of the 1970s – East Coast versus West Coast – hammering away at or soaring over one another. "Yeah, that would have been nice," says Hammond. "But I don't even know where Raymond Lewis is anymore."

Few do. Lewis, a 1973 first-round draft pick of the Philadelphia 76ers, seems to have disappeared, vanished down a darkened street. Some say he's still in the Watts neighborhood where he grew up; others say he moved away long ago. And some say that, for the right amount of money, they can put you in contact with Lewis. What is clear, though, from the recollections of hordes of players who went up against him, is that during the 1970s Raymond Lewis was the best basketball player in all of Los Angeles. Better than any Los Angeles Laker, any UCLA Bruin, any USC Trojan.

"No guy who ever touched a basketball was as good as Ray," says Dwight Slaughter, a high school All-American and a teammate of Lewis's at Verbum Dei High in South Central. "When you looked at him, you'd think, 'I'm gonna kill this skinny dude.' But when the ball went up it was like he was nine feet tall and everybody else was two."

"I watched Raymond Lewis when he was in high school," recalls

Sonny Vaccaro, a representative for Adidas who ran the Dapper Dan basketball tournament out of Pittsburgh in the late 1960s and early 1970s. "He was the greatest player I ever saw in my life, Calvin Murphy not withstanding. Raymond Lewis was the best – there's no question about it. I saw him eat up Calvin on the playground, and I saw him get sixty-eight as a freshman for Los Angeles City College to beat Jerry Tarkanian and Long Beach State when Tark had five future pros on his team."

At six-foot-one and 175 pounds, Lewis did in fact look as malleable as Gumby. But that was part of his charm. He looked so mortal, so beatable, so much like everyone else, that people were inclined to root for him. Aside from his glory on the playground, though, Lewis gave his supporters precious little to cheer.

His career started well: In both his junior and his senior years at Verbum Dei, Lewis was the area's player of the year. After seeing Lewis play, Tarkanian, who got to watch from his perch at Long Beach State, offered this scouting report: "He combines tremendous shooting ability with total control over the basketball and was best at beating his man off the dribble." This isn't just heavy breathing from an enraptured college coach. Everyone recruited Lewis, from Tarkanian to John Wooden to nearly every coach in the East. Lewis surprised them all by accepting a scholarship to Los Angeles State, where he led the nation's freshmen in scoring. In his second season Lewis finished second in the nation in scoring behind Austin Peay's Fly Williams, a street legend himself from Brooklyn.

After two years in college, Lewis believed he was ready for the NBA and declared himself eligible for the 1973 NBA draft. At this point, though, Lewis's pride got in the way. Instead of hiring an agent to negotiate his contract, Lewis thought he was better off doing it himself. For nearly a decade he had dealt with street agents who had tried get him to play for money on the playgrounds, and he was fed up with their back-handed ways and their selfishness. For whatever reason, Lewis didn't recognize the difference between a street hustler and a legitimate financial advisor. The mistake would prove fatal to his career.

Philadelphia, which had the first and last pick of the first round in 1973, selected Lewis with its second first-round pick. Lewis was no Kissinger in the negotiations. "In retrospect, you could say he could have gotten a better agreement," says agent Don DeJardin, who was the 76ers' general manager at the time. "I ended up spending a lot of time on the phone with his father. Not trying to convince them of anything – it was time spent explaining."

Lewis signed a three-year deal worth $50,000, only half of which was guaranteed. The contract was chicken feed compared with that of the Sixers' top pick, Doug Collins out of Illinois State, but the team's first rookie camp made it clear who was worth more. Recalls one scout who watched the two duel at the camp (and who wishes to remain anonymous), "Collins wasn't as impressive. He walked more than he ran, and his passes, while fancy, missed more than they hit. So did his shots. Lewis, on the other hand, was doing everything but talk. You watched him closely for flaws. You saw absolutely none. He was in a class by himself."

Lewis's teammates and coaches were saying much the same thing, as were the Philly papers, and the youngster started to believe what he was hearing and reading. Before the season began, he demanded that his contract be renegotiated. Sixers management laughed, and Lewis left, heading back to the playgrounds in Los Angeles. He would never return to Philly, never play a minute of basketball in the NBA. Call it opportunity wasted, on an epic scale.

Raymond Lewis, like Hammond, squandered his talent and lost his chance to push a wheelbarrow of money to the bank. But both elevated the quality of the street game in the 1970s – and, though they may not have realized it, the game's marketing potential. People came to see these smooth, natural athletes run the floor, and, as a byproduct, the gear they wore – sneakers, shorts, shirts – became hip. It was hardly Jordan Incorporated, but the era of basketball commercialism was slowly being ushered in. And in 1972, Scott Miller became the first to sink a well into the oilfield.

Miller was a 26-year-old advertising associate working for Humphrey, Browning and McDougal in Boston. He had played football at Washington and Lee University and was an avid playground basketball player. Before he got to Boston, though, Miller had rarely played alongside black players. When he stepped onto the court at Boston's Washington Park for the first time, he was amazed – stunned – at what he saw. "The first thing that struck me was the powerful language the black guys would use when they would talk about their equipment and their game," says Miller, who is now an advertising consultant in Atlanta. "It seemed like it all came from Ali at the time, this poetical approach to talking about basketball. It was an intense awareness of their surroundings that I had never seen before. The total focus on every aspect of the game fascinated me."

Shortly after Miller arrrived in Boston, he learned that he would be working on the Converse account. Converse wanted something new, something fresh, and Miller immediately thought of his experience on the playground. But how, he wondered, do you capture the playground essence in an advertisement? "I struggled with that for a long time," he says. "You had to make it authentic, and I figured there were two ways to do that. One, you could try to capture the guy in Indiana shooting baskets on his farm when it was ten below outside with snow on the ground. Or two, you could try to capture the inner-city playground. Since I had no experience with the Indiana scenario, I chose to work on the playground concept. To capture the playground, I knew I had to give it poetry. I always heard guys saying things like 'I'm all over you like a skin disease' or 'like a cheap suit,' so I just went out and listened."

One day in Boston Miller heard the golden words that perfectly captured the playground, that glamorized it while staying true to its character: *limousines for the feet.* This was exactly the poetic hyperbole Miller was looking for. He doesn't remember who uttered the phrase or where he heard it, but when he did he knew he had a perfect catchphrase for Converse, one that would appeal both to the playground and to the masses. Miller wrote a thirty-second ode to the shoe, a poem that ended with the phrase *limousines for the feet.* "You had to put the shoe on a pedestal, like you were worshipping it, if you were going to stay with the playground theme," he says. "It took me about thirty seconds to write the poem, but I was afraid it would sound too much like a white guy trying to be like a black guy. So we took it to Harlem and did some market research."

Converse shared Miller's concern. But when the commercial was tested, everyone in Harlem loved it. The poem, recited by a young man in Ali's familiar rhythmic style, went as follows:

You're the greatest and that's no jive,
You're standard equipment on the B-Street Five.
As I fly through the air doing my famous slam-dunk,
I'm flying First Class and that ain't no bunk.
My shoes will be wearing the Converse name,
Till they bronze my feet for the Hall of Fame.
Converse All-Stars
Limousines for the feet.

The commercial won a Cleo, the advertising industry's top award, but it caused barely a ripple in Converse sales. It was, nevertheless, the first commercial aimed at glamorizing the playground, and it unquestionably had a direct influence on the growing popularity of the game. During the mid-1970s, playground tournaments grew exponentially all across the country.

Nowhere, though, was the basketball boom more in evidence than in California, particularly in Venice Beach, the eclectic boardwalk community nestled against Santa Monica Bay ten miles west of downtown L.A. Not until the early 1970s did the playground fulfill its manifest destiny with a major westward expansion. The Venice Beach Tournament today draws the top talent from all over the west. Right now, one man above all others rules that tournament by the sea.

◆ ◆ ◆

In the early evening, as the Southern California sky blushes a soft shade of pink, John Staggers steps onto Oceanfront Walk at Venice Beach. He weaves his way through the crush of humanity congregated here on a postcard-perfect Saturday, his six-foot-five, 240-pound frame lumbering through a gaggle of surfers and sunbathers, past a chainsaw juggler, past an electric guitarist wearing a turban and teetering on roller skates, past a stall from which the smell of mango-banana incense wafts gently through the cool, salty air, until he finally arrives at a slab of concrete. Framed by splintered wooden bleachers on the east and the azure Pacific on the west, this stretch of Venice Beach cement is, to any inveterate hoopster, a pure picture of paradise, a snapshot of pickup basketball that belongs in the Louvre.

"This is where it all starts," says Staggers, flipping his right wrist in the direction of the court. "If you want to make yourself a reputation in this city or on the West Coast, this is where you come. This is where I've been coming for years." Indeed, this is where John Staggers cultivated his reputation as a towering force in L.A. street basketball – the top street player on the West Coast, according to the locals. The 1988 Los Angeles high school player of the year, Staggers has been making the fifteen-mile pilgrimage to Venice from his home in South Central since he was a teenager. This court may not play host to the best pickup basketball in the city – that distinction certainly belongs to the gym at UCLA, where pro players frequently visit – but the overall quality of ball here isn't far from what you'd find in the CBA. At Venice Beach reputations are made, enriched, and lost, a place where the game is two parts theater, one part basketball.

"I have all the stories," says Frank Williams, thirty-six, a Venice elder who has been playing on the beach four times a week for more than twenty years. His body is pockmarked by three bullet holes and four knife wounds. The scars on his chest map a life lived on the edge, a life lucky not yet to have been extinguished. "Everyone from Michael Jordan to Malcolm-Jamal Warner has been here. And let me tell you something. I've seen 'em all, and John Staggers is as good as they come. That's what anyone who knows anything about Los Angeles basketball will tell you."

Staggers really should not be here. He should be somewhere else, somewhere where his immense ability can truly be challenged. But Staggers, like so many other players coming out of high school, was abused by a recruiting system in which the rules of the game are broken more commonly than anyone in the NCAA will admit. In the end, John Staggers's involvement in two separate recruiting scandals would put a scarlet letter on his chest. He would never be looked at in the same way by scouts or coaches – and Staggers himself would never have the same feeling about the game.

"There is no question that John should be in the NBA right now," says Joe Weakly, who runs a pro-am summer league in Los Angeles and has known Staggers since John was in the eighth grade. "He is one of the best scorers to ever come out of Los Angeles. You get him the ball, and somehow, some way, he's going to score. That's why he's an absolute marvel on the playgrounds. It's just too bad he didn't show more patience and have better instincts when it came to dealing with college recruiters and college coaches."

"The experiences I had with college coaches and boosters definitely have left a bad taste in my mouth," says Staggers. "I can't help but wonder what might have been if everybody I dealt with had been honest and just let me play basketball. That's all I ever wanted."

So this is what he has now, this court, this game, this place that affords him fame, if only a fraction of the fame that at one time seemed to be his birthright. It's something, at least. "John Staggers has arrived!" Williams yells the moment he spots Staggers approaching the court, offering up the kind of welcome every street player craves. "You're already signed up on my team. We got next."

Staggers watches the game unfold. "This is so much of a show," he says, shaking his head. "Guys are more interested in showboating for the people in the stands than in winning. That's the hardest thing about playing here. If you're a real serious player who is competitive and loves to win, it's so easy to get pissed at your teammate if he's just trying to be flashy. And it's gotten worse in recent years."

The game ends. As the players on the court try to organize the next game – it takes fifteen minutes of arguing to decide who actually has next, a maddening ritual here – an apple-cheeked midwesterner on vacation puts a $20 bill at the base of one basket and says whoever can come up with the most creative dunk can take the money. Seven guys line up to show their stuff. The winning flush, a 360-degree windmill slam by a player who stands about six feet, draws a smile from the tourist. "Doctor J would have been proud," he says. It's true: Some of the players here *would* impress the likes of Doctor J with their mid-air creativity. But Staggers does not fall into this genre of players. He's a banging, low-post Charles Barkley-clone who could probably outmuscle many of the weightlifters working out at Muscle Beach, lying adjacent to the court.

Without stretching or taking a warm-up shot, Staggers steps onto the court. His first touch is a tip-in basket. His second touch is a fadeaway jumper from fifteen feet that splashes the bottom of the net. In all, Staggers scores eight of his team's eleven baskets, all but singlehandedly defeating a team that hadn't lost for more than three hours. On Staggers's final score he cut left to right along the baseline, hopped between two defenders, jumped, pump-faked on one side of the rim, cradled the ball, then scooped it up to hit an impossible reverse layup. He is silent after the game, but Frank Williams keeps yapping, yapping, yapping. "Next time," he screams to the other team, "pick a better dynasty."

Staggers's team wins the next two games. For their fourth game, his team picks up a white player. He is the only white player to have played in any of these games. Though Staggers scores 8 points, it is not enough. His team loses after the white player – who refused to give his name – turns the ball over three times in his team's last three possessions. "That's what happens when the homeboys try to take over a game at the end," Staggers says with a smile, sweat dripping from his brow. "That dude needs to learn how to pass."

With that, John Staggers takes off his shirt, wrings it out – causing a small lagoon of sweat to form on the pavement – and walks off the court. He leaves Venice Beach to become completely anonymous again. He drives his 1987 Volvo wagon to his home in South Central, to the place where his problems began.

John Staggers is twenty-seven years old and still living at home with his mother, Gloria. Sweet and dulcet-voiced, she holds a Master's degree in business from National University's Los Angeles campus and works as a contract administrator in the aerospace division of Northrop Grumman. John is her only child – she never married John's father – and she has dedicated practically all of her time and energy toward making John's life better than hers.

"The most important thing I taught John growing up was to be honest and respect himself," Gloria says. "Being an only child, he loved to be around other children and he was very giving. He didn't buy his friends, but people would hang around him for who he is."

South Central Los Angeles does not have the rundown look of other low-income neighborhoods, like Harlem and Chicago's South Side. South Central isn't as old as these other neighborhoods, and on appearance an outsider wouldn't necessarily judge it to be a dangerous place. The street John Staggers lives on is lined with two-, three- and four-bedroom houses sporting healthy, robust front lawns. Aside from the cackles of the kids flying kites and the occasional bark of a dog, this is a quiet, sedate street. Standing on the Staggers's porch, it's hard to fathom that the L.A. riots of 1992 erupted just a quarter-mile from here, at the corner of Torrance and Normandy.

"I can't explain why the riots broke out," says Staggers. "There was just so much anger, so much bitterness over the Rodney King verdict, and now South Central has this reputation for being a bad neighborhood, when it really isn't. I blame the media, but I also blame myself for not being stronger during the riots. I hate to admit it, but when all the looting was going on I didn't exactly not participate. I ..."

He stops, lowering his hard eyes to the ground. Staggers doesn't need to finish the sentence. The guilt is palpable. "I was wrong," he says softly.

Unfortunately for Staggers, that was not the only time he exhibited poor judgment. During his senior year at Crenshaw High, Staggers, who played three different positions, was Mr. Everything. He averaged 25 points a game and was named the city player of the year. Considered one of the top twenty recruits in the nation, he was offered scholarships to more than thirty schools. Louisville, DePaul, UCLA, Texas – all wanted a piece of Staggers. That year he led Crenshaw to a 28–0 record and into the regional final against L.A.'s Manual Arts. In the last thirty seconds of that game, with Crenshaw trailing by 3 points, Staggers called for the ball. Standing some twenty-five feet from the basket with a defender draped all over him, he launched a shot as the buzzer reverberated throughout the gym. The ball hit nothing but net. Crenshaw would lose the game in overtime, but the game added yet another layer to the Staggers mythos.

Of the many college coaches who sat in the Staggers's living room and promised John everything under the sun, the words of one would resonate with Staggers. His name was Don Haskins, and he was – and still is – the head basketball coach at the University of Texas, El Paso. "I wanted to get away from home, away from all the influences of Los Angeles. UTEP seemed like the ideal place. It was the only recruiting trip I ever made. Haskins promised me I was their number one guy, and that he would do anything possible to make my life as comfortable as it could be." In November 1987, after making that single recruiting visit, Staggers signed a letter of intent with UTEP. As soon as he signed on the dotted line, however, Staggers essentially quit attending his high school classes. He had made it, right? His transcript, according to one college coach, was dotted with so many unexcused absences that it "looked like a checkerboard."

"We just took a chance on a guy who was going to be a nonpredictor [a player not expected to be eligible his freshman year] all the way," UTEP coach Don Haskins said at the time of his decision to sign Staggers. "They do that all over the United States."

By the end of the spring semester of his senior year, Staggers had missed so much school and so much schoolwork that he was not awarded a diploma along with his classmates. Staggers doesn't like to talk about this dark period of his life, but he attributes his carefree attitude to the toxic influence of a group of friends who were already out of school. It is a mistake that still haunts him, one that undoubtedly will haunt him forever. "He isn't a dumb kid," says Joe Weakly. "At the time he just lacked maturity. You know what they mean when they say, 'Young in the mind'? That was John – just young. He just wanted to fool around."

"Not getting my high school diploma was the most embarrassing experience of my life," says Staggers. "But at the time I thought I could work everything out once I got to UTEP."

Ah, UTEP. The school would be the magic solution to all his problems. And why shouldn't he think that? The plan the UTEP coaches had mapped out for Staggers was that he would come to El Paso in August, earn his GED at a local community college, and be ready by the winter term to enroll, possibly playing for the Miners as early as the second half of the 1988–89 season. It sounded so easy.

On August 13, 1988, Staggers drove to LAX, where he went to a certain airline ticket counter and said to the attendant simply, "Hi, I'm John Staggers." Magically, a one-way ticket to El Paso appeared. Once he landed, Staggers was met by Russ Bradburd, then a UTEP assistant, who drove Staggers to an off-campus apartment. "You'll be staying here," is all Bradburd told Staggers as he dumped him off. Exactly who paid for this apartment is a great mystery to Staggers, who lived there rent-free. It takes very little imagination to venture a guess. "I came out to El Paso with money," says Staggers, "but I never had to spend any of it because they gave me everything for free. At the time it seemed real nice. When they were recruiting me they said I'd be taken care of, and they sure meant that."

According to Staggers, if he ever wanted a meal or small amounts of money in the range of $50 or $60, all he had to do was ask one of the assistant coaches. Always the assistants. That way Haskins could plead ignorance and avoid getting tarred and feathered when the NCAA bloodhounds came sniffing. UTEP would, however, eventually pay for its transgressions. In 1991 the school was slapped with two years' probation and a reduction of scholarships for those two years stemming from the recruitment and treatment of John Staggers. Violations ranged from a UTEP coach's tutoring of Staggers for the GED to Staggers's receiving free meals and transportation from UTEP coaches. Two assistant coaches, Russ Bradburd and Greg Lakey, were fired. Haskins, who was inducted into the Naismith Hall of Fame in 1997, failed to return any phone calls.

One of Staggers's housemates at El Paso was a skinny, inconsistent point guard named Tim Hardaway. The Chicago product had yet to explode into the player he is today – an NBA All-Star – and Staggers and many of his coaches felt that John had a brighter future in the NBA than Tim. To prove the point, John and Tim would spend hours under the wilting Texas sun on El Paso playgrounds, playing one-on-one on any open court they could find. Staggers won most of the games, a fact that infuriated Hardaway to the point where, Staggers says, their friendship was nearly severed.

While Staggers's play continued to progress on the court, his classwork stagnated. He had hoped to pass the equivalency test, which consisted of five sections, before the fall semester, but was unable to do so. The coaches, fearing they might not be able to get a return that season on their investment – and make no mistake, that's what Staggers was to them – instructed Staggers to enroll in UTEP's Equivalence High School Program, a federally funded operation for migrant workers and their families. J. Ray Johnson, a graduate assistant at UTEP at the time, often gave Staggers rides to his classes. Staggers was not exactly the type of person the program was intended to help, but sly winks can move mountains when you're talking about the future of a basketball player.

"When I wasn't playing ball and taking those GED classes, it's like all of a sudden I became a forgotten man," says Staggers, his voice rising. "Coaches said they'd help me get a job. They didn't. And then I find out that they started talking behind my back, saying I'm gone if I don't pass my GED real soon. What sort of support is that?" Frustrated by his coaches' indifference, Staggers left El Paso. "Don't worry about this UTEP shit," Hardaway told Staggers right before he left. "You're a better player than how you've been treated. You pass that test, get on with your life, and I'll see you in the NBA."

Those words hurt. Then. Now. Always.

Staggers was driven to the airport by an assistant coach and put on plane back to Los Angeles. To this day, he doesn't know who paid for that return ticket.

This strange little tale had just begun to unravel. As soon as Staggers got home, he called his friend Anthony January, who had briefly played for UTEP and was now attending Salt Lake Community College in Utah. At the time, the basketball program at SLCC was only in its third year and had fashioned itself as something of a safe harbor for wayward players. Staggers fit the mold. He asked January to talk to coach Dave Osborn about the possibility of Staggers's someday playing at SLCC. "The next thing you know," says Staggers, "I had a ticket at the airport waiting for me. I'd never even spoken with the man."

Staggers arrived in time for the fall semester of 1988, but he still wasn't eligible. He took the GED a few more times, and the results were the same. "They wanted me to play so bad," says Staggers, "that they actually had a guy take the test for me. He passed and I played."

Everything seemed fine and dandy at first. Staggers played in five games and averaged 25 points. The team was winning. And everyone was wondering how Osborn had unearthed this gem of a player named Staggers. Slowly, though, fissures emerged in the grand plan. First, both the school and the NCAA launched investigations, prompted by the dramatic improvement in Staggers's test score. After the investigation, the NJCAA, the governing body for junior colleges outside of California, placed Salt Lake Community College on a year's probation. It also ruled that Staggers was ineligible to play at any NJCAA school. Osborn resigned under heat.

The school seemed to want to wash its hands of Staggers. "He's like a lot of young men who [haven't] figured out what life's all about," said

Ron Gerber, the SLCC athletic director, at the time. "He didn't lie to me. When I found out about [the fraudulent test score] I approached him and he admitted what happened. He did what you or I would do at eighteen if basketball was your whole life. The guy wanted to play ball. He had his eye on the NBA. To him, school was a handicap, a hindrance."

Staggers left school once again. His plane ride home to L.A., was, as always, paid for anonymously. He finally did receive his GED at a junior college in Northern California, and after flirting briefly with Jerry Tarkanian, then at UNLV, Staggers ended up playing his final two years of eligibility at an NAIA school, St. Martin's University in Olympia, Washington. Predictably, Staggers dominated there. He averaged 27 points a game and was named NAIA All-America both years.

Not that it mattered much. Staggers's dream of playing in the NBA had long ago ruptured. He had talent, yes. But the scouting report on Staggers also said he was undisciplined, a head case, and that problems followed him like a stale odor. Consider it a case study in one method by which a potential NBA player ends up a playground player.

"I paid big-time for allowing myself to believe what everyone was telling me," says Staggers. "But I still got the playgrounds." A smile lights his face. Staggers's reputation as the city's top blacktop player stems not only from his awesome ability, but also from the fact that not many kids with chances at Division I scholarships in Los Angeles slip through the cracks anymore and wind up solely as street players. With so many youth programs and youth leagues having taken root all over the area, any kid who shows the slightest bit of ability by the age of ten or eleven is immediately chaperoned into a structured league that, in theory, should carry him all the way to a college scholarship.

"There are so many programs and leagues now for kids in the Los Angeles area that it's almost like the kids have a foster parent," says Weakly, who has started playground leagues for youngsters in the past. "We're still losing kids to the streets, but it's nothing like it used to be. Perhaps it's not good for the quality of ball on the playgrounds, but it's good for all the kids who get involved early and don't get swept up by the streets."

Give John Staggers credit: He has not been swept up by the streets. For a few hours every day, he works as a guidance counselor for a group called the Woodcraft Rangers, a nonprofit organization in Los Angeles that offers courses such as conflict resolution to children throughout the L.A. area. Staggers stays in shape by playing at Venice a few times a week and at a playground court at Lomita Park. He's planning to travel to China to play in the fledgling China Men's Basketball Allowance League. His coach will be Joe Weakly – the one person who has stuck with Staggers through all his trials and tribulations.

"John is really ready for China," says his mother, Gloria. "As a younger kid with the publicity of a superstar, he couldn't handle it, but he's grown and matured. This is something he really wants."

"I want people to learn from me," says Staggers. His face has softened now, and his eyes are aflame as he sits on the bed in his bedroom looking at the ceiling, studying it as if it were a complex piece of art. "I lost out on my chance because I was naive and I let people take advantage of me. I hope someone will read this and think twice about believing what everyone tells you without thinking about what they're saying. I know I'm partly responsible for what happened, but not totally responsible."

So in the morality play that is John Staggers's life, we now have our moral. Perhaps in China things will be different. Perhaps Staggers will find what he never could in the United States. Perhaps, finally, he will find contentment on the court. Then again, perhaps not.

◆ ◆ ◆

Lowell, Michigan, is a one-stoplight town a universe away from Venice Beach. Far from the cutting edge of fashion or bohemian culture, Lowell is a 1950s kind of place, where you are quite likely to bump into Opie Taylor and Huck Finn types. But during the 1970s and continuing into the 1980s, Lowell became a Holy Land of sorts for those who worship pickup hoops. The story of basketball in Lowell is an unlikely one that begins in the most unlikely of places: on Scott McNeal's driveway in 1974.

While sitting at home during spring break of his junior year in high school, McNeal was feeling a little restless. He enjoyed playing basketball to kill the time, but he was getting bored with just going up against his friends, with nothing more than pride on the line. McNeal, a gregarious sort with luminous blue eyes and a big smile perpetually glued to his face, came up with an idea. He gathered seventeen of his closest friends and told them that it was time to make the game of basketball a tad more interesting. To do so, he proposed that everyone throw a buck into a hat and then they could divide up into teams of three and hold a tournament. His friends agreed, and they went at each other at the hoop above McNeal's driveway. The winning team split the $18 kitty.

"We were sick of playing each other for no real reason other than the competition," says the five-foot-seven McNeal, who played shooting guard at Lowell High. Though no great hoops talent, he had always been a meticulous planner. "So we decided to make things more interesting by throwing some money around. As soon as we did that, the intensity picked up. We held a draft. We made up brackets. The buildup of the thing was much bigger than the actual tournament itself. I thought it would die after that first year."

For that first tournament, McNeal asked his mother, who was an executive secretary at Amway, to make some photocopies of a tournament program that he had put together, containing the bracket, the teams, the captains and some corny sayings. When Scott handed the information to his mother in their living room one evening, one of Scott's friends told him that they needed a name for their tournament. "It's gotta be the Gus Macker," said one of Scott's friends in the living room. "That's perfect."

Who is Gus Macker? That's the sobriquet given to McNeal by a classmate named Rick Thompson in the seventh grade. Thompson and McNeal had shop class together, and one day Thompson scrawled the nickname on a piece of paper and taped it to McNeal's locker. So it began. "Rick doesn't even know why he called me that," says McNeal. "There is no real reason behind it, other than it sounded a little funny."

In the second year of the tournament, thirty players participated. The next year, 1976, thirty-six players again participated. At this point McNeal sensed that the enthusiasm for his tournament was waning. So in 1978 he made some changes. Instead of inviting only his friends to play, he opened the tournament to anyone. If you could dribble a ball, you could play. In the first year of open admission, a few people from out of town came. Crowds slowly started to get bigger. The McNeals, sensing they were on to something, began selling T-shirts and buttons. Then they started awarding trophies. In 1979, ninety teams participated. The local press began to take notice, and the growth of the monster was now unstoppable.

Just a few years after it had become an open event, the tournament grew so large that the one court in the McNeal driveway would no longer suffice. Some of the McNeal's neighbors were less than thrilled to have basketballs slapping the pavement in his driveway until 2 a.m., so McNeal constructed two hoops in the street to accomodate the growing interest. One basket was attached to a forklift, and another was coerced from the local high school. By 1980, crowds had swelled so much that folks climbed trees to get a glimpse of the action. In 1986, 1,100 teams played in the Gus Macker.

"We had a hundred thousand people in town for the tournament, in a town of thirty-five thousand," says McNeal. "The city fathers started to get a little upset. But I think it got popular because people started to play in it just to say they did. I can't take credit for the explosion. We're a grass-roots type of tournament that isn't overly commercialized, and we like to make it a spectacle and have as much cornball fun as possible."

Indeed, the spectacle of the Macker is its charm. It's now played in Belding, Michigan, and the McNeals have taken their act on the road as well, organizing about eighty-five tournaments a year across the country. But wherever the Macker takes place, it still is played as if it's in the McNeal driveway. McNeal still presides over the tournaments, and things are as wacky as ever. Each team, for example, has to fill out a questionnaire and list its team colors, team rock and team bird.

And then there are all the extraneous events attached to the Macker. There is the Miss Macker beauty pageant (the winner tosses up the opening tip), an opening ceremony where a celebrity hoists an opening shot (note: Dolly Parton is oh-for-two), a slam-dunk contest, and a goofy motto that eloquently sums up McNeal's life philosophy: "Wear a Macker smile for all the world to see; Macker makes the world a better place to be."

Though there is a lot of silliness associated with the Macker, it all feels right, the way a backyard tournament should. The biggest problem the tournament has had to deal with over the years has been the physical and often boorish behavior of some participants, so in the early 1980s McNeal added court monitors – so-called "Gus Busters" – to help make the games more civilized. This, in turn, helped the Macker attract top talent, guys who otherwise might have been deterred from playing because of the chance of getting hurt. Over the years, Chris Webber, Grant Long and numerous other future NBA players have participated.

In the grand scheme of things, the Macker helped bring pickup basketball to the suburbs, and served as a sort of national championship of playground basketball as it is played in the 'burbs. It also started the wave of three-on-three tournaments, competitions that are now nearly as ubiquitous as inner-city summer leagues.

If you scanned the stands at a big-time inner-city basketball tournament in the mid-1970s, you more likely than not would come across a plump, pasty man with droopy brown eyes, watching intently. Sonny Vaccaro first became a figure on the national basketball scene in 1965, when he started one of the first of the high school basketball all-star tournaments, the Dapper Dan Classic in Pittsburgh, Vaccaro's hometown.

Vaccaro had been a scholarship football player at Ohio's Youngstown State, but during his sophomore year in 1958 a knee injury ended his football career. Vaccaro had made an impression on the coaching staff with his enthusiasm and his ability to bring his teammates together. He was a good schmoozer, making friends with the most ornery of players and tactfully settling disputes among his teammates. It would prove to be a handy skill later in life. When Vaccaro's football career ended, an assistant football coach who was also Youngstown State's head basketball coach told Vaccaro he could stay on scholarship if Vaccaro would help him recruit basketball players in the Pittsburgh area.

"I hadn't been involved with basketball before that," says Vaccaro. "I started forming these club teams and going to the playgrounds and high school tournaments. I was basically putting together kids and putting them in tournaments, then recruiting them to go to Youngstown."

After college, Vaccaro took a job on the basketball staff at Wichita State, but he still spent a lot of time in western Pennsylvania, where he would watch players at the Sharon-Hoyle, a tournament in Sharon, Pennsylvania, on the Ohio border just across from Youngstown. For seven years Vaccaro sweet-talked players at the Hoyle – which, in the late 1950s was the top showcase for high school–age players from the Philly and Pittsburgh areas – into attending Wichita State. One day, though, he decided he could organize a competition that was bigger and better than the Sharon-Hoyle.

For the Dapper Dan Vaccaro added perks like T-shirts and gym bags for the players. He provided transportation to and from the tournament for some of the better players along the Eastern seaboard, broadening the reach of his tournament beyond that of the Sharon-Hoyle. He ingratiated himself with coaches all over the country, who had no other choice but to attend the Dapper Dan if they wanted to see the best high school players in the country.

"There was no nationwide recruiting in the sixties and seventies, so everyone used to come for the weekends and watch the games," says Vaccaro. "The Dapper Dan used to have three hundred coaches attend the games. Reputations and scholarships were won and lost. I can remember Jerry Tarkanian coming from Long Beach State and looking at a kid named Les Carson. He was supposed to be the greatest player in America, and Jerry had all but offered him a scholarship based on word of mouth. He plays in the Dapper Dan, doesn't score all weekend, and Tark and everyone else loses interest in him."

The constant hard sell required to run a high school all-star tournament put a strain not only on Vaccaro but on his wife. Despite the prestige the Dapper Dan, and consequently Vaccaro, achieved, and the connections he had cultivated in the community, he found it difficult to make ends meet. Ten years after the tournament began, Vaccaro was all but jobless, separated and on the way to a divorce. The father of four children, whom he saw only sporadically, was adrift in life. Nearing middle-age – he was thirty-eight – the man with the boy's name was also nearing the end of his rope when he got an idea. Vaccaro, who had been living in Las Vegas to find work in the casinos, went back to Pennsylvania and approached a shoemaker named Bobby DiRinaldo. Vaccaro asked him to design a pair of sneakers with air vents, a pair without any backs, like sneaker-sandals, and a pair that used Velcro instead of laces. When DiRinaldo came up with the designs, Vaccaro put them in a bag and headed to a nascent shoe company in Beaverton, Oregon, named Nike for a meeting that would shape the future of the sports apparel industry – indeed, of the entire sports world.

Vaccaro went to lunch with about a half-dozen Nike managers one fall afternoon in 1978. They laughed at his designs. ("Just for the record," Vaccaro says, "those shoes were on the market in a few years.") But the brass at Nike was impressed with Vaccaro, whose message was that the company needed to pay attention to the playgrounds and to the colleges if it was going to sell athletic shoes. Vaccaro also told them that Converse, which ruled the athletic shoe market at the time, was vulnerable for the very reason that it had never had to deal with competition. He, Vaccaro, was just the guy Nike needed, Vaccaro told them. Thanks to his involvement in the Dapper Dan, he had connections to all the coaches and playground players in the East, and that was where Nike had to start.

"That gave me entrée into every college in America," says Vaccaro. "At that time there was no Nike, no Reebok, all that other bullshit. I had my place pretty much established back then." Nike bought the spiel hook, line and sinker, and chairman Phil Knight gave Vaccaro a job in the promotions department, where Vaccaro's philosophy was "everything starts with the playgrounds in the inner city."

"When I went to work for Nike full-time," says Vaccaro, "they had a bunch of white people from the Northwest who had absolutely no concept of what the East was like and what playground basketball meant in the grander scheme of things. I told them something that is still true today – in fact, it's a billion dollars true today – that everything comes out of inner-city America. And that means that the playgrounds play a crucial role in how companies like Nike should do business."

"I was charmed by Sonny," Knight has said in the past. "We had been beating our brains in trying to get a foot in the door in this game. Then this little portly Italian fellow comes around and says he's going to burn down the walls for us. When we saw his relationships with coaches in action, that he could produce ... And then these massive orders for shoes began pouring in. We gave him all the room he wanted."

On his first trip across the country to sign up coaches for Nike, Vaccaro netted a dozen, ranging from a little-known coach at Iona named

Jim Valvano to Vaccaro's buddy Tarkanian at UNLV. He would pay coaches to get their players to wear Nike, and donate shoes to other programs all to build Nike's name recognition among the players. "I had twelve years' experience in the business, with the all-star games and the camps I was running," says Vaccaro. "So these coaches were my friends. And I got 'em all. College teams were our first priority. Tarkanian was the first one we signed. Then I got involved with the high school teams in the late seventies, continuing until this very minute. Obviously, I never thought it would become this big." The momentum had been generated, momentum that would push Nike to the dominant position in the athletic wear industry, from which it exerts its enormous influence, through the hundreds of millions it spends on marketing, licensing and sponsorships, on American sports.

Vaccaro's influence at Nike spread to the playground. To the coaches he was trying to recruit, he preached the virtues of playground basketball, and they listened. College coaches began turning up at playgrounds to see if they could find that player with the big-time ability who had somehow fallen through the cracks. Vaccaro also gave shoes and apparel to street agents like Rodney Parker in New York, who would in turn hand them to the top players on the playground in exchange for friendship and a loose contractual agreement similar to that between a player and an agent in professional basketball. And such was the power of the playground star, and anything associated with him, that when other players saw the top guy on the court wearing Nikes, they wanted the shoes, too.

By the time the kids who wore Nike as teenagers got to deciding which college to attend, the shoe that the team wore – believe it or not – played a major factor in shaping their decision. The result, is that, despite his somewhat cartoonish – and some would say unsavory – quality, Vaccaro played a major role in the growing prominence and credibility of the playgrounds in the world of college recruiting.

"In the seventies the playground became a place where every white recruiter in the country was going to find kids in the inner city," he says. "There were no recruiting guidelines in those days, so all summer long you'd get college guys coming to the playgrounds and the parks. This is where the game expanded because now you had guys from everywhere getting a chance to play college basketball. The New Mexicos of the world, all these small schools, were coming back east to these playgrounds to watch the players."

By the late 1970s, the forces were in place to launch playground basketball to new heights of popularity and to a once-unthinkable place in the American consciousness. But despite the newfound prestige of the playground, and the potential money it promised, all too many playground players in the 1980s would discover that this paradise had its dark side.

6

Blood on the Ball

They were just lying there, brand new, expensive, shiny red hi-tops. To leave playground jewels like those on the feet of a dead boy would be a waste of good leather. So after his friend Shatik pumped a bullet into seventeen-year-old Tyrone Hampton's head at the Kingston Playground in Bedford-Stuyvesant, Brooklyn, sixteen-year-old Anthony Lee ripped the shoes from Hampton's lifeless feet.

The shooting occurred at 1:30 a.m. on August 27, 1980. Hampton and twelve other boys were playing a late-night game of pickup basketball. From June to August, the games at Kingston begin only as the stifling summer sun goes down, and they continue from dusk until long past midnight. On those summer nights you can always find teenagers shooting tattered balls through netless rims under one dim light of a flickering lamppost. The setting that late August evening was no different: The court had been busy for nearly six hours. Most of the players had no doubt been there the whole time. Guys were tired, and tempers were short.

A player from Tyrone's team pushed Shatik out of bounds. Shatik pushed back. Tyrone's teammate punched Shatik. Then the fighting stopped. Shatik stepped away and gathered himself. Why fight with my fists if I don't have to? he thought to himself. "I'm going to get my gun," he said to the crowd as he stormed away. When Shatik came back to the playground with Anthony, most of the players had scattered, including the one who had punched him. But there stood Tyrone, alone, still shooting hoops. He was one of the punks on the other guy's team, Shatik thought. Shatik didn't need to knock off the guy who hit him to sate his hunger for revenge; anyone on the other team would do. After Anthony pummeled Hampton, Shatik eased the gun to Hampton's head and shot him point-blank, execution style.

If not for the macabre detail of his shoes' being swiped after he had been killed, Hampton's murder would have earned no more than a three-line notice in the New York newspapers' police blotter. Just another shooting in the ghetto. But when Shatik and the Lee brothers robbed Hampton of his life, his future and his sneakers, it was a warning of the status symbol basketball shoes would become in the 1980s, and the violent lengths to which some would go to acquire them. From the Kingston playground in Bedford-Stuyvesant, the epidemic of killing for basketball shoes would spread across the country. The old, canvas Chuck Taylors – *limousines for the feet* – weren't good enough anymore. The player didn't make the player – the shoes did. By 1980 the basketball shoe had begun its ascent from a mere piece of athletic equipment to a badge of wealth and success.

On a broader scale, the shooting foreshadowed the events that would shape the decade. The playgrounds of the 1980s were dangerous places where violence had become a way of life, and drugs – more than ever before – had become the common currency. Most distressingly, a crippling sense of hopelessness had crept onto the court. Those who couldn't find jobs would, in the parlance of the playground, chill by the chain-link fences that surrounded the courts. At first they relaxed there only after a day of job hunting. But for all too many, that hobby unspooled into an alternative to looking for work at all. The blacktop, with its alluring sound of bouncing balls, became a home for the displaced. For older men who couldn't find work, the playground, with its simplicity, offered a place to experience again a carefree youth. There was, however, one difference: When they were children they went to the court to have fun; now they were wasting their lives.

"The fortunes of inner-city America in the 1980s were dire, to say the least," said Tom McMillen, a former Maryland congressman who played in the NBA from 1975 to 1986. "The despair level for people in the inner city was almost unfathomable. We saw a retrenchment of life in urban areas across the country in the early eighties. Simply put, people couldn't find jobs." Indeed, the rising unemployment level in urban centers across the country ripped apart the the soul of inner-city America in the mid-1980s. And the escalating unemployment triggered a foreboding trend that manifested itself on the playground.

"The drug and cocaine problem hurt the inner city to the point that playground basketball became a place of last refuge for a lot of inner-city residents," McMillen says. "On the court, there was an element of hope that was so strong that it almost ameliorated some of the problems in the inner city. There wasn't a lot of hope in inner-city America in the eighties, and the playground was one place people went for outlet, a place where hope seemed real."

In the early 1980s, the illicit drug business rode a bull market like that enjoyed by Wall Street throughout much of the decade. In general, two factors accounted for cocaine's remarkable rise in popularity: greater availability, because of the Latin American drug cartels' ability to deliver to major cities across the country; and a price drop due to more effective means of production. In the late 1970s a gram of cocaine cost $125; by 1980 the price of a gram had plummeted to $65.

By conservative estimates, some 10 million Americans used coke on a regular basis in 1981. According to the President's Commission on Organized Crime, requests for treatment for cocaine abuse increased by 600 percent between 1983 and 1984. Upon leaving his position as the administrator of the Drug Enforcement Administration in 1981, Peter Bensinger remarked on the drug's newfound foothold in once unlikely places: "We see coke sales in suburbs, in recreational centers and in national parks," he said. "It is an unrecognized tornado."

The playground thus became the turf of drug dealers. And as a cheaper but more lethal form of cocaine called crack became readily available in the mid-1980s, the atmosphere on the playgrounds – in the inner cities and the suburbs alike – became increasingly combustible. In cities as varied as New York, Philadelphia, Detroit, Omaha and Austin, drug dealers emerged from the shadows to become the dark angels on the playground.

At the St. Cecilia's Church recreation center in Detroit, drugs and guns combined to shut down one of the most popular summer basketball programs in the country in 1989. The basketball program at St. Cecilia's was founded to give kids an escape from the tensions that triggered Detroit's 1967 riots and over twenty years it had established itself as a safe haven from the drugs and the crime that permeated the West Side of Detroit. Future pros such as Magic Johnson and Spencer Haywood had played in the league at Ceciliaville, as the recreation center was known, and over the years the program had swelled to eighty-five teams and 850 players. But on August 5, 1989, what took more than two decades to establish was torn asunder by a hail of gunfire.

"I'd say 99 percent of the guys who come in here are trustworthy," church pastor Thomas Finnigan said in 1989, "but you have that element around St. Cecilia's now – drugs, alcoholism, poverty." According to most accounts, it was the drug element that led to the fateful gunshots. On that late summer afternoon, in a game between two college-level teams – Steve's Big Shots and Players – a fight erupted on the court. When the fans joined in, league director Ron Washington tried to cool the situation by calling the game and ordering everyone out of the gym. But the fight rolled out into the parking lot, where Steven Dale Goodwin, coach of Steve's Big Shots, began arguing with another man, reportedly over a $37,000 bet Goodwin and the man had with each other. The man shot Goodwin twice. Goodwin – who had been previously convicted of armed robbery and of carrying a concealed weapon, and had had three charges of intent to deliver cocaine dismissed – fully recovered. But the stain left on the St. Cecilia basketball program was indelible.

During that same summer in the Melrose section of the South Bronx, the Hot Rod Classic – a tournament named after Rod Strickland, who grew up in the nearby John P. Mitchell Housing Projects – attracted some of the Big Apple's top street stars. But the tournament also drew some of the top drug dealers in the city, many of whom placed side bets on the games. When a fight broke out over a contested call early in the tournament, an anonymous member of the crowd boldly pronounced that he was going home to get a gun. The crowd of nearly 300 scattered, and the tournament was never completed. No shots were ever fired, but the incident left tournament directors scratching their heads over how a meltdown of order like that could have been averted.

How many playground players never reached their potential because of their involvement with drugs or guns? How many Michael Jordans or Magic Johnsons or Larry Birds never bloomed because their games withered prematurely? In the 1980s, more so than in any other decade, drugs were a major player in shaping the destiny of street stars. So perhaps it is appropriate that the demise of the top street player of the 1980s would be linked to drugs, his life a sad microcosm of his generation. His name is Lloyd Daniels.

"They'll write the history of guards and start with Jerry West, Oscar Robertson, Magic Johnson and Lloyd Daniels," Jerry Tarkanian, former coach of UNLV and current coach at Fresno State, said while he was recruiting Daniels to UNLV.

"When Lloyd was sixteen," says former NBA reserve Sam Worthen, "he had the knowledge of the game to play in the NBA."

For better or worse – and for him, it has undoubtedly been worse – the legend of Lloyd Daniels started early in his teens. Once when playing as a teenager at a tournament in Harlem, so the myth goes, Daniels grabbed 42 rebounds and scored 42 points in two games. And there was the time Daniels made Strickland, a future NBA point guard, look like a Washington General during a game in the Bronx.

Like all legends, Daniels was tagged with a sobriquet. His friends called him "Swee'pea" after noticing that Daniels' oval-shaped head, high cheek bones, and millimeter-length hair gave him a striking resemblance to the baby-faced character from Popeye. On the court, however, Swee'pea's skills often left people comparing him to Renoir or Rembrandt. But the problem for Lloyd Daniels has always been the same: Away from the playground, the only thing he painted for himself was a picture of utter despair.

"I probably should be dead," Daniels said in 1992. "After all the stuff I've been through, I know I should have been a statistic."

He grew up in the depressed neighborhood of Brownsville, which ranks among the worst in the world in the number of drug-related deaths. By the time Daniels was three, his mother was dead and his father had abandoned him to the care of relatives. By the time he was ten he was regularly dealing and doing drugs. Though he never applied himself in school – one year he was marked absent 152 days – in basketball he committed himself with the dedication of a graduate student during finals week.

Hailed as the most talented New York City basketball player to come along since Lew Alcindor, Daniels was coddled by coaches and recruiters from the time he was in eighth grade. But he had little self-discipline, and he suffered from dyslexia, main reasons why Daniels either quit or was kicked out of four high schools, one junior college and one college.

It also didn't help his cause that he was a drug addict and an alcoholic. In May 1989, Daniels was on the wrong end of a drug deal gone sour. Two men came to his grandmother's house in Queens to collect $8 that Daniels owed from a crack purchase. When Daniels didn't pay up, he was shot three times – twice in the chest and once in the neck. He fully recovered, but his game never did. He played parts of four years in the NBA with three different teams and averaged 7.4 points, 2.3 rebounds and 1.6 assists over the course of his career, never fufilling the promise that he displayed on the playgrounds. As far as his legend goes, he would have been better off if he had never played a second of professional basketball.

At his best, Daniels the player in the mid- to late 1980s simulated the smooth rhythm of the silkiest rap lyrics. With sonic riffs and electric booms blaring in the background when he played, Daniels at times seemed to be rap-in-motion on the court, the economy of his moves strikingly similar to the economy of lyrics in the most succinctly written rap song.

At his worst, Daniels the citizen was a charter member of a lost generation of inner-city black males. In 1989, 23 percent of black males between the ages of twenty and twenty-nine were under the supervision of the criminal justice system, incarcerated, paroled, or on probation. According to a 1989 study published in the *Journal of the American Medical Association,* a black male was six times more likely to be a homicide victim than a white male. Marc Mauer of the Sentencing Project, a nonprofit group concerned with disparities in the administration of criminal justice, summed up this situation in 1989: "We now risk the possibility of writing off an entire generation of black men."

Like that of Daniels, the story of Gregory Vaughn typifies this generation, though in more tragic tones. In the 1970s, gun-toting drug dealers began wagering on basketball games in Harlem and Brooklyn, but not until 1988, until the case of Vaughn, did the phenomenon of drug dealers wagering thousands of dollars on playground games become fully, and painfully, exposed.

Basketball was Vaughn's life and livelihood. The dream of making it to the NBA first entered his mind while playing on the playgrounds of New York City in the late 1960s and early 1970s. After a distinguished career as a street player, Vaughn attended Queens College, where he became the school's all-time leading scorer. While he quickly realized he was not an NBA-caliber player, Vaughn never lost his love for the game. From Queens College he went on to teach at P. S. 140 in South Jamaica, Queens, coach basketball, and at times referee games on the playground.

On July 30, 1988, Vaughn was asked to lend a hand in refereeing a game on the asphalt basketball courts of Baisley Pond Park in South Jamaica. The game was his passion, so of course he would help ref the game. Vaughn thought he had agreed to officiate a friendly neighborhood competition. He was unaware that drug dealers, sitting silently in the shadows, were betting thousands of dollars on the outcome. One estimate put the total amount wagered at $50,000.

Vaughn knew that cocaine was the scourge of his South Jamaica neighborhood, and so he had dedicated his life to trying to get kids to stay in school and away from drugs. But Vaughn knew that everyone was vulnerable to being knocked over by the powerful and deadly wake of a drug deal. He saw it every day. But he could not have known or seen, not even in his nightmares, that the place where he was most vulnerable, at least on this day, was the playground basketball court.

With about ninety seconds remaining in a tied game, the 33-year-old Vaughn made a call that angered some of the drug-dealing gamblers. Ten minutes later, after the game had ended, he was followed off the playground and fatally beaten by a known thug working for a dealer who had lost money. Somehow, street basketball changed that afternoon.

◆ ◆ ◆

To really understand the paramount role basketball can play in a person's life, you must venture into the thickly wooded foothills of the Allegheny Mountains in northwest Maryland. You need to go five miles west of an old mining town called Cumberland and enter what looks like an industrial complex that houses a cluster of buildings encased by a barbed-wire fence fifteen feet high. Before you enter the complex, take a deep breath and prepare to cross into that river of darkness that every creature fears almost as much as death itself: the fear of freedom lost. After you exhale, enter a federal correctional institution known simply as FCI Cumberland. This is where you will find inmate 27812-037, surely one of the most talented incarcerated basketball players in the world.

FCI Cumberland is a medium-security prison nearly filled to its capacity of 768 inmates. Of all the men moldering away in Cumberland and other prisons across the country, it is Derrick Curry and his troubling story that speak most eloquently to the power of basketball. It is a tale that embodies most every element of Greek tragedy: Curry is a man of high basketball renown who was brought down by a tragic flaw that was part hubris, part naiveté, and part plain bad luck. During his years in prison he has undergone a certain amount of introspection that has led to a self-discovery and moral revelation about his life. Ultimately even he admits that without spending time in prison a catharsis would not have been possible. Yes, somehow he's a better man now.

If Derrick Curry's appeals are not granted, he will be in jail until the year 2013, serving nineteen years and seven months for possession and distribution of crack cocaine. He is still allowed to play basketball, and that is his only consolation. A person who enjoys freedom simply cannot fathom how important Curry's moments of court time are to him. They give him the ability, albeit momentarily, to fly, fly away.

"The only time I feel free is when I'm on the basketball court," says Curry, as he sits in a cinder-block interview room. The late afternoon sun sits atop the Alleghenies, sending streams of bright white light through the room's only window and straight into Curry's face. He does not squint as he speaks.

"Freedom is something that most people take for granted, but not me," he says. "It's like for those few minutes when I'm on the court everything is OK again. People are respecting me, looking up to me, counting on me, and rooting for me. For those few minutes it's like I'm not even in prison. I wish I could play basketball twenty-four hours a day, seven days a week. But I know I can't."

He pauses, his deep brown eyes staring out the window at the reddish sunset spilling over the mountaintops. "I just hope I can get out of here so I can give the NBA a shot. That is, if I can get my freedom before it's not too late."

Freedom is a concept that is difficult to define. After spending years in prison, Lord Byron's prisoner of Chillion eventually concluded, "My very chains and I grew friends," so twisted had his notion of freedom become. The astonishing rate of recidivism in the United States offers reason to believe that Byron may have been on to something. Yet Curry, like all athletes, yearns for freedom. And in some respects, athletes are the people who need freedom the most: freedom to create, to run, to jump, to be physical. For those reasons, basketball is Derrick Curry's sole salvation as he struggles with life in prison. It is a struggle shared by thousands of basketball players/inmates across the country.

Derrick Curry was born on New Year's Day, 1970. He grew up in the quiet town of Mount Rainier, Maryland, a wooded place flecked with refurbished homes and manicured lawns and filled with hard-working, upper-middle-class folks. Derrick's father, Arthur, holds a Master's degree and a Ph.D. in education. He has spent more than thirty years in the field of education, as a high school teacher, a high school principal and a college professor. Derrick's mother, Darlene, is a middle school teacher. Though his parents divorced when Derrick was eight, they both played active roles in their children's lives. Derrick's older sisters, Jennifer and Melanie, went to college and are now working professionals. Arthur, in fact, has dedicated his career to saving children – young African Americans mostly – from the pitfalls of drugs and street life. You can hear the agony swell in his voice when he reflects on the dark irony of his inability to save his own son.

"Now part of my mission," says Arthur, who is a professor at Bowie State in Bowie, Maryland, "is to make sure there aren't any more Derrick Curry stories."

Curry, who is six-foot-one, played shooting guard at Northwest High in Washington, D.C. In his senior year he averaged 20 points a game, displaying a tremendous vertical jump (recently measured at 43 inches), soft, quick hands and powerful play in the paint. "He could really shoot, but what struck me about him was his rebounding ability," says Cornell Jones, Curry's coach at Northwest. "He had Division I potential written all over him. But aside from being a terrific basketball player, Derrick was a terrific person. He was very quiet and cooperative with everyone. He seemed to run with a good crowd of friends and, really, he was a perfect gentlemen."

And on the playgrounds of Washington, Curry became known as one of the city's most gifted players. What makes D.C. basketball distinctive is that it's one of the few big cities in the country where the jump shot didn't go out of style with the hula hoop. Some locals attribute this to the abundance of young, predominantly white suburban kids who work on Capitol Hill and play basketball in the District. They bring a suburban style, which places a higher emphasis on long-range marksmanship, to the inner-city courts. Though this is no doubt an oversimplification, if you tour some of the courts in D.C. you'll find the unmistakable influence of suburban ball.

Curry thrived in this atmosphere. He could drain a 25-foot jumper just as easily as he could play with his back to the basket down in the pivot. In many ways, his game translated into more success on the playground level than on the competitive level because at his height he was a little short to be considered a pure shooting guard.

But Curry had bigger problems than his height to deal with as he was finishing high school. He failed to qualify academically for a Division I school, and so attended Pratt Community College in Pratt, Kansas, for a year. In his one season at Pratt, Curry averaged more than 20 points a game playing against teams that had future NBA players such as Shawn Kemp, Stanley Roberts and Larry Johnson on their rosters. But toward the end of his freshman year Curry caught a serious case of homesickness and decided to transfer to Prince Georges Community College in Largo, Maryland. In retrospect, the move was the worst Derrick Curry ever made.

It was October 1990. Derrick was in his first year at Prince Georges and was hoping that with an impressive basketball season he could earn a scholarship to Georgetown. He talked on a few occasions with Hoyas coach John Thompson, who told him that if he could get his grades in order-something that had always been a problem – there might be a spot for Derrick on the Georgetown roster in the fall of 1991. That dream exploded on October 17.

During this period, Derrick was spending a lot of his time with a friend named Norman Brown. Arthur Curry saw that Norman drove a brand new Volvo, which sent up a red flag of suspicion because Norman didn't come from a very affluent family. Derrick's father feared that Norman's affluence came from dealing drugs, so he decided to investigate Norman's background. He did this by simply calling Norman's mother and asking her about the car. She explained to Arthur that when Norman was child he was burned over 75 percent of his body in a fire, and as a result Norman had come into a large sum of money when he turned twenty-one. Norman had recently celebrated his twenty-first birthday by purchasing the Volvo. This made sense, so the explanation allayed Arthur's worst fears.

A few weeks after that conversation, Derrick was driving another car owned by Norman Brown – a station wagon – when Curry noticed that he was being followed by a black-and-gold sedan with tinted windows. He began to get nervous when he noticed a grove of antennas sprouted from the car's roof. A flash of fear shot straight to his soul as he concluded that he was being followed by the FBI. He panicked. He drove the station wagon into a recreational center parking lot and ran, sprinting as fast as he could. When he found safety in a house in Mount Rainier, Curry called Norman's beeper. Norman beeped back. The conversation was caught on a wiretap. Arthur's instincts proved correct.

"You get outta there?" asked Norman.

Derrick was sucking his thumb, a habit of his when he is confronted with a dicey situation. "I can't hear you," commanded Norman. "Take your hand out of your mouth."

Then the incriminating words were uttered, the words that would be replayed in court and forever shape Curry's destiny.

"Where the shit at?" asked Norman.

"In the car," said Derrick. "I parked it in the rec center."

Inside the station wagon, under the passenger's seat, the FBI agents found a single, opaque rock of crack cocaine that weighed a little more than a pound. Curry contends that he had no knowledge that there was crack in the car, that he was unwittingly duped by Brown into transporting the crack. He also contends that the conversation caught on tape by the FBI was the second conversation that he had with Brown after he ran from the car. Curry says that in the first conversation, the one that according to Curry the FBI didn't get on tape, Brown told him for the first time that there was crack in the car, giving him the knowledge that the "shit" was at "the rec center."

"I am an innocent man," says Curry. "They offered me a plea bargain and I turned it down because I'm not guilty. My own attorney even told me to cop a plea because of the evidence against me, but I wasn't guilty, and it didn't seem right to admit to something that I didn't do."

"I knew what was going to happen," says Arthur. "I've seen too many cases in my life to think that my son was going to get off. Once the FBI agent testified about the wiretap, I knew that my son was going to be sent to prison."

The trial took five days, and the jury deliberated for less than two hours. The result was just what Arthur had anticipated: A federal jury convicted Curry of conspiracy to distribute crack cocaine. "I had never even been in trouble at school before this," says Curry. "You could say that I was at the wrong place at the wrong time."

Curry was sentenced to nineteen years and seven months in prison – with no chance of parole. According to Curry, the judge who presided over his sentencing hearing "apologized before he handed down the sentence. He said I deserved parole, but because of mandatory sentencing he had no choice but to give me the sentence he gave me."

So as it stands, if Curry does serve his entire sentence – and, since he has no possibility of parole, he would need to win an appeal to be released – he'll serve three times the sentence of the average murderer in America, four times the sentence of a kidnapper, and five times the sentence of a rapist. Because of the harsh terms, many who have followed Curry's case wonder aloud if justice is being served in this instance.

"The punishment must fit the crime, but this is just unbelievable," says Arthur. "I have no problem with the fact that Derrick was found guilty by a jury of his peers and that he should be punished. But this is crazy. What kind of society do we live in?"

If you walk into a prison and start talking to inmates about basketball, the legends of players past will emerge. One such ghost that materializes in the minds of many inmates is Richard "Pee Wee" Kirkland. Kirkland, a playground star from Harlem, was drafted out of Norfolk State by the Chicago Bulls in 1968, with a reputation as flashy off the court as on it. His style didn't mesh with that of then Bulls coach Dick Motta, who limited Kirkland's playing time, frustrating the player to the point of quitting. By 1971, Kirkland was back in New York and running with his old gang. That year he was arrested and convicted of conspiracy to sell narcotics and sentenced to ten years in prison.

In prison, he flourished in a way he never had on the playground or in the NBA. The waterbug of a guard averaged more than 70 points a game for the US Penitentiary at Lewisburg, Pennsylvania, the only prison team in a basketball league composed of "outside" squads at approximately the junior college skill level. In one game, Kirkland scored 135 points while being guarded by Wali Jones, who had played for the Philadelphia 76ers.

"I hate to say this," says Kirkland, who is now an educator and a coach in Manhattan, "but I was at my best when I was in prison. I added a dimension to my game there. You had to if you liked to penetrate like I did. It was a physical game beyond what you were used to on the playgrounds, where you never took your life into your own hands. You go to the hole in prison and that is exactly what you are doing. You are in danger of losing your life. I added a jump shot because I had to."

Kirkland continues. "When I first got there I didn't want to play. I didn't think the competition was going to be very good, and who knew how these guys would react to a little guy like me. But when I started playing, and we were winning, you could see a change in the guys. They were treated better by other inmates, and they felt better about themselves. It was something positive happening that never happened in the prisons. People just felt differently about themselves. They felt better. It made being in prison easier."

Curry knows what Pee Wee is talking about, and he is quickly becoming known as the "next Pee Wee Kirkland," a demigod to prisoners all across the country. At Cumberland the inmates organize their own summer basketball league of seven teams. The inmates act as coaches and player personnel directors. To form the league, the inmates hold a lottery to determine the draft order. Curry has been the first person selected in the draft every year he has been at Cumberland. The team that has drafted him has won every championship, and he has averaged roughly 36 points a game. But, he says with a sly little smile, "It could be more if I really tried."

"I think I do get treated a little differently by the inmates because of my basketball ability," says Curry. "I really don't have a problem with anyone in here, and no one, I think, has a problem with me. There's a certain level of respect I get because of my basketball talent that I wouldn't have if I didn't play basketball."

The role sports play in prison cannot be overemphasized. Sports today are more important than ever to the inmate because prison life has become so much harsher in recent years. In Mississippi, weightlifting equipment, private televisions and radios were taken away from prisoners; in Louisiana, legislators passed a law banning martial arts; in New York, North Carolina, South Carolina and Ohio, legislators have at one time or another proposed bans on basketball courts, weight rooms, boxing and wrestling.

In 1994, Mike Quinlan, the director of the Federal Bureau of Prisons from 1987 to 1992, warned, "If inmates aren't kept busy when you take away all those activities, they will find something to do with their time, and it probably will not be in the best interest of staff trying to monitor their activities."

Indeed, prison experts universally tout the benefits of sports – and basketball in particular, because of its popularity – in prison management. Sports are a way to control the behavior of the inmates, to instill order and calmness in a group of people that, collectively, is a powderkeg waiting to erupt. Sports, and access to them, can encourage proper behavior. And, perhaps most important, because many inmates come to prison with a history of drug and alcohol abuse, sports can help an addict recover by providing a needed outlet. "We would go crazy without sports," says Curry. "Basketball is, like, the only thing I got to hang onto while I'm in here. I can't imagine what it would be like if that was taken away from me."

Surprisingly – despite Pee Wee Kirkland's claims – basketball in prison is less physical than you might expect. True, there have been instances when a game called "murder basketball," in which there are no rules, has been played and inmates have gotten hurt. (In 1990 an inmate named Richard Gain in London, England, sued for damages when he broke his arm during what he said was a murder basketball game being played on the instructions of the prison guards. The case was dismissed.) But for the most part, prison basketball players exhibit more restraint than street basketball players.

This pleases Curry to no end. He does not want to get hurt and perhaps jeopardize a chance to play professionally if his appeal should ever go through. And he certainly doesn't want to jeopardize the special status he carries in prison. He recently added to his legend by ripping down a rim with a monstrous dunk during a game. Even though Curry has never lifted a weight in his life, he boasts a powerful, barrel-chested build. He often plays inmates in games of one-on-one and horse, but he eschews wagering money, opting instead to play for push-ups.

"If I win and we bet two hundred pushups, which is what we usually bet, then I can tell you to do those pushups whenever I want," says Curry. "We can be sitting in the cafeteria, and I can make you do fifty or two hundred or whatever it is right there in front of everybody. We try to embarrass each other."

Curry's typical day starts at 7 a.m., when he wakes up in the lower bunk of his 10-by-10-foot cell, which he shares with another inmate. Each has a nightlight and a desk; they share a toilet and a sink. Curry has one of the prime-location cells at FCI Cumberland. His window looks out onto the entrance of the prison, so he can monitor who comes and who goes. On Curry's desk is his Bible and a collection of John Grisham novels. Before he was incarcerated, Curry rarely even picked up a newspaper; now he is a voracious reader.

"That's been the biggest change in my son," says Arthur. "He has become much more intelligent since he went to prison because he reads so much. And he's gotten much more spiritual, too. He never went to church before. Now he goes almost every day. He used to walk that fine line between good and evil, but now he knows he can't take that risk. And he won't when he gets out."

After Curry awakens, he has a half-hour to get to his job in the gym, which was recently renovated and now houses a regulation-size basketball court outfitted with glass backboards and break-away rims. From 7:30 to 3:30, he checks out equipment to other inmates who are using the gym facilities. This also gives Curry a chance to slip away for a few minutes and shoot hoops by himself. These are the windows of freedom that sustain him: paradise found.

After he's done with his job, Curry attends classes taught by professors from Allegheny Community College in Cumberland. Curry acknowledges that he probably never would have taken school seriously had he not been sent to prison. "That's one good thing," he says. "Can't think of much else that's been good about this, other than the fact that I've matured and become a man."

The catharsis? "The biggest realization that I've come to about life since I've been here is how to value freedom and how to respect freedom. And also that you've got to be your own man and not let others influence you. You have to be strong to succeed in life. I never fully understood that until I spent time in prison."

If obtaining his degree is the high-water mark of his life in prison, the low-water marks have undoubtedly been the days that he has spent in solitary confinement. "The Hole," as solitary confinement at FCI Cumberland is known, is a room in which an inmate spends twenty-two hours in a day. When you're in the Hole you can't mingle with the other inmates, you aren't allowed to watch television and you can only talk on the phone for fifteen minutes a week. "It tests you," says Curry. "It teaches you to rely on yourself."

From the beginning of 1995 to the end of 1996, Curry had been thrown in the Hole three times. Before each of his trips to solitary confinement, Curry's father had somehow been highly visible on Capitol Hill, either testifying in front of Congress about the unfairness of mandatory sentencing or protesting the mandatory sentencing law. Both Derrick and Arthur allege that Derrick was thrown into solitary confinement as an act of retribution for Arthur's defiance of the law. And, in fact, each time Derrick has been released from solitary confinement, he says, "They told me all charges against me [that had put him in the Hole] were dropped, and that I'd been cleared of all wrongdoing."

One time, Derrick says, he was placed in the Hole because prison guards thought he had stolen a pair of shoes. The missing pair was a size 8; Derrick wears size 14. Another time he was thrown into the Hole because, it was alleged, Derrick warned an inmate who was watching sports on a television that was designated for non-sports viewing only that guards were approaching and that he should change the channel. The third time Derrick was sent to solitary confinement came after a prison strike to protest a tough crack law that had been signed by President Clinton in October 1996. Curry, it was alleged, organized the boycott while working in the gym.

"The shoes were a joke because first of all they wouldn't have fit me. And it's not like I need the money, so I wouldn't steal them to sell them. I would guess I'm one of the most well-off prisoners here because of my parents. They'll send me money whenever I need it, but I work so I don't really need it. Each time I was released and cleared, they didn't even apologize for throwing me in the Hole. That's when I really started to think that something strange may be going on."

Officials at FCI Cumberland would not comment on any of the alleged incidents, but they say that the notion that there is a conspiracy to punish Curry is absurd. "When Derrick is in the Hole he just lays there, with no contact with anyone, and waits for his three meals a day," says Arthur, who has spoken with more than fifty members of Congress about mandatory sentencing. "If he's lucky they'll let him have a book. They let him exercise one hour a day, and they won't give me any information on why he's there or when they're going to let him out. It's a feeling of total helplessness.

"This is either a backlash for what I've been doing on the outside or just a tremendous coincidence – a coincidence that I'll remind you has happened three times."

When Derrick talks about being in the Hole, he repeats again and again that the worst part is not being able to play basketball. As a prison guard comes into the interview room to announce that visiting hours are over and Curry must return to his cell, Derrick reiterates how important basketball is to him. "Just the thought of playing makes me smile," he says. "Life is hard here, but I can get by as long as I have basketball. I need basketball."

The guard leads Curry out of the interview room. He walks slowly back to his cell, his head gently bowed. The sun has dropped below the mountains. Darkness fills the cool autumn air.

◆ ◆ ◆

G. Van Standifer was a private man. He didn't like people interfering in his life and, reciprocally, he didn't interfere in the lives of others. After leaving the army in 1954, Standifer attended technical college in Washington, D.C., where he learned the basics of business management and typesetting. By the time he graduated from college, he had a family to support. While he would have liked to have gone back to his home in Nashville, he had to go where the jobs were. So in 1955 he accepted a job as a systems analyst with the Federal Aviation Administration in Washington, D.C., and he moved his family to Glen Arden in Prince Georges County, Maryland.

At the time, Glen Arden was no more than a bedroom community for D.C., a sleepy burg ten miles northeast of the White House with a population of 1,200 that was slowly growing larger as government workers moved in. But in the mid-1970s, low-income housing projects began going up in Prince Georges County. Over the next ten years the population of Glen Arden increased by 3,000, and crime rose concomitantly. When G. Van Standifer retired in 1985 after thirty years with the FAA and became the Glen Arden town manager, he still steadfastly believed in the tenets of privacy: Whatever problems there might be in the community should be handled by parents in the home. Take care of your own. To Standifer, that's what community responsibility implied.

A year into his stint as town manager, Standifer came across the crime statistics for the small town that he always considered a bastion of safety for his family. What he saw frightened him into taking action. In 1985, 4,500 people lived in Glen Arden, and there had been 1,900 violent crimes committed there, including homicide, rape and armed robbery. The statistics revealed that most of these crimes were committed between the hours of 10 p.m. and 2 a.m by males age seventeen to twenty-one.

Standifer had raised two boys of his own, and he knew that no matter how many straps he laid on their butts, the most severe punishment was taking away their chance to play basketball. That's the way it was with just about any teenager growing up in Glen Arden. Putting these two factors together – the crime statistics and what the absence of basketball meant to teenagers – Standifer suddenly developed a civic consciousness and a plan that would hatch midnight basketball.

"You could open a gym up anywhere in the country for twenty-four hours a day, and I guarantee someone will be playing there the entire time," says Nelson Standifer, thirty-nine, G. Van's youngest son and the commissioner of the Prince Georges Midnight Basketball League. "These guys love the game so much they'll stop doing just about anything for it."

G. Van began meeting with any town or county official who would listen to his plan, which entailed opening the local rec center during the crime-time hours of 10 at night and 2 in the morning for organized basketball games. First came Prince Georges County commissioner Parris Glendenning, who went on to become the governor of Maryland, then Glen Arden mayor Marvin Wilson. The politicians were easy. Even the residents of Glen Arden were amenable to having potentially dangerous kids traveling their streets late at night, if the kids had somewhere constructive to go. The toughest task was convincing the players themselves to show up. So as though he were running for office, Standifer pounded the pavement, knocking on doors to get the word out about the league. With an almost evangelical verve, he sold his idea as an alternative to gangbanging. Some listened, but most kids slammed the door on him as if he were selling them their own funeral insurance.

The week before the league was scheduled to begin in July 1986, Standifer and his family tried one last promotion. A carnival was in town, so why not set up a booth and raise money there? It rained for five of the carnival's seven days, and Standifer raised only $150. It looked as if his idea would founder on inaction. Yet on July 6, 1986, Standifer opened the doors at the Glen Arden rec center and – almost magically – players came. Three times a week, for four hours a night, the players arrived in bunches. Sixty that first year. Seventy-two the next. In 1988 there were eighty-four players. "Our target group is young men who don't respect authority and more than likely don't respect themselves," says Nelson Standifer. "They have a bad taste in their mouths from people telling them what to do. So getting kids to come in at all was a big deal. And when you get them here, they'll follow the rules or else they get booted. And they'd rather play than mouth off."

In the meantime, the players were drawn into programs that educated them. GED programs were offered, as were scholarships to technical colleges in and around Prince Georges. They heard sex education talks, and speeches by personnel directors on how to interview for a job. "The last thing midnight basketball is about is basketball," said President George Bush when he visited Glen Arden after honoring G. Van as one of his "thousand points of light" in 1991. "It's about providing opportunity for young adults to escape drugs and the streets and get on with their lives."

The statistics show that there are some golden nuggets of truth in that statement. In the first four years of midnight basketball in Prince Georges County, crime dropped 60 percent. So successful was the program that more than fifty cities duplicated the concept and joined the National Association of Midnight Basketball Leagues. G. Van Standifer, the man who believed his basic communal responsibility extended no further than rearing responsible, law-abiding children, was indirectly educating thousands of kids who didn't think they'd live past twenty-five.

A couple of days after the 1992 season ended in September, Standifer, who suffered from congestive heart failure, went down to his basement to finish up some paperwork from the season. He slept upright every so often, which helped to keep fluid out of his lungs and allowed him to breathe more easily through the night. Normally he'd work in the basement until late in the evening and then crash in his favorite chair so he didn't wake up his wife, Martha. On September 16, Martha went down to get him for breakfast. In his favorite chair, surrounded by midnight basketball paperwork, Standifer sat still. His heart had finally given in. "It surprised all of us when my Dad became so passionate about the problems outside our front door," Nelson Standifer says while sitting in his father's basement, which still serves as home office to the Midnight Basketball League. "But despite what he did and how the program has succeeded, he'd say midnight basketball is not the real answer for crime and the drug problem. It's just an alternative."

Despite the positive influence of programs like midnight basketball, by the mid-1980s some communities were actively attempting to diminish the role of playground basketball. In Birmingham, Alabama, in 1984 the city council made an unprecedented move: It made basketball illegal in the city streets. The six–three vote split the council along racial lines, with all the white council members voting for the measure and all the black members opposing it. Those who supported the measure decreed street basketball to be a traffic hazard that if allowed to persist would open the city to lawsuits if someone were to get hurt. Said William Bell, a black city councilman, "Being one who honed his skill in basketball on the asphalt surface of our streets, I'm opposed to it. Passing a law like this is stealing part of our children's childhood."

In 1989, the town of Fairfax, Virginia, ruled free-standing basketball goals to be in violation of a county ordinance that restricted "accessory structures" in the front yards of homes. Pink flamingos and flag poles were deemed acceptable front-yard structures by the local government, but the basketball goal was viewed as a nuisance by many of the Fairfax County legislators because of the noise that emanates from a pickup game. Sane minds eventually prevailed, and the ban on basketball was short-lived.

Just down the road from Fairfax, in the town of Alexandria, the recreation department confronted a persistent problem in 1987: How do we keep playground players from slamming the basketball? Though the slam is the most beloved of maneuvers on the court, to those charged with the upkeep of the playgrounds, the dunk keeps them in a funk. To fix one droopy rim cost the Alexandria recreation department $65 or more. Their solution? Raise the rims. Between 1987 and 1989, the department began a covert mission of raising the height of playground baskets by about six or seven inches, in the hope of making the hoop too high for most would-be dunkers. Until a *Washington Post* investigation uncovered the basket-raising scheme in 1989, the plan worked. Before the rims rose, between twenty-five and thirty rims were being ravaged and bent each week in Alexandria. Only a handful were damaged after they were raised.

"We wanted to stop all these guys who come out here pretending to be Michael Jordan or Doctor J and hanging on all the rims," Richard Kauffman, Alexandria's director or recreation, said in 1989. "Broken rims are our number one form of vandalism."

Is it any wonder that the players on the streets of Alexandria, or any other playground for that matter are – as Kauffman says – "pretending to be Michael Jordan or Doctor. J?" After all, who gets the glamorous commercials, Jordan or a streaky jump-shooter like Jeff Hornacek? The hang-timing, 360-dunking, monster-slamming players on the playground are the guys who get respect. They're the ones other players want on their teams, the ones even grandmothers leave their apartments to watch. On the playground, you're only as good as your image and your attitude, and a rim-wrecking jam elevates both.

No industry tapped into this macho vulnerability better than the athletic shoe companies. As a matter of fact, the footwear folks did whatever they could to perpetuate the notion that a certain image will give you attitude as well as altitude.

The sneaker wars began in earnest in 1985. At first the battle wasn't over who'd wear what on the meager plots of asphalt that dotted the inner cities. Nike, which had dominated the athletic footwear market for the previous six years, had fallen behind in profits and sales to Reebok, a nascent company that emphasized fashion over performance, and whose revenue had gone from $4 million in 1982 to $900 million three years later. The running boom Nike had capitalized on in the 1970s was fading, and the company was looking to expand into niche markets – aerobics, walking, tennis, baseball and basketball, among others. In all likelihood, Nike believed the walking and aerobic shoe markets would be the ones to put it back on top. After all, that's how Reebok had taken over the top spot. Almost as an afterthought, Nike, on the advice of Sonny Vaccaro, signed a skinny kid out of North Carolina named Michael Jordan as the front man for their basketball shoe efforts.

Though Jordan hadn't gone to any Nike basketball camps, and North Carolina wasn't a Nike-sponsored school, Vaccaro finagled a meeting with Jordan through former USC coach George Raveling when Jordan was in Los Angeles as a member of the 1984 US Olympic basketball team. They met at Tony Roma's Place for Ribs on Santa Monica Boulevard. Jordan, who knew almost nothing about Vaccaro, showed up only at the behest of Raveling.

During dinner Vaccaro turned on the charm that since his days as a recruiter at Youngstown State in the late 1950s had been his greatest asset. At the time Jordan showed no wildly extraordinary promise; though he had been named college player of the year in 1983 and 1984 and had built a reputation as a spectacular dunker, he had never averaged more than 20 points a game during his three years at North Carolina. While other companies had offered Jordan more money to endorse their products, Vaccaro told Jordan that Nike would go the distance with him, offer Jordan something different, something new: his own shoe.

The prospect intrigued Jordan, but he was skeptical.

"Why should I believe you?" Jordan asked Vaccaro about Nike's committment to him.

"Just trust me," Vaccaro responded.

Nike's first commercial featuring Jordan changed forever the way sneakers would be viewed. For that spot in 1985, Jordan stood at the center of a playground court as a beat-up ball rolled toward his Nike-adorned feet. As the sound of jet engines revved in the background, Jordan moved in slow motion toward the basket. As he took off and soared toward the basket, the sound of the engines grew to a scream. In all, just ten seconds passed from Jordan's slow-motion takeoff to landing, but in those ten seconds Jordan had propelled himself from mere basketball player to potential demigod. Schoolchildren in China would one day vote him as one of the two greatest men in history, along with Zhou Enlai, the first premier and foreign minister of Communist China. The man was grace personified. Sinewy muscles, handsome smile, wholesome-as-milk demeanor. But he could also fly. And, apparently, he could do so because of the shoes: Air Jordans.

In 1989 more than 150 million pairs of brand-name sneakers were sold in the United States – more than twice as many as in 1984, the year before the first Jordan commercial aired. Athletic shoe sales jumped from just under $2 billion in 1984 to more than $4 billion in 1988. Companies went berserk with options. By 1989 Reebok offered 175 models of shoes in 450 color combinations. Nike marketed shoes for twenty-four different sports, a total of 300 models and 900 styles. Shoes now would be marketed in the same way the fashion industry sells its clothes – changing products, colors and styles every six months, in spring and fall, to keep the lines fresh.

Basketball shoes were the brightest cluster in this footwear galaxy. In 1988 that niche accounted for $230 million in sales. One company that didn't exist in 1986, British Knights, made close to $100 million in 1988 marketing only basketball shoes. Where were the advertising dollars – which for Nike and Reebok grew from $23 million and $12 million, respectively, in 1987 to $50 million and $60 million in 1989 – targeted? Inner-city playgrounds. As cars had been to teenagers in the 1950s and 1960s, shoes had become the youth status symbol of the 1980s.

As much as the shoes were coveted for their look and their prestige, footwear represented the inner-city kids' marker in the bigger game, the game of life. These kids heard the message being sent out about style over substance. "A man's got to have style, or he's half a man," eighteen-year-old Harlem resident Brian Washington told the *Wall Street Journal* in 1988. All too often, it was the shoes that made kids feel whole.

"The uneducated inner-city kids feel the system is closed off to them," University of Pennsylvania sociologist Elijah Anderson told *Sports Illustrated* in 1990. "And yet they're bombarded with the same cultural apparatus that the white middle class is. They don't have the means to attain the things offered, and yet they have the same desire. So they value these emblems, these supposed symbols of success. The gold, the shoes, the drug dealer outfit – it's all a symbolic display that seems to say things are all right. The shoe companies capitalize on this situation because it exists."

Are the shoe companies, therefore, responsible for exploiting the despair of the inner city? Responded Nike's chief marketer at the time, Tom Clarke, "Our higher-end shoes are basketball shoes. And basket-ball is the highest art form in the inner city. The fact that our shoes sell well there is a function of how important basketball is in those com-munities."

Nevertheless, by the late 1980s, playground basketball wasn't just a sport anymore. It had become a marketing tool. At least 80 percent of the athletic shoes sold in the US during this period were not used for their intended purpose. Even Nike officials admitted that six of ten people bought its shoes because they were fashionable. "Brand names possess a totemistic power to confer distinction on those who wear them," Paul Fussell wrote in his book *Class: A Guide Through the Ameri-*

can Status System. "By donning legible clothing you fuse your private identity with commercial success, redeeming your insignificance and becoming, for the moment, somebody."

On the playground, in the streets, the somebodies were the drug dealers and the gang members. Some gangs wore Adidas, others wore Reebok. School principals in Atlanta, Detroit, New York and Chicago began banning various shoe brands in school because of the potential for violence. British Knights prospered when the Crips – a Los Angeles gang whose rivals are the Bloods – bought the product en masse and gave the BK logo a new meaning: Blood Killers.

Yet during this period when gangs ruled the playground, there were rays of hope. An owner of three sportswear shops located in and near New Haven, Connecticut, tried valiantly – and relatively successfully – to stop the rampaging flood of drug money into his business. Throughout the decade, sports apparel, especially basketball shoes, had been the clothes of choice for drug dealers across America. Aware that approximately $2,000 a week in sales had come from drug dealers, Wally Gringo, a New Haven store owner, put a sign in the front window of his inner-city store that read If You Deal Drugs, We Don't Want Your Money. Spend Your Money Somewhere Else. "Our industry is sick, addicted to drug money," Gringo told *Sports Illustrated.* "We're going through the first phase of addiction, which is total denial."

After Gringo put the sign up, a representative from a small shoe company came to his store and told Gringo, "Wally, we're thinking about giving you the line. But, you know, I can't do anything until you cut out the crap and take that sign out of your window. The bulk of our business is done with drug dealers. Wake up!"

Gringo saw the real problem: Drug dealers were the ones setting the fashion trends. While they have the money to afford high-priced apparel – the higher-end basketball shoes easily top $100 a pair – most inner-city kids don't have that kind of cash. Simply put, that explains incident after incident of kids killing kids for clothes or shoes. Some items from the apparel blotter:

- In 1983, fourteen-year-old Dewitt Duckett was shot to death in the hallway of Harlem Park Junior High in Baltimore by someone who apparently wanted Duckett's silky blue Georgetown jacket.

- In 1985, thirteen-year-old Shawn Jones was shot in Detroit after five youths took his Fila sneakers.

- In 1988, seventeen-year-old Tyrone Brown of Hapeville, Georgia, was shot in the head and killed, allegedly by two acquaintances who robbed him of money, cocaine, and his sneakers.

- In 1989, sixteen-year-old Johnny Bates was shot to death in Houston by seventeen-year-old Demetrick Walker after Johnny refused to hand over his Air Jordan hi-tops.

The small opening Nike hoped to make for itself in the basketball shoe market had over the course of time become a gruesome gash. Backlash against the companies followed the random deaths over shoes, shirts, and hats. But that didn't stop Nike and its competitors from basing their marketing campaigns on urban appeal. They realized that fashion trends in the suburbs were set by what kids in the inner cities were wearing.

In 1988, 30 percent of all sneakers in the US were purchased by people between the ages of fifteen and twenty-two; studies found that that demographic spurred an additional 10 percent of sales through word of mouth. In 1986, as Nike was attempting to reclaim market leadership from Reebok, the company held a convention of sporting goods store owners from around the country in Chicago to ask one question: How can we get inner-city kids interested in our product?

"We'll put our shoe in the inner city and see how it catches on," said James Solomon in 1988, when he was marketing vice president of Avia, a Reebok subsidiary. "Within ninety days we'll get an indication of what's going to happen with that shoe." Never forgetting that basketball is the reason for making the shoes they do, Reebok rebuilt playground courts in the cities where the shoes were market-tested. Essentially, it created its own marketing laboratory under controlled conditions. "The fact is," said eighteen-year-old Brian Washington in that *Wall Street Journal* article, "in the inner city, you are what you wear – on your feet."

By 1989 the values of the decade had distorted the essence of the sport. Playground basketball had divided into a multitude of disturbing dichotomies: Playground basketball was a sport and a fashion. Playground basketball was a crime deterrent and a reason for killing. Playground basketball was a way out of the ghetto and a reason for staying. The playground itself was a drugstore, a shoestore, a swap meet and a conference center for the community's "businessmen." What playground basketball was not was a mere game.

7

Money Game

On a hot summer New York night, a coach in a loud Hawaiian shirt paces up and down the sideline of the court at Jackie Robinson Playground in Crown Heights, Brooklyn. As a half-moon glows in the sky, the only illumination on the dark asphalt court, the action in front of him is nonstop, as intense as you'll find anywhere in Gotham. The jerseys the athletes wear have the words Community Peace emblazoned on the front – ironic, because there is nothing peaceful about the coach ranting on the sidelines.

You would never guess it, but nothing more is at stake in this game than pride and reputation, the basics. But that's exactly why the coach is screaming feverishly in his rumbling, Barry White voice. "Hey man," he yells, snagging the attention of the refs. "Make that fucking call." As the words fly from his mouth like poison darts, he immediately puts his hands to his face, trying to hold back whatever might be left. He realizes his mistake and wishes his language were not as colorful as his shirt. For he knows the gravity of the mistake he has has just made: He has incurred the wrath of Richard Green.

One icy stare and a terse "watch your mouth," from tournament director Green, and the coach cowers and takes a seat on the bench. Green will not tolerate bad language, taunting or fighting at his tournament, staged in Jackie's park across from the Ebbetts Field Housing

Projects. "Jackie used to hit home runs out here," says Green. "We will respect the ground he broke."

Green claps his hands at the end of every game and implores the players to "show some love, shake each other's hands." He pays as much as $200 a night out of his own pocket, covering the costs of jerseys or referees. For twenty-two years Green has been running the Crown Heights Youth Collective – the local rec center – as well as this basketball tournament at the park. His hair is styled in dreadlocks, which are wrapped in a rubber band and drape down his neck. He wears nylon army fatigues and shoes that – remarkably – bear no discernible logo. A graying beard covers his face in tight curls of whiskers. Although he served two tours of duty in Vietnam, he looks more like a militant from the 1960s, the kind who protested war and oppression. But this is just appearance. When Green returned from Southeast Asia to the "war at home," as he calls the racial tensions he encountered back in the US, he had grown tired of fighting. He is now the peacemaker of Crown Heights. And when the battle had reached its most violent and deadly stage, his plan for calm was to teach basketball. On the playground. It may not be the best ball in New York City, but Green's tournament embodies everything that is right about the city game.

In 1991 Crown Heights was a cauldron of tension. Blacks and Jews lived side by side but rarely spoke. The divide was deep, and it had cost lives. In August of that year, a Hasidic man driving his car in Crown Heights lost control of the vehicle and killed a seven-year-old black boy who had been playing on the sidewalk. The police ruled the death accidental, sparking four days of riots. In the midst of the upheaval, a twenty-year-old Hasidim was attacked by a group of twenty black men and stabbed to death.

New York City Mayor David Dinkins called on community leaders to quell the storm. The two men he turned to were Dr. David Lazerson, a teacher in the Hasidic community who grew up in Buffalo, New York, and Richard Green. Lazerson brought his Jewish students and Green brought his black students to meetings over the next couple of weeks. For the first time anyone could remember, the students openly discussed their sterotypes of each other. Slowly, because of the dialogue, their perceptions began to change and tensions started to ease.

Then one afternoon at P. S. 167, two black kids who were new to the group began to walk out without ever saying a word. Dr. Laz, who peppers his conversations with words like *bro*, *yo*, and *man*, asked them to offer something to the group before they left. "I want to do something, man. I don't want to just sit here and talk," said one of the boys. Lazerson asked what the two wanted to do. "Play ball," they answered.

Simple enough. Green had been running the Community Peace tournament at Jackie Robinson Park for sixteen years, so he knew something about organizing a basketball tourney. A new series of games was started, dubbed "Increase the Peace." T-shirts were printed, with logos depicting black hands and white hands interlocked. The Jewish kids sometimes played in dress shoes and long black pants. Often the blacks were better. But the games fostered relationships and bonds where once there had been indifference and incomprehension. "You wouldn't see fighting," says Green, who now wears a Star of David around his neck. "Everything was a negotiation process. We wanted to teach diplomacy as much as how to play, and that can all be done through this game, more effectively than talking."

At the start of each game, all players – black and white – would come together in a circle, hold hands, and say a prayer for peace. Years of hatred and anger were washed away with the sweat of these games, along with innumerable perceived snubs and misunderstandings. "They got to know each other," says Lazerson. "They would walk past each other on the streets and say hello. I can remember one time a black kid named Henry Rice heard that one of the guys he played with in the games got engaged. It is Hasidic tradition to leave your doors open for a celebration when you get engaged. Friends and relatives come and greet you all through the night. Well, Henry comes into the home, whose door is open, and immediately this kid's parents start screaming, afraid Henry is going to rob them. All of a sudden, the kid comes out of his room. Henry picks him up and hugs him. That never would have happened before the games."

"It was amazing," says Yudi Simon, a former player who, at twenty-one, is now a youth leader with Project Cure, a community program that is an offshoot of Increase the Peace. "I was a victim in the riots, and although I was raised not to be a racist, after the riots I had a different view. My parents had friends in the neighborhood who were black, and after the riots I could not look them in the face. When I was finally convinced to go to a game, I brought orange juice as a weapon to spray in someone's eyes, just in case. I ended up just drinking it. There was a sense of belonging between blacks and Jews that I had never felt before."

The games survived the sternest tests, such as when the man accused of killing the Jewish student during the riots was acquitted despite overwhelming evidence against him. Or when a homeless black man was allegedly beaten by a mob of Hasidim in Crown Heights. Through it all, the games continued. As always, they were the common denominator, the home base, a place where blacks learned about Jews as persons, and vice versa. No longer were these strangers drug dealers or money grubbers, but Shmuli and Yudi and Derrick and Henry. It is playground basketball at its best.

"Athletics has proven to be one of the best areas in which to lift people beyond fences," the Rev. Jesse Jackson said when he heard about the Increase the Peace games in Crown Heights. "The ball goes through the hoop, it's two points. When you get a rebound you go back on defense. We have seen more public embracing and neutral support among athletes than in about any other area of American life. Even churches can't compete with athletics in this regard."

Jackson's point – that athletics and athletes have transcended racial and societal boundaries – is especially true with regard to basketball. The success of Increase the Peace is evidence enough of that. But playground basketball has always been as much a mirror for society as a harbinger of change in the social order. The style of play on the court reflected the dominant cultural phenomena outside those caged theaters. It's always been that way, but a new dynamic emerged in the 1990s.

This decade added a dimension to the relationship between street ball and the world outside it. The playgrounds these days no longer merely mimic what is happening in the world but serve as the epicenter of chic. Rather than shun the hip-hop, gangster culture epitomized by the inner city, and specifically the blacktop, America began to embrace it. Shoe companies romanticized the ghetto. Clothing companies lured playground kids into their threads, knowing the world was watching to see what young black men were wearing. Niche magazine and television shows sprang up to capitalize on street ball's new credibility, and Hollywood turned playground hoops into mainstream entertainment. Finally, the NBA, long the goal for any kid who ever played in a pickup game, embraced the playgrounds. Fashion, media and professional sport itself became windows through which mainstream America could view and ultimately partake in – vicariously, safely – the gritty life of the inner city.

The 1992 film *White Men Can't Jump* featured Woody Harrelson and Wesley Snipes as two street ball hustlers scoring big on the playgrounds of Los Angeles. In 1994, Tupac Shakur starred in *Above the Rim*, which took the trash-talking machismo of *White Men Can't Jump* to a more violent, confrontational level. These movies opened the eyes of the viewing public to a language and a lifestyle that may be hyperbole on the surface, but is unabashedly honest at its core. "This is a place in the world where the criticism is relentless and funny and so politically incorrect that it's liberating," says Ron Shelton, who wrote and directed *White Men Can't Jump*, of the playground court. "Nothing is out of bounds in terms of comments, but relationships are born out of that. I trust the people I play ball with a lot more than most Hollywood executives."

Those two movies, combined, also grossed more than $100 million at the box office. After years of subtly advertising to the urban set in the hope that fashion trends would grow out of that, shoe and apparel companies finally had proof of the street game's mainstream appeal. Soon thereafter, two documentaries, 1994's *Hoop Dreams*, chronicling the lives of two high school players from Chicago's West Side seeking a shot at college, and 1997's *Soul in the Hole*, about playground basketball in New York City, created instant legends – the kind of reputation that once took years to build.

There is a danger in elevating street players this way. Their legends are formed before their time on the court has run its course, and their great moves – and great missteps – are on display to millions. The element of exaggeration, so vital in playground lore, is lost.

For better and for worse playground basketball has transcended the cages that once held it in. The breakthrough into the mainstream left the world awaiting, anticipating, the next great street player: "The

Goat of the Nineties." Someone whose brilliance existed in fact, not just in legend.

Worthy or not, Booger Smith is it.

On an early evening in August 1997, just before the premiere of *Soul in the Hole*, director Danielle Gardner organized a basketball game at Brooklyn's Tillary Park in which all the principals from the film would play. It was a promotional gig, and Gardner sent out notices to media outlets all across New York City. The skies thick and mottled as marble threaten rain, but nearly fifty members of the press show up to check out Booger Smith. As the game is about to start, the skies open with a fury, spitting down inch-size raindrops and daggers of lightening that illuminate the low-lying clouds. Of course, the rain doesn't really matter, because Booger, the star of the film, the man who once and for all was to have the spotlight squarely trained on him, fails to show up. Small wonder that Booger has never made it off the playground and onto a college or pro court.

"He promised he'd show," Danielle says, shaking her head with the frustration of a mother whose son is out past curfew. "I don't know what to tell you other than he usually doesn't back out of things. But deep down inside, he really is a warm, caring kid and a terrific basketball player. Just give him chance."

A makeup game is scheduled for two days later, and Booger does in fact bless everyone with his presence. In a game in which both teams score more than 130 points, Booger scores exactly zero. He takes four shots, all layups. Two are blocked, and two he just plain misses. But Booger shows the dazzling ball-handling of a Bob Cousy. True, on three of every five plays he throws the ball away or dribbles it off his foot – but they are the most breathtaking turnovers you'll ever see. Smith does things with the ball that a stick-thin, five-foot-nine human being shouldn't be able to do. Some of his moves must be seen to be believed. He seems to control the ball as though it is secretly attached to his hand, like a yo-yo. On one trip down the court he pulls out his special move, perhaps the most magical that any playground player in New York City can perform today. He calls it his wraparound shot: Booger wraps the ball around the head of his defender with his right hand, catches it in his left, and dishes it off. The move seems utterly impossible.

On a subsequent trip down the court, Smith catches a pass, bounces the ball between the legs of his opponent, spins around the man and catches the ball blindly behind his back, and continues dribbling toward the basket. The move happens so fast that most people standing around the small blacktop court are left gazing at each and asking, 'Did that really just happen?'

Most of the moves Booger cannot replicate if you ask him to. They are unplanned, unrehearsed responses to the ebb and flow of action on the court. A basketball magazine once asked Booger to perform some of the moves for a photographer. He failed miserably.

Everyone associated with the documentary honestly believes Booger is the best thing on the New York City playgrounds since the great Earl Manigault, but in reality he's just a great ball-handler who wouldn't stand a chance on the proving ground where New York City playground legends are forged: one-on-one money games. In parks all across the city, nearly every playground player who was asked said he could name two dozen players who had stronger local reputations than Booger Smith. Go to Holcombe Rucker Park in Harlem, and nine out ten players will tell you they've never even heard of Booger Smith.

"If Booger played college ball," says Charles Jones, "he'd be one of the best point guards in the nation if he wasn't counted on to score." Jones, who grew up with Smith, was the leading college scorer in the nation in 1996–97, averaging 30.1 points a game for Long Island University. He's leaning against a chain-link fence at Tillary as he scratches his fuzzy face and ponders Booger's talent. "The problem with Booger is that he sometimes can be too much of show player," says Jones, perhaps unwittingly defining the essence of the playground player. "Most of the time when he's dribbling over people's heads or passing the ball between people's legs he never loses control of what he's doing. But if he does lose control, it will make a coach crazy. And that's been his problem."

Actually, Booger has had other, larger problems to deal with in his life than incurring the occasional wrath of a coach. They started almost the moment he was born to a fifteen-year-old girl in the Fort Greene section of Brooklyn. His mother, Booger says, was incapable of administering discipline. He does not know his father. Most of Booger's childhood was a perpetual recess composed of basketball, parties and girls.

"I didn't have anyone to wake me up to go to school," says Booger. "When I didn't want to go, I didn't go. I didn't have anybody on my case, telling me when I be doing things wrong. And I was getting into trouble too much, fighting all the time."

When Booger was fourteen, the trouble became more serious: He started selling crack. With no one to keep Booger from straying, he drifted ever further into the abyss that swallows so many young black men in New York. Booger was playing basketball at Westinghouse High in Brooklyn when, one night after a game, he was with some friends who beat up a man. Booger was swept up in the police dragnet. "I thought I was going to jail," he says now.

He didn't, but the arrest hardly eased things at home. One night when Booger was sixteen, he got into an argument with his mother and walked out of the apartment. He considered running away – to where, who knows – but instead spent the night at the apartment of Kenny and Ronetta Jones in Bed-Stuy. Kenny had been Booger's coach in various leagues since Booger was eight, so the two were close. Eventually, Kenny adopted Booger, who became the star of Jones's neighborhood team, a team called Kenny's Kings that competes in playground tournaments across New York.

"His mother was going to send him away to a job corps program, and Booger didn't want to do that so I accepted him into my home," says Kenny, who appears to be a good influence on Smith. "Booger is at a real disadvantage right now because he never finished high school, and it takes a lot of discipline to go to junior college or a community college. I think he has the skills to get to the NBA, but he'll probably have to go to Europe or somewhere like that."

No one, in fact, knows where Booger is going. Not even Booger himself.

The most glaring blank spot on Booger's application for legendhood is that he hasn't proven his wares Uptown. "BK" – Brooklyn – is OK, but Uptown, as in Connie Hawkins's day, is still where it's at. Stepping onto the court at Holcombe Rucker Park, the proof is all around you. You can't turn your head at the Entertainers Classic without seeing the confluence of commerce surrounding the game. Literally. Every portion of the chain-link fence encircling the court at 155th at Eighth Avenue is adorned with corporate banners. The Entertainers is, after all, the premier playground tournament in New York City, and therefore the world. About 250 people show up four nights a week, Monday through Thursday. They begin arriving at three o'clock in the afternoon, waiting in line for three hours for the games that begin at six. On a given night, such NBA stars as Allen Iverson, Stephon Marbury and Joe Smith (nicknamed 911 by the hometown crowd because he shows up in an emergency) or top college players like Arkansas's Kareem Reid and Long Island University's Charles Jones and Richie Parker will showcase their basketball stylings here. In 1994, ESPN broadcast a game at the Entertainers Classic that was announced by Dick Vitale, but even he sounded sedate compared to the juiced up, high-voltage play-by-play of Thomas "Duke" Hill. Every player gets a nickname from Hill; every shot, good or bad, earns a comment. He is the ringmaster of this circus, shouting out the score, the time left and where to eat after the game (the Rucker Cafe, of course). When Mike Tyson, who still sponsors a team in the league, walked through the park's gates the week after disgracing himself by biting Evander Holyfield's ears, Hill led a rousing ovation.

If Hill is the Classic's ringmaster, Greg Marius is its P. T. Barnum. He started the Entertainers Classic while he was an aspiring rapper in 1980 when another local rap group had challenged his to a game of basketball. A New York City DJ announced the grudge match on the radio, and when both teams showed up, 200 people were waiting to watch. The next year more groups, including Grandmaster Flash, joined the fray. By the mid-1980s rappers were bringing in ringers like former St. John's All-American Walter Berry and former Syracuse All-American Dwayne Washington. Eventually the rappers took a backseat to the athletes, and the tournament grew big enough to move from 139th Street to its current home.

By the late 1980s Marius knew things were getting out of control on the playgrounds. Because he ran a playground tournament, he says, people naturally assumed he was a drug dealer. In 1992 Marius invited some of the old Rucker Pro League stars to come up to be honored at the Entertainers Classic. Many refused. "They said it was too wild up there now," Marius recalls. "Everyone was afraid to walk around here because it had gotten so dangerous in the area." Hill adds, "In those days people were getting paid. And I mean getting *paid.*"

Thus, in 1992, Marius asked the New York City Police to assign officers to his tournament. They obliged and came in force with blue police barricades to control the crowds. Then in 1995, Marius hired security guards, who frisked every person who entered. "At first people stayed away," he says. "They were angry. Then they realized this was a safe place to be." Even Tyson and his prodigious posse got patted down. Over the course of the summer of 1997, Marius spent $36,000 on security.

Bernard Bell remembers the way things were with little fondness. The 35-year-old Bronx construction worker is a member of a union local that the government cracked down on because one of its members was taking illegal kickbacks. He likens the episode to Marius' effort to clean up street basketball. "It's just like basketball now, baby," he says as he sits on the court in Rucker Park, his knees tucked under his chin. "They are just trying to weed out the corruption."

As Bell watches the game in front of him, the Sugar Hill Gang is taking on the Crusaders in a midseason Entertainers game amid a woolen blanket of humidity. Even after the sun dips beneath the Polo Grounds housing projects across the street, the heat is unrelenting; Charles Jones says that sometimes, after playing in these summer games, he will go days without urinating. The play is erratic and spectacular – a carnival of fastbreaks, dribble drives, taunts and dunks that have the crowd screaming like they did in the Rucker's heyday, twenty-five or thirty years ago. The game epitomizes the testosterone-charged, showtime style that is street basketball. Sugar Hill applies the full-court press, and the Crusaders' coach screams to his point guard, "Take him to school." When Lamont Jones, Charles's older brother, swipes the ball, Hill bellows out, "Somebody call the cops! The ball has been stolen!" Later on, while being guarded on the wing, Lamont makes a dribble move so quick he actually hesitates afterward because he can't believe how badly he has beaten his defender. When he is subsequently fouled from behind, he cups his hand over his ear and thumps his chest, encouraging the crowd to give it up for such a fine display. Bell takes it all in. Unlike the old-timers who wax nostalgic about a better game in better days long past, Bell is only encouraged by what he sees.

"It's a lot more professional now," he says. "Before, if you were a drug dealer and you had the money, you got out your crew and you played. Now that's all being weeded out. Players respect the game more. They respect each other more. I'm not saying this place is weapons-free or that stuff like that doesn't still happen here. I'm sure some of these games are sponsored by drug dealers." He pauses, sweeping his hand across the darkening blue sky. "But I bet it's ninety percent weapons-free, and that makes it better for everyone. Every kid that is here now is a kid who isn't out there committing a crime."

Bell watches a hard foul and continues. "A play like that in the eighties – well, that's a bench-clearing brawl, with shots fired. Now it's over and done with quickly because the refs can step in and feel comfortable they won't get clocked for breaking up a fight or making a call."

There is another reason for the beefed-up security, beyond the noble aim of making the playground safe for the neighborhood. NBA guys are coming back to play in tournaments like these. Not has-beens who have been out of the league, guys who come by to prove they've still got it, but guys who represent the future of the NBA: Iverson, Marbury. More than ever before, the NBA's players are products of the city game. They developed their games on the blacktop, and when the NBA season is over, that's where they go to keep sharp, keep it real. Even after you establish yourself in the NBA, proving you've got game on the playground carries heavy weight.

Says Pee Wee Kirkland, who began coaching at the Dwight School on Manhattan's Upper West Side when he was released from prison, "People in the inner city like to see their folks make the NBA, but a lot of them don't keep up with it. When you come back, you still have to show you've got it against the guy who has been making a name for himself while you've been away."

"At NBA games now, the African American players from the inner city – which is a large chunk of the league – don't see people who represent them," says Tony Gervino, managing editor of *Slam* magazine. "That's why they play in the playgrounds in Harlem or wherever. They want to get their props from there. The NBA sometimes looks like a cartoon. Playground ball is always more tangible."

More tangible and more rebellious. The game these days is not about technical fouls, the three-second rule or even winning. It's about manhood. Playing playground basketball is cool. And a guy like Allen

Iverson, who spent four months in jail in 1993 after being convicted of malicious wounding, is an idol to many who play it. Violence may be cooling down in playground leagues, but the attitude is hotter than ever.

With so many playground stars now reaching the NBA, the league's elder statesmen – Michael Jordan, Karl Malone, even Charles Barkley – sense the changing of the guard. The next generation of superstars are brasher and more street-wise. Iverson, Gary Payton, Chris Webber, and so on – they play by their own rules, with little regard for the hierarchy of the league. "It's this macho mentality that says, 'I made it, and I want it all now,'" Michael Jordan has said.

Which offers yet another reason for high-profile corporations to sponsor these playground tournaments. The Michael Jordans of the NBA are reaching the final stages of their careers. The new consumers identify with the younger generation, guys who play in the streets, not the stratosphere. "The big companies have to embrace the street game because they see how important it has become," says Marius. "It's like rap music. In the beginning, people were afraid of us, and we made our own stuff. Then one guy broke through, and another, and all of a sudden it was mainstream. The big corporations need us now."

Unlike the 1980s, when marketers targeted the inner city through subtle means, the 1990s have been a coming-out party. The Entertainers Classic is brought to you by Mountain Dew, Tommy Boy Records and Boss Clothing. The heaviest presence at the Entertainers, though, is that of Reebok. Nevermind the banner that is visible from two blocks away, or the color-coordinated uniforms with the Reebok insignia adorning every jersey. Listen only to the riff of announcer Hill. In between yelling "oxygen" when a player shoots an airball and dubbing this game the "real NBA" because it's "nothing but action," Hill provides gentle nods and winks to the big sponsor. "Give a shout out to Reebok," Hill frequently implores the crowd.

"Companies realize they have to be a part of it now, that it's a positive in the community," says Marius. "[African Americans] are the main buyers of fashion, records and sports products. Trends are set in the inner city. Companies see that and need to be involved."

In 1996 wholesale revenues for athletic footwear companies hit $7.5

billion, and Marius is right – African Americans make up a large portion of that market. Every player at the Entertainers Classic is black. All
but 6 of the 300 or so fans are black. If a clothing company or shoe
company is popular on the street, it has credibility, and a million-dollar
ad campaign cannot equal the cachet that goes with being considered
real. "There is a style people in the urban marketplace have that is
inspirational," says Peter Roby, director of brand marketing for Reebok. "That cannot be ignored."

According to Northeastern University's Center for the Study of
Sport in Society, 66 percent of black males between the ages of thirteen
and eighteen believe they can earn a living playing professional sports,
a figure more than twice that of white males in the same age group.
Logic dictates that the group most likely to buy what the pros are
wearing would be those who believe they can be a pro. "David Stern
has taken a game that is eighty percent black and put it on TV in America," says Thomas Hill, "and it is now on the top, if not the number
one, sport in the country. Corporate America sees this and will hop on
at the first stop – the black playgrounds – to take advantage of the
popularity."

Hill is right, almost. The playground game is no longer solely the
domain of the black man. Gus Macker proved that in the mid-1980s,
and Terry Murphy capitalized on it shortly thereafter. Murphy read an
article about the Macker in *Sports Illustrated*'s July 8, 1985, issue, and the
next year, as publisher of *D Magazine* in Dallas, he hosted a street basketball tournament to benefit the Special Olympics. Two thousand
people showed up, and Murphy had found his pickup pot of gold.
Within three years he had quit the publishing business and was running
the Hoop-It-Up tournament and a sports marketing firm, Streetball
Partners International, full-time.

The Hoop-It-Up is everything the Macker isn't and everything playground ball in the 1990s is. It's not grassroots basketball, where conversations are peppered with basketballese. It is a money-making venture.
"A lot of consumers could play in a league with three buddies and have
some fun," says Murphy. "But this guarantees they will play in a
bracket where they are competing against like competition."

Murphy systematically sold an A-list of sponsors on the idea of
street basketball as revenue generator, and in 1990 NBC signed on as a

partner to televise the Hoop-It-Up tournament twice annually. A year later the NBA sanctioned Hoop-It-Up as its official three-on-three playground tournament. Games sprang up on the streets everytime Hoop-It-Up came to a town: Everyone wanted a piece of the street game.

In the summer of 1997, the tournament made stops in more than forty-five US cities. Approximately 180,000 people took part, and another 2 million watched on television. Throw in ninety tournaments in Europe, and Hoop-It-Up was expected to generate close to $13 million in revenue in 1997. These are not big-name NBA players taking part – just regular people who like to play pickup basketball. Nevertheless, Gatorade, Nike, Southwest Airlines and Foot Locker are among the sponsors that see how potent a marketing force the pickup game can be.

There are about 125 summer-league tournaments in New York City, and sponsors vie for a piece of the "nothin' but action" at almost every one. The Rucker Pro League is long gone, replaced in terms of high-profile talent by the Entertainers Classic. The Rucker's namesake successor, the Holcombe Rucker Community League, is for kids of high school age and younger, and can't compare in talent with other summer events. Although sponsored by Nike, the current Rucker charmingly retains the qualities found in a neighborhood pickup game rather than a sophisticated sports marketing event.

The relationship between the tournaments and the sponsors is reciprocal. Marketers make money and promote products, while players, coaches and refs take part in a reputable tournament that attracts top competition and top scouts. "Everyone feels good playing in these tournaments," says Byron Irvin. "People feel safe playing there, and there is something to be said for being involved with an event that is credible, legit."

The action hasn't been for men only. In 1996 Tisa Key, a former basketball player at Broward Community College in Florida, began the Do Your Thang women's basketball tournament at 139th Street and Lenox Avenue in Harlem. Leagues like the Sonny Hill in Philadelphia have long sponsored girls' and women's teams, but the men garnered all the attention, and women's leagues suffered because of it.

"I've played in tournaments with women's divisions, but they are all geared toward the men," Key says. "Everything for women is disorganized, even the prizes."

The Do Your Thang league began with eight teams, including one sponsored by rapper Queen Latifah, and has attracted talent not only from New York but from all along the Eastern seaboard. Yet despite the success of the US women in the 1996 Olympics and the launching of the American Basketball League and the Women's NBA, sponsors have been slow to realize the opportunity of women's playground ball. What the women's summer league needs is the allure of legends. Now that more women are playing, the legends can't be too far off.

◆ ◆ ◆

Gail Doughty walks onto the basketball court at 11th and Lombard in South Philly. Soft leather Reeboks, bought that morning, cushion her feet. She wears flame-red nylon pants that billow when the wind blows, exposing a neon yellow beeper hanging from her pocket. Rings adorn three fingers on each hand, and gold hoop earrings dangle from her ears. She looks more like a showcase for everything you can buy at the mall than a basketball player looking for a game.

At one end of the concrete court stands Don Levon, a North Philly guy who has apparently lost his way, shooting by himself with an underinflated ball. His shirt is off. His shoes are untied. Slim blue jeans cling to his thighs. His long, striated muscles have the look of someone who has spent years hustling games on the asphalt. Gail, however, appears undaunted. As she approaches, he flashes her a look that says, "You don't belong here." But she just smiles, her sweet round face hinting devilishly that she knows how to handle a bonehead like Don. She has played here before, with Philly's best: Mo Cheeks, formerly of the 76ers, ex-Villanova star Jason Lawson, former LaSalle All-American and NBA player Lionel Simmons. Gail has always held her own, and skinny Don Levon with the shaved head will not be a problem.

"Can I shoot wichya?" Gail asks.

"What?" he answers increduously

"You mind if I join you?" she repeats, with less softness in her voice this time – more a declarative statement than a question.

As Gail says this, she grabs a rebound just outside the lane and, in a fluid motion, dribbles through her legs, takes one step, and lays the ball back in the hoop, tapping her fingers on the bottom of the backboard on her way back down.

You can always tell a basketball player by the first touch of the ball. The first shot means nothing. Any fool can sink a 10-footer. It's the way a player corrals a pass, grabs a rebound or just picks a ball up off the ground like it's the most natural thing in the world. That is the telling thing. These are the most minute of first impressions, unnoticed by those who aren't players themselves but impossible to ignore by those who are. The player controls the ball with grace, spinning it in the palms, leisurely hoisting shots or dribbling with nonchalance. Such moves say, I've done this before and I've done it well. Those who haven't just look clumsy. With her one layup and without uttering another word, Gail has let Don know that she is a player. Confused, all he can do is shake his head and say, "Yeah, you can shoot."

Of course she can shoot. And she can dribble and pass and rebound and, occasionally, she can play defense. Thirty-three years old, and Gail can do just about everything she did at twenty-three. Gail is a product of the playground, running on the courts at 11th and Lombard or 23rd and Reed or the rec center at 34th and Haverford since she could tie her shoes. If she wasn't going to the court, her grandma wouldn't let her out of the house. It was too dangerous in Philly – South Philly, West Philly, North Philly – to let little Gail walk the streets with nothing to do. She would play ball with the girls, although she'd rather play with the boys. That's how you got better. Take an elbow to the kidney – that's how you made a name for yourself around the city. No respect comes from earning a spot on the girls' All-Public League first team.

"Even the simple games, horse or whatever, if you win against the guy it builds confidence," says Doughty. "Besides, when you win, that's just one more guy who believes there are some girls who can compete."

So when Don Levon tires of the monotony of passing the ball back to Gail after she sinks yet another twenty-footer, he innocently asks, "You wanna play 21?" Gail can't help but smile. Another convert coming up.

The Philly rules for 21 are simple: Sink a shot from the top of the key for 2 points, make a rebounded shot for 1 point and then back up to the top of the key. For a few minutes neither player seems to have the range to consistently sink a shot from the top of the key. Their legs seem tired, the wind is swirling, and a bunch of kids playing hooky on another court keep letting their ball interfere. Then Don breaks the seal on the basket: 2 points. He grabs his rebound off the make and sinks the layup: 1 point. He goes through this routine three times. Before Gail has the ball again, she is losing 9–0 and Don is holding a bony hand up to his mouth to hide his snickering.

They begin trading three-point plays. Don 12, Gail 3; Don 15, Gail 6; Don 18, Gail 9. Then Gail gets hot. She reels off six in a row. Don then nails a two-pointer but chokes on his layup. He is ahead 20–15. Both players are screaming with each miss, contorting their bodies to direct the ball through the hoop. A small crowd has formed around the fence along 11th Street as Gail lines up for a chance to win. Trailing 20–18, she lets fly from the top of the key. If the net had been hanging by more than a shred of twine Gail's jumper would have made a beautiful sound as it went through the hoop. But the soft wisp of the dangling net says enough: game over. After Gail casually sinks her layup, Don grabs the ball and leaves. As Don Levon walks away, he mutters, "Nice game."

When Gail reaches the exit to the court, a man with a nappy beard yells out, "There she is, Miss Gail, still conquering the court." Gail laughs and mutters, mostly to herself, "Around South Philly, everyone knows me. I just can't seem to get known anywhere else."

Loneliness and frustration are the reward for a legendary player destined to be considered among the greatest who never made it. That status has long been the exclusive domain of men. Guys like Earl Manigault, "Helicopter" Knowings and Lamar Mundane have yearned for a shot at the big time, at the million-dollar contracts, the crowds, the women, the cars and – most alluring – the fame. Instead, they were condemned to obscurity while their legends continue to grow years after their last airwalk or thirty-foot jumper.

Now the kings of the court will have to make room for its queens. Before now, the greatest women players in the world disappeared to Europe after college. Now that the women's game has hit it big on American soil, there's more at stake, more to gain – and thus more to lose. At the playground level are the female versions of the wouldas, shouldas and couldas. Count Gail Doughty as one of the first.

"Gail Doughty has all the skills to play at the next level," says Philadelphia native Dawn Staley, a 1996 Olympic gold medalist and an all-star guard with the ABL's Philadelphia Rage. "She's explosive, like Charles Barkley, and she could intimidate people the same way. She is as good as anyone I've played with. No question, she's capable of playing in the pros. But who knows why some people don't get the opportunity and others do."

It's a little bit timing and little bit luck. "Five years ago I know I would have been one of the first people getting a tryout for a pro league," says Doughty. "Now I can't even find out where or when one is."

"So much of it comes down to having a name," says Linda Page, a four-time All-American at Philly's Dobbins High School in the late 1970s and a two-time All-American at North Carolina State in 1982 and 1983. "Gail's a playground player. Even though she could play with anyone, no one outside of Philly knows her."

When Gail was growing up, wandering from court to court looking for a game, she was always the first girl picked, the one everyone wanted to be like. She studied the game as a coach would, videotaping the Sixers and watching them over and over late at night with the sound low and her face inches from the screen. She wanted to see the rotation on the ball when Julius Erving shot his free throw. She needed to know how Mo Cheeks planted his foot on the entry pass. Every night she crammed, because every day on the court was a final exam. "She's from the old school," says Staley who, at twenty-six, is a decade younger than some of the women still haunting the Philly playgrounds. "If someone were to describe me as a player, I would want them to say I could play with Linda or Gail. They're smarter than players today. They have the sweet skill, but they also have great basketball knowledge."

For women, conferring upon someone a professorship of the playground is the highest compliment. The standard is different for men. What matters in the male game are get-backs, facials, hard-core retaliation and Globetrotter-like exhibitions. Can you pick a quarter off the top of the backboard from a standing jump? Do you make the guy guarding you wobbly at the knees when you snap a fresh move that proves you've got the juice? That is how men are measured on the playground. Style over substance is the rule, and the flashier a player is, the bigger the legend. Put Dick McGuire and Earl Manigault on the same playground today and, unless Dick's brother Al is watching, every spectator would pick the Goat as the NBA great – yet Dick is the one in the Basketball Hall of Fame. Somewhere along the way, the team game became lost out on the boys' playgrounds. For women, though, the team game is the only option. Move the ball, find the open player, set the pick at the top of the key. That's how women players survive among the men in the street game.

"When I went to the playground I would have to set picks for my teammates if I ever wanted someone to consider letting me play," says Carol Blazejowski, who finished her career at Montclair State in 1978 as the leading scorer in the history of women's college basketball, was elected to the Hall of Fame in 1994 and is general manager of the WNBA's New York Liberty. "And I would have to develop a great out-side shot because no one would let me drive. I'd be smart and let the guys worry about showing off."

Doughty was indoctrinated into the game early. She was playing ball with two of her older brothers, Meechie and Sandy, when most other girls were playing with dolls. When recess came during grammar school, Gail headed to the playground inside the fence while the other girls stayed outside the iron gates playing hopscotch. Every time she got into a game, if only for one play, she gained confidence and made believers of her male classmates. In one game, she recalls, she was pushed from behind, fell face-first onto the concrete, and chipped her tooth. But she came back again the next day. If she was the first one outside, she'd hold the ball until the boys had no choice but to let her into the game.

"I stayed out there on the basketball court so when they got out there and wanted to play full court, they couldn't get rid of me," says Doughty. "Every now and then someone would Bogart [hit] me, and when they did that I would just push them out of the way. Some guys don't want to see a woman beat them, and they will do whatever it takes to beat 'em. But I'm not gonna let a female take advantage of me, and I am not gonna let a male take advantage, either."

By the time Gail was in the eighth grade at Pierce Elementary, only a handful of boys could outplay her. When the girls' season ended that year, the boys' coach invited her to play on his team for the last two weeks of the season. She said yes, knowing her biggest challenge would come not on the court but off. Her teammates whined that she was getting more playing time than they were. Then she had to deal with the nasty looks from opposing players and fans when she was the sole figure trotting out of the girls' locker room to join the guys' layup line. "Gail was always strong," says her oldest sister, Diane, "mostly because of who raised her."

Grandma Francis was the best rib-cooking ordained minister south of Market Street. The woman could preach fire and brimstone during her sermons, but none of the listeners could ever envision an apocalypse with her around. Grandma Francis was strong enough, and loved enough, to shield her flock from all things evil. And Gail was her chosen one.

Gail's mother and father had fourteen children, two of whom died in infancy. Gail was third from the youngest. By the time she was born, neither her mother nor her father could quite handle the idea of raising another child. They sent Gail off to live with Grandma Francis down the block. "I guess my mom needed a break when I was born," Gail says. "I knew my mom because she was always around, but I was closer with my grandmother. She was my pride and joy. She made sure I did everything right. Besides, I knew I would get more spoiled living with her than with all my brothers and sisters."

The deal Grandma offered was straightforward: Do right, which meant going to school, and Gail would never have to worry about having spending money, new shoes or anything else a kid wants but doesn't always get. Besides, considering Gail's other leisure time options, a bribe or two to keep her in line made sense. The gangs were always out there, ready to grab a malcontented young kid wandering the street. Though she was strong, Gail was impressionable, and if it took a bidding war with the gangs to keep her safe, so be it. But Grandma Francis had an ace in the hole. If Gail ever faltered, if she didn't live up to her end of the bargain, if she didn't go to school, she knew there would be no basketball. The gangs never had a prayer: Gail went to school. And afterward, she went to the Mantua Rec Center.

The corner of 34th and Haverford, where the Mantua is located, is called "the Bottom." The way Philly's West Side is laid out, that section of the city happens to be at the bottom of a hill. "But," Gail adds, "it also happens that a lot of the people living here have nowhere to go but up." Tacked up to a bulletin board just inside the Mantua's doors is another reminder of the grip basketball has on the area. A flyer advertises the first annual alumni basketball classic: legends of the 1970s, 1980s and 1990s. One team is called "Evens" and the other "Odds," and the players are a collection of guys who made their mark at the Bottom but never made it to the top.

Every day after school, Grandma Francis gave Gail two options: come straight home or go to the rec center. Either way, there was no stopping in between. "She kind of adopted me as her friend," says James Wright, the director at the Mantua. "That way she could stay as late as she wanted, and she knew I would take her home." Wright became Gail's personal basketball coach. The lessons extended beyond the confines of Mantua. On the drive home from the rec center, the two would stop for cheesesteaks, Wright diagramming pick-and-rolls on greasy napkins. "The difference between ballplayers and people who think they are ballplayers is attitude," says Wright. "The ballplayers know what the game is about. They understand the moves and the rhythms of the game and how to work those into the team. Those who think they are good because they make an individual play – well, they might be talented, but they aren't ballplayers. Trust me: Gail was and is a ballplayer."

That much was obvious once Gail entered University City High in 1978. Along with William Penn, University City boasted the top girls' basketball program in Philly. When Gail arrived her sophomore year, the school was the defending public league champs and featured Yolonda Laney, the best player in the city. Yolonda and Gail had been playing with one another for years on the playground. With them together, there was little doubt that University City would repeat. "There was something special about their chemistry from the first practice," says Lurline Jones, who has coached University City since 1974. "They knew each other inside and out. But they were also fierce competitors with each other. If one made a great play, the other one had to make a better play. Usually, though, Gail was the consummate playmaker."

University City rolled through the regular season undefeated, and Gail and Yolonda were both named to the All-Public League first team.

The girls were so sure of their talent that Yolonda, who also was editor of the school yearbook, which had a deadline in February, dedicated a full page to the girls' back-to-back championships, even though the yearbook closed a full month before the finals. "I called up Yolonda the night before the championship game after I heard about this from one of the other teachers," says Jones. "I was freaking out. But when Yolonda was on the phone, I heard Gail in the background singing the song 'Ain't No Stopping Us Now.'"

No one did. University City beat William Penn 73–58 to win the Public League title. Yolonda, a senior at the time, went on to become an All-American at Cheyney State in Cheyney, Pennsylvania. Gail dominated the Public League for the next two years. Every school along the Eastern seaboard clamored for her services. "What she could do with a basketball for someone her size was unnatural," says LaRue Fields, who was the coach at Morgan State in Baltimore at the time. "Everyone said she played just like a guy, whatever that meant. I just thought, 'What a talent.'"

Gail was equally impressed with Fields, and she chose Morgan State without visiting another school. "It's not like I had to worry about going to a big school and impressing some NBA scouts," says Gail. "They offered me a free ride, and it was close to home. I didn't want to be too far from my Grandma in case I wanted to come home."

Almost immediately, though, Fields and Doughty clashed. "Gail was a street–ball player, probably the best around, but usually those players don't have the discipline to stay within a structured game plan," says Fields. "She didn't like me much, I got angry at her a lot, and she just wanted to go home from the first week." Even at eighteen, Gail was still a grandma's girl. Although she was a starter and averaged 12.5 points and 7.3 rebounds in 1982–83, Gail was miserable. She'd call home every night, crying because she missed the city, the neighborhood, her grandma's barbecued ribs. She hated the school. She didn't get along with the coaching staff. The team was full of first-year players, and they never won. Grandma Francis would listen and quietly issue the same response every time, "You know you can't come home, Gail."

"Me and my grandma, we talked about everything," says Gail. "We were more like mother and daughter than my mother and I. That's why I looked up to her so much. She didn't have to raise me but she did. I love my momma to death; I just love my grandmother more."

When she needed her support the most, however, Grandma Francis wasn't there. Gail could handle being away from home and playing on a bad team as long as her grandma was around for a reality check. She would remind Gail about the education she needed if she wanted to move on. Basketball was nice, but school made it happen. It turns out, however, that Gail didn't so much learn the lessons her grandmother taught her as simply follow along. Gail thought she was a strong woman who struggled her way out of the ghetto, but she was actually pushed out against her will. The shell she thought was so hard turned out to be delicate as a robin's egg – apply even the slightest pressure, and she would crack. Unfortunately for Gail, she didn't learn this until Grandma Francis died.

Toward the end of the first semester of her sophomore year, a call came into her dorm room one evening shortly after practice: The cancer that for the past few years had slowly been attacking Grandma Francis had run its course. Until that point, Gail's motivation for staying in school had been her grandmother's constant prodding. "You went there for a reason," she would tell Gail. When Grandma Francis died, Gail realized the the biggest reason she stayed in school was to make her grandmother proud. With her gone, what point was there in staying? Gail left school that day and she never went back. "When my grandmother died, I lost interest in everything," says Gail. "Nothing mattered. All my focus was on her. It's hard when you're around someone your whole life, and then you don't really know how to deal with them not being there the next day."

"Basically, she was gone once her grandma died," says Fields. "I don't mean from the team, which was obvious, but from a mental standpoint. Her grandma was the thin thread keeping her in school. When she died, that snapped."

For thirteen years since then, Gail has floundered. She lived with cousins in Pittsburgh for five years, playing ball in women's night leagues there. She came back to Philadelphia and worked for UPS until she threw out her back. A cycle of self-pity that begat bad luck that begat more self-pity left her occupying the third floor of her younger sister Tanya's house in South Philly, living off money her brothers gave her. She never started a family of her own because she didn't want to miss time on the court by getting pregnant. Then the new women's professional leagues started popping up, and Gail thought maybe they'd be her shot. "I haven't had anything to hold onto for a long time," she says. "This is something to shoot for."

Though still in its infancy, the women's pro game in the US is morphing to match the NBA's penchants for showmanship and poor fundamentals. Lost in the bustle of becoming famous is the team concept that made women's hoops such a welcome departure from the gotta-get-my-shot attitude permeating the NBA. As Dawn Staley says, the "throwbacks" like Page, Doughty, Lytle and Laney play a style of ball that produces wins anytime, anyplace.

"Here is the biggest problem with today's women's game," says Staley. "We are getting too much hype. The game used to be about the team working as one. That's why people started watching us. They found it refreshing compared to all the individual play in the NBA. We weren't superstars, just good ballplayers working together, playing the game as it was meant to be played. Now, with all the publicity, some girls are coming into the league and changing that. Some of these girls think they're Michael Jordan and want to get famous. Both leagues are going to suffer because of it."

"I used to be a ballgirl for the pro team in Philly when the first women's league was around," says Linda Page of the Women's Basketball League, which ran from the late 1970s through the early 1980s. "It broke my heart to see that first league fold. I dreamed about it. When I didn't have the opportunity to play in the States it hurt."

Gail adds, "You see Lisa Leslie and players like that – they're good, and I give them their props, but I see some of them who aren't good, and how they got the opportunity I just don't know. I'm not knocking nothing from nobody. But if we get a fair chance, we can go out there and prove ourselves. I can take five players from Philly who can go out there and beat anybody."

"I honestly feel I can still compete," says Page. "A lot of the nineties ballplayers – except for the Olympians – are hotdogs. They don't have the discipline, the fundamentals, that we old-fashioned players have."

Page was a high school All-American for four straight years at Dobbins Tech in North Philly. She had a sweet jumper with a quick release spawned from years of playing against bigger, stronger boys. After high school, she went on to become a three-time All-American at North Carolina State before playing two years professionally in Spain and Denmark. She is thirty-four years old, hasn't played organized ball in ten years, and, like Gail, wants her shot.

"I see this as a dream I never got to fulfill," says Page. "If you want it you can motivate yourself to get it. I feel like a new woman because of it."

Page has been Gail's backbone in Gail's quest to stretch beyond the playground. She makes Gail work out. She tells Gail she can make a team if she has some discipline, gets in shape, commits herself to it. No one has offered her such guidance since Grandma Francis died. "Gail is the perfect playground player," says Page. "She knows where all the games are, and she knows she'll get on a court there. It's comfortable for her. She wants to be recognized, but she may not want to work for it."

Adds Fields. "All she has to do is get conditioned, and she'd be playing for money in a pro league in the United States right now. But she doesn't understand that working hard is not a seasonal thing but a yearly thing. She has all the talent. But what about the drive? Maybe she's just paying lip service to the idea of playing pro."

Fields may be right. Even with something, literally, to shoot for, Gail still seems directionless. Laney had a tryout in the pros. Page had one set up for late 1998. Gail talks to both of them almost daily, yet somehow she says she can't figure out how to get a tryout herself. She is a walking contrast, contending that she'd like to play, then in the next breath emphasizing that she doesn't need vindication. Gail once said, "I walk around here and get compliments for my play all the time. I don't worry about the WNBA or ABL because I know I could have been there. If only someone gave me a shot."

As different as the men's game is from the women's, a common thread binds every player who shines brightest and burns out on the playground: All are certain sure they could have made it at the next level if they hadn't somehow been slighted. It's never their fault. Gail has the excuse. She wouldn't be a legend if she didn't.

◆ ◆ ◆

Fernwood Park on Chicago's South Side is where the luminaries hang out during the summer. The NBA's Antoine Walker and Juwan Howard work against each other. Byron Irvin, who now plays in Europe defends against Tim Hardaway's killer crossover. These are Chicago guys, born and bred, practicing their craft on a hometown court. Each could play in a pro-am league at Malcolm X College or at an indoor league at Leclair Courts. But when they want to get back to the basics, away from the gym and onto the street where the game began, they go to Fernwood.

On those nights the little park rocks like the United Center during the last game of the NBA finals. As many as 300 people will circle the court, high-fiving each other when one NBA star makes another look silly. There are no sponsors here, and no scoreboards. No refs, no rappers and no supplementary entertainment. Just pure, hard-core basketball, one of the last bastions of such a style. Casual pickup games on the blacktop are fading away like so many legends who spent their best days playing on it. Nowadays it seems, every game is organized, paid for and scouted. Trips are arranged, coaches draw up plays and use substitution patterns befitting an NBA game. Teammates wear matching uniforms. Shirts and skins have given way to mesh and rayon.

"Pickup games like you knew are a thing of the past," says eighteen-year-old Nick Irvin, Mack's son and Byron's brother. "It's all AAU or all-star traveling teams. That's what is in vogue now."

Mack sponsors an all-star traveling team, taking it to tournaments all over the country every summer. The roster is littered with kids who have been playing on the team since they were eleven years old. Coaches snap up the best players as soon as they show the first sign of developing a sweet finger-roll. It's hard to find anyone on the playground who hasn't been discovered. No one can sneak up on anybody anymore. The late Roger Brown went from Harlem playground star to first pick of the Indiana Pacers in the 1967 ABA draft as a 25-year-old. That will never happen again.

The mystery has been lost in large part because of a change in NCAA regulations regarding recruiting. In 1982 the NCAA instituted the early signing period, meaning that recruits could make their college decision in November of their senior year in high school. In the early 1990s, the NCAA then reduced the time in the summer during which college coaches can evaluate high school prospects to twenty-three days, from July 8 to July 31. The impact on summer basketball, and consequently playground basketball, has been tremendous.

The new regulations means college recruiters now do almost all of their recruiting in July. Tournaments have popped up all over the country to accommodate them. In the inner cities, always the most fertile ground for talent, all-star and AAU teams have sprung up even faster. Players need to be seen during the summer if they are to land a scholarship at a big-time school. That means playing organized ball, which means fleeing the local parks for one of the burgeoning number of new, organized teams.

"To me, your playground today is nowhere near what it was," says Boston Celtics patriarch Red Auerbach. "There's too much organization. In too many leagues, if they are organized, they don't worry about getting in that extra workout. They are already playing two or three times a week."

Adds Izzy Washington, who has coached AAU teams in Southern California since 1967, "It's not just horse-and-buggy playground games anymore. These tournaments have shoe contracts and sponsors. It is sophisticated stuff."

Washington sponsors the Slam and Jam basketball tournament in Los Angeles every summer. His is one of the few major events that doesn't carry a shoe sponsorhip – "Not that I wouldn't like the money," he says. But the biggest showcases are never at a loss for cash. The National Prep Basketball Classic boasts Nike as a sponsor, and the Big Time Classic in Las Vegas has Adidas as a benefactor. In 1996 these two events drew more than 400 college coaches to watch 259 teams. At least 2,000 players from thirty states and four foreign countries participated.

"The early signing period has created a lot of changes in college basketball," says University of Oklahoma coach Kelvin Sampson. "All of a sudden you see guys in these summer leagues before you see them in high schools."

The high school basketball coach has been replaced by the summer league private team owner as the man with the connections to and the influence on the top basketball prodigies. This is a new breed of coach – renegades who are free to recruit whomever they want for their teams, unencumbered by the rules governing school districts and residency requirements. A traveling team based in New York might have players from Florida, Texas, Illinois and California. One coach, Leo Popile of the Boston Amateur Basketball Club, has proven so adept at finding talent for his all-star team that Celtics coach Rick Pitino hired him as a scout.

Placing such importance on coaches who operate in a regulation-free environment sets a dangerous precedent. Players as young as seven years old have been recruited for summer league teams, and often these kids earn accoutrements usually reserved for the country's top schoolboy basketball players. Some have their tuition to private schools paid for by their all-star coaches; others get a handout here or there, or have access to cars whenever they need them. They learn early on that basketball is a game of give-and-take, as much off the court as on. "Basketball is definitely a business," says Stephon Marbury, who played for New York's renowned Gauchos as a teenager. "They use you, and you use them."

"AAU programs and all-star teams are a problem on the playgrounds," says *Slam* magazine's Gervino. "Players learn the commerce of basketball. They are treated like a piece of meat from the time they are seven years old."

"I'm not a Father Flanigan," says Tom Sicignano, who coaches the Brooklyn USA All-Star team. "I don't want to be a Father Flanigan. I want to be a coach. But yes, I'll pay tuition for a kid's prep school."

Sicignano started his club in 1990. He has nine teams, with kids ranging in age from nine to eighteen. He knows the parents of all the kids who play for them. If they say their son can't play, he doesn't play. But if the boy is doing poorly in school or skipping his summer-school classes, Sicignano, unlike coaches in sanctioned high schools and colleges, still allows the kid to travel with the team, though he won't play. In 1995, when Lawrence Phillips, a star running back for the University of Nebraska football team, was arrested for dragging his ex-girlfriend down a flight of stairs, Nebraska coach Tom Osborne allowed Phillips back onto the team. He reasoned that, without the structure and comraderie of the team, Phillips would be a far greater threat to society.

Sicignano subscribes to the same theory.

Many of his recruits come from the playgrounds of New York City. Basketball is, as it always has been, a savior: Without the incentive of playing, many of Sicignano's athletes would be subject to the perils of the street. Every six weeks he holds an open tryout for players from all over the city. No one ever gets cut from the program. Kids who don't make a team in their first attempt are invited back for every tryout thereafter, until they make it or just decide they don't want to come back. Eliminating the option would be eliminating the avenue to opportunity.

That opportunity comes from being seen. In the summer of 1997 Brooklyn USA competed in ten tournaments across the country. Popile's Boston Amateur Basketball Club played more than 100 games in 1996, practically the same number that the Chicago Bulls played in each of their five championship seasons. The competition is fierce, not just between the players, who represent some of the top talent in the country, but among the coaches. Sicignano once falsely accused his rival, Lou D'Almeida, who owns the New York City Gauchos, of kidnapping one of his players at a tournament in Las Vegas (it turns out the kid was just walking the strip).

Such accusations underscore a problem facing colleges and the playgrounds alike. Pickup basketball, as an artform that developed such talents as Earl Manigault and Joe Hammond, is disappearing as these all-star team coaches raid the blacktops for the undiscovered talent. "I don't think you will ever find a talent like Ray Lewis just wandering on the playgrounds ever again," says Izzy Washington. "Some traveling team will snap him up long before he develops a street rep."

College coaches suddenly have a new middleman to deal with in the person of the all-star team coach, who, unlike the high school coach, is free of the traditional restrictions. "A lot of AAU coaches want to be a liaison," says Mack Irvin. "But when you do that, someone has to wonder, why does this guy want to play the big-shot role? What's in it for him? There has to be some ulterior motive."

Some say fair complaint; others cry foul. The coaches say they're giving these kids a chance. But from the aerial shot, the view isn't so clear.

On the one hand, coaches have an enormous amount of prestige riding on the success of their young charges. If you find a kid and win a championship with him, and that kid becomes a college All-American, you are indirectly the hero, the savior and the stud NBA-caliber talent evaluator. Other guys want to play for you as a result, and that breeds success for your team. Success for your team attracts ... shoe company dollars. Which are not insignificant. The top summer-league and AAU teams hook deals as high as six figures with Nike, Adidas or Reebok.

But if it pays to be a big shot, it also costs. In 1995, the Gauchos' D'Almeida told *Sports Illustrated* he spent about $100,000 a year on tuition for the twenty or so players he sends to private schools. He says he also supplies SAT and ACT tutoring, meals, clothing, and money for rides to practice, and has paid legal expenses, bailed kids out of jail, covered overdue bills for his players' families, and helped relatives and former players find jobs or start businesses.

The Gauchos practice in a $2.5 million gym in the South Bronx and have traveled to the Bahamas, Israel, France and Hawaii. A sweltering playground bustling with kids can't compete with those perks. No wonder everyone is deserting the blacktops at the first invitation. Heck, most AAU teams, high schools and even colleges have a hard time equaling such luxury.

"A couple of teams have all the toys," says Southern California's Izzy Washington. "I've seen good programs fall by the wayside. I do think the shoe companies should contribute something, since so many of the kids who play are buying their shoes. But this is getting a little out of hand."

If Washington wants to call for some kind of regulation of the street game, he had better not do so in front of Sicignano. "Why should we be restricted?" Sicignano says. "A high school coach gets paid by the school. He get certified. He gets a pension. When you give me a pension from some higher organization, you can start restricting. Otherwise, stay out of my business."

So that's what playground basketball has become. After decades of developing, refining and creating, of suffering sieges and reinventing itself, the game is now a cash cow. Ask most fans, and they'll tell you they'd rather have a real, hard-core game, played on a cracked and uneven blacktop. No sponsors. No shoe deals. No scouts. Ironic, isn't it, that the neighborhood pickup game is garnering such mainstream attention at the very time it is fading out as a major event in inner-city neighborhoods?

On a sunny Saturday afternoon, the kind of day Holcombe Rucker would have reveled in while watching his tournament, Bob McCullough offers a tour of Harlem's great playground spots. He cruises the streets in a brand new Mercedes, past excavated lots, burned-out buildings and winos sipping from bottles hidden in paper bags. McCullough stops at the Charles Young Playground on 145th and Lenox, where the Rucker Community League holds court. Then he travels south thirty blocks to the Milbank court at 116th and Lenox, the site of the memorable New York–Philadelphia all-star game in 1961. Finally he turns the car around and heads back up to 155th and Eighth, back up to Holcombe Rucker Park, home of the Entertainers Classic. He is asked if he can believe how the game has changed. The sun glares off the roof of his Mercedes as he nods his head. "People are figuring out what I've known for a long time," he says. "This can be a big business."

He has captured the moment perfectly.

THE HAYMARKET SERIES

Mike Davis and Michael Sprinker, Editors

Recent and Forthcoming Titles

THE RISE AND FALL OF THE WHITE REPUBLIC: Class Politics and Mass Culture in Nineteenth-Century America *by Alexander Saxton*

UNFINISHED BUSINESS: Twenty Years of Socialist Review *edited by the Socialist Review Collective*

WRITING FROM THE LEFT: New Essays on Radical Culture and Politics *by Alan M. Wald*

BLACK MACHO AND THE MYTH OF SUPERWOMAN *by Michele Wallace*

INVISIBILITY BLUES: From Pop to Theory *by Michele Wallace*

PROFESSORS, POLITICS AND POP *by Jon Weiner*

THE LEFT AND THE DEMOCRATS: *The Year Left 1*

TOWARDS A RAINBOW SOCIALISM: *The Year Left 2*

RESHAPING THE US LEFT: Popular Struggles in the 1980s *The Year Left 3*

FIRE IN THE HEARTH: The Radical Politics of Place in America *The Year Left 4*